AROUND THE WORLD IN 80 COUNTRIES

Travel Experiences of a Lifetime

David Linton

AROUND THE WORLD IN 80 COUNTRIES
Travel Experiences of a Lifetime

David Linton

First published in 2021

David Linton has asserted his rights under the Copyright, Design and Patents Act 1988 to be identified as author of this work.

ISBN: 9798711936022

All rights reserved. No part of this work covered by the copyright hereon may be reproduced or reused in any form or by any means - graphic, electronic, or merchandised, including photocopying, recording, taping or information storage and retrieval systems - without the written permission of the author.

Every effort has been made to obtain the necessary permissions with reference to copyright material, both illustrative. We apologise for any omissions in this respect and will be pleased to make appropriate acknowledgements in any future edition.

Cover Design - Christopher Steel

To my parents

John and Grace

who first took me travelling

'Life is what happens to you while you're busy making other plans.'

"Beautiful Boy"
John Lennon

80 Countries

Introduction	7	Germany	85	Portugal	177
		Greece	87	Qatar	179
Andorra	9	Guatemala	89	Romania	181
Antigua and Barbuda	11	Honduras	93	San Marino	183
Argentina	13	Hong Kong *	95	Scotland	185
Australia	17	Hungary	97	Serbia	187
Austria	23	Iceland	99	Singapore	189
Barbados	25	India	101	Slovakia	193
Belgium	27	Indonesia	109	South Africa	195
Belize	29	Ireland	111	South Korea	197
Bermuda *	33	Italy	115	Spain	199
Bosnia and Herzegovina	35	Japan	119	Sri Lanka	209
Brazil	37	Jordan	121	Sweden	213
Cambodia	39	Kenya	125	Switzerland	215
Canada	41	Laos	133	Tanzania	217
Cayman Islands *	43	Latvia	135	Thailand	221
Chile	45	Lithuania	137	Tunisia	225
China	47	Malaysia	139	Turkey	229
Costa Rica	53	Malta	141	Uganda	233
Croatia	55	Mauritius	143	United Arab Emirates	239
Cuba	57	Mexico	145	United States of America	241
Czech Republic	61	Monaco	149	Uruguay	255
Denmark	63	Morocco	151	Vatican City	257
Dominican Republic	65	Myanmar (Burma)	157	Vietnam	259
Egypt	67	Netherlands	161	Wales	261
El Salvador	71	Nicaragua	163		
England	73	Norway	165	Where Next?	263
Estonia	77	Oman	171	Acknowledgements	265
Finland	79	Panama	173		
France	81	Poland	175		

* Territories covered but not counted as countries

Introduction

This book is for me! Well, that's how it started. A large box of photos, some picture frames and albums from a pre-digital age had been bugging me for years and then came 2020, the year of lockdowns in a pandemic. So, I embarked on the epic task of sorting through this huge pile of random pictures and quickly decided that they were best sorted by country. This willed me to delve into an even more disorganised archive of digital pictures. At least I knew where the physical photos were stored.

As I pieced together this visual puzzle, I started to recollect the stories and experiences these pictures told. My intention was to liberate the most important images and create some sort of order by making a photobook that I could pick up from time to time to relive my travels. But after staring at so many pictures and trying to recall the past, I realised I would need some commentary for them to be of value to me, or anyone else, in the future.

My first travels were as a child. My parents took my younger sister and me travelling around Europe for six months in 1976. I was thirteen years old. Given we were all born and bred on the far southern coast of mainland Australia, this was quite a thing to do. But travel for Aussies is a rite of passage. Both my parents did their grand tours to Europe on passenger liners in the sixties. They were hooked. I became hooked. I blame them!

A few years later we moved from Australia to England, from the end of the line with the nearest country several hours away to a global hub for travellers with different cultures on our doorstep. My student years and relatively impoverished twenties were mostly about interrailing trips to Europe. New York also beckoned, so I went. And a trip back to Oz afforded a big trip to China and south east Asia.

My thirties and early forties were mostly about shorter, but still very memorable, trips around the UK and to continental Europe. There was the occasional trip back to Oz and a couple of explorations to North Africa. Around this time, I developed the habit of going away for about a month every Christmas, when it would be less noticed at work. This allowed for the bigger trips to Asia, Africa, the Middle East, and South America.

About a decade ago, I moved to New York for a year with work. I lived there, some 40 floors up in the clouds, but probably spent more time on airplanes above them. That year I flew all over the world covering the equivalent miles of London-New York 42 times.

I visited half the states in the US, some of them on weekend road trips. Living in the Americas allowed for trips to the Caribbean and Central America as well. The last ten years have mostly been about big annual Christmas trips to new places that I always wanted to visit.

So, this book tells the story of my 80 countries, in alphabetical order, as I have experienced them. Some visits were fleeting. Half the countries have been visited more than once and half of those a few times or more. Nowadays we all have a camera on the phone in our pocket, so the evidence of more recent trips is better. And the three countries I have lived in, Australia, England and the USA, inevitably have many more pictures and stories behind them, though I have endeavoured to confine my descriptions to travelling, not living, in these home nations.

Most lists of countries count the United Kingdom as one, but I have argued (quite rightly I believe!) that England, Scotland and Wales each deserve their own country status. And, while I have included three territories, Bermuda, Cayman Islands and Hong Kong in this book, I have not counted them. So, I have gained two and lost three, making 80 countries in all.

There have been many people along the way in my travels. For the most part I have mentioned those that I have travelled with, rather than those I have met up with. My photos roughly follow the text.

I am often asked, 'which is your favourite country to visit?'. That is a hard one and my usual answer is, 'one I haven't been to,' as there is nothing quite like arriving somewhere new. But maybe you will guess my favourite place from the pages that follow.

I hope you gain some insight into each of my 80 countries and that my experiences in those that you have also visited chimes with your own. Most of all, I hope this book inspires you to go somewhere you have not been. Safe travels.

Cowes, England
March 2021

Andorra

I have been to Andorra twice. The first time was with my parents in 1976 when we braved the icy mountain passes in the Hillman Hunter that took us all over Europe. Good on hills this car was not! Andorra is a tiny country in the middle of the Pyrenees that might just have the highest capital city in Europe, Andorra le Vella. Your only way in, is by road. My memory from that time is that Duty Free seemed to be Andorra's 'raison d'etre'. We were travelling from the French Riviera to Spain. We were curious, so we made a detour and stayed the night.

My second visit was decades later where it was necessary to drive through. We had set out from friends on the French Mediterranean coast on our way to skiing in the Spanish Pyrenees. Andorra does offer skiing but it's not very challenging. That, and its relative low cost lends itself well to school ski trips. Our route doglegged through the principality and we stopped briefly for fuel and food. This short revisit confirmed that the main centre – more of a town than a city, lying in a cold, grey valley – remained a fairly drab place. I suspect the alpine scenery might be better in the summer and there must be some great hiking. Every place has its charms and I accept I was not there long enough to find any. It is unfortunate that the alphabet dictates that my first country is among the least memorable for me. Sorry Andorra.

Would I go back? No.

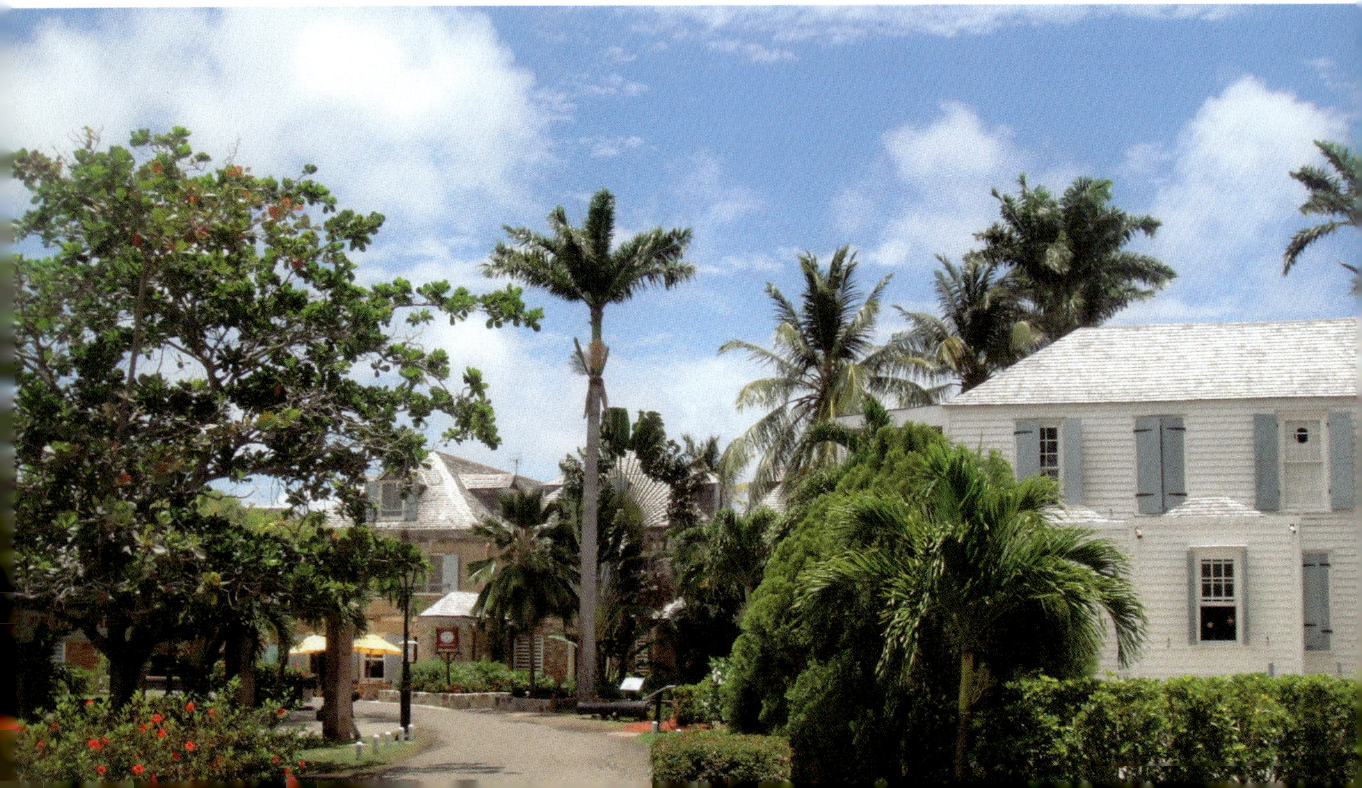

Antigua and Barbuda

It will become apparent that sailing is a passion of mine. I have sailed in the waters of a quarter of the countries in this book. But Antigua is the only country I have been to specifically to sail. I was living in New York and got wind of the fact that a throng of my English sailing friends were making their way to Antigua Race Week. Fear of missing out got the better of me, so I jumped on a plane and headed due south.

The first things I noticed arriving in Antigua were how lush it was and the disproportionally large Sir Vivian Richards cricket stadium. The Oz in me felt a little at home. As I rode in the taxi from the airport in the welcoming warm air, I was transported back to a time when the 'Windies' were the dominant force in cricket. My target destination was regatta HQ in English Harbour. I had no plan, no place to stay, no boat to crew on. But I was not worried. My inner compass told me that the friendly sailing community would somehow come good.

English Harbour must be one of the most historic British colonial outposts in the Caribbean. It is a small collection of smart stone and whitewashed weatherboard buildings set around a sheltered palm tree-lined small harbour. Here, lies the lovely Admiral's Inn with its white and grey shutters and the historic dockyard right in its waterfront grounds. At reception I asked the lovely French lady, Catherine, if she had a room for the night. I learned a long time ago just get your first night sorted. Better to book online, but I did not know the lay of the land, prices were very high in regatta week and a first night somewhere allowed me to find my bearings. They had a small loft room in the roof that was free just for that night. But once ensconced in this lovely place, I built a rapport with Catherine and miraculously the hotel moved me from room to room as they juggled their way through what must be their busiest week of their year. Anyone who has spent any time in English Harbour knows Catherine from the café that bears her name on the other side of the harbour.

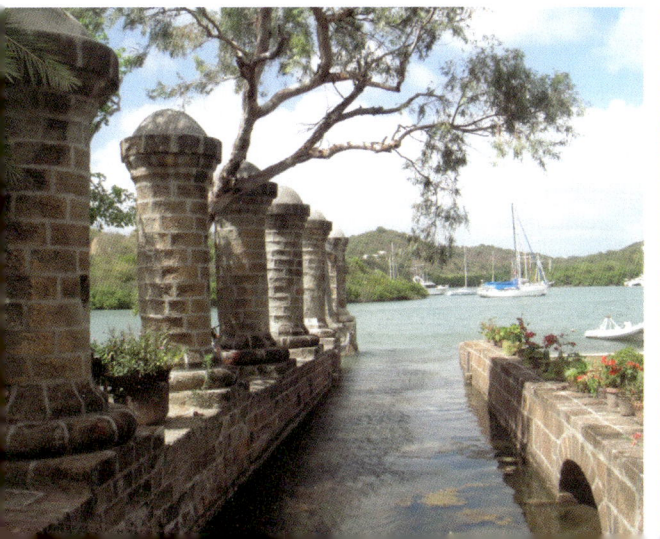

My next mission was to find a boat to crew on for the regatta. I headed out and walked round the harbour front where all the boats were tied up. The iconic Steinlager, winner of Whitbread Round the World Race years earlier, was there along with a group of boats readying themselves in the pre-regatta excitement. I ran into loads of friends, had beers onboard, progressed to rum cocktails and partied on into the night. I did find a crew the next day on a boat called Skyhunter II, a J122. It was great to be out on the water again. Yacht racing in the warm waters of Antigua is a real treat. In England, you spend your time on the rail dodging buckets of water from a freezing grey sea. Here, on the pristine blue green sea, you are quite glad to be refreshed by a wave hitting you fair and square.

Skyhunter II was berthed in the much larger Falmouth Harbour just across a narrow neck of land from English Harbour. This was where the big boats docked, including the world's biggest sailing yacht, Maltese Falcon. At 289 ft long she is a modern sailing ship. The walk back to hotel each night was an assault course of navigating friends in bars. A quick beer at Cloggy's bar after sailing, leads to expresso martinis at Skullduggery's café followed by a much-needed pizza at Paparazzi before rum and cokes at Life on the Corner. Rum is cheaper than coke in Antigua, so the bar owners wince every time you ask for more coke in your rocket-fuelled drink. By this time, you have no hope of escaping the last pitstop, Rasta shack, a grass hut on stilts about fifteen feet square, packed with all comers strutting their stuff to local tunes. Back to the hotel to bed, wake up, repeat!

Every night at Antigua Race Week is party night but none more so than the Tuesday night, high up on the Shirley Heights lookout that towers over both harbours. The whole of Antigua joins the party. At 500ft you are just above the top of the big masts down in Falmouth Harbour, which are lit up as a warning for airplanes. You can't really talk against the thumping Rasta beat, but soon the rum cocktails kick in rendering intelligent conversation mostly useless anyway. Sailors go for it on this night, due to the inspired idea of having a regatta lay day on the Wednesday.

We did manage a big lunch table of friends at the exclusive Carlisle Bay resort the next day. The last two days of the regatta were a race through turquoise seas to Jolly Harbour for a regatta BBQ and then back the last day. We won our group and held a load of silverware at the prizegiving to end a great week. I did manage a lovely relaxing day on the beach at Willoughby Bay looking across to Eric Clapton's Crossroads clinic on my last day. All in all, a great week!

Would I go back? Yes. Almost certainly for another race week or the Caribbean 600 race as well as to stay with friends who spend the winter there.

Argentina

I had always wanted to go to South America, my last continent save Antarctica. I had to wait until my early forties to do it. Buenos Aires was my arrival point and I was captivated instantly. It is always great to be in the southern hemisphere for an English winter and BA provided the ideal tonic. Bright blue skies and warm nights sitting out in this cultural city was the perfect escape. I was lucky to make a new friend on the plane, so I was guided in by a local.

I found a room on the top floor of a hotel on the 9 de Julio Avenue where I could lean out the window and marvel at the bustle of the city's heart. With 14 lanes of traffic, this is the widest street in the world. An enormous Argentinian flag furls and unfurls against its huge weight in the summer breeze that wafts down this vast boulevard. Wandering around, there is no escaping the European influence that comes with the scale of beautiful old buildings. If it were not for the palms in front of the French embassy, you would guess you were in Paris. The opera house is a homage to Argentina's favourite daughter, Evita. I went to see her ornate grave in a crowded cemetery, but was more impressed by the buttress roots of the trees outside. So much in Buenos Aires feels old, but the regenerated Puerto Modero district with its waterfront restaurants provides a great contrasting modern buzz.

I did not really eat red meet for a couple of decades. It was an overhang of travelling in China where you never quite knew what was on the plate. I went off it and did not really got back into it. Everything changed in Argentina. The secret here is strips of char-grilled meat are served on big, tasty salads. It cushioned the blow for my return to bloody flesh and I was a fully reformed carnivore by the time I left the continent. You imagine they eat big hunks of cow. Maybe a horseman on Las Pampas does, but it did not seem to be the rule in the Capital. In the San Telmo district, famed for tango dancing in the squares, lies the footballers' restaurant "La Brigada." There are pictures of heroes of the pitch everywhere, including, in pride of place, 'God with the hand', Diego Maradona. I remember there was little pretence and lousy service, but the piece de la resistance is when they bring a thick grilled sizzling steak to your table. With little ceremony, they pick up a tablespoon and cut the steak in two. The flesh parts like a palm tree split down the middle. They left the spoon on the plate and I was compelled to check how sharp it was. It was blunt.

Tango is at the heart of nightlife in Buenos Aires and watching it is arresting. Purposeful moves are executed with precision to the accompanying tunes in such a way that Tango becomes the music. In one tango hall I visited, stunning young women would form a queue to dance with an experienced old man. He would effortlessly take the girl through a quite dramatic routine, all the while placing just a pair of a fingers on the strap of the dress across her back. It was all about making the woman shine. We would sit out in squares late at night chatting and being distracted by tango constantly.

Argentina is the world's eighth largest country so, with the limited time that I had, I needed to fly. Patagonia beckoned so I flew two hours south to Trelew, only half way to the far south. I hired a car and hit the road. Driving across this barren landscape reminded me of Australia, barring the occasional llama. Peninsula Valdes is famed for its sea life and the beaches were covered in sealions, penguins and gulls. The noise was deafening. I had sort of hoped to witness the gruesome spectacle of killer whales swimming up the beach to poach young seals but, fortunately for the seals, that didn't materialise. I had also missed seeing humpback whales by a day. But I did see Wales. I drove through a valley to the Welsh settlement of Y Wladfa the following day. I stayed a couple of nights in Peurto Madryn. On the vast beaches nearby, I would sip sundowners and watch kids playing touch rugby, presumably introduced by the Welsh. There was an array of fish on the menu here with fewer people to eat it. This far south, the sea was cold and there was a chill in the air at night. The stars where incredible. The Milky Way is so much better in the southern hemisphere and I felt comforted always seeing the Southern Cross beaming at me. While waiting for my return flight at Trelew airport, I studied a wall covered with blue faded photographs of the airman who flew sorties from there in the Falklands War. I know I need to explore Patagonia further one day and I probably will on my way to Antarctica.

After a short trip to Uruguay, I was flying to Mendoza in the heart of wine country, where the Malbec is to die for. It is a friendly city with lovely squares and a modern feel. Apart from some great food and wines my objective was to catch a bus from here across the high Andes and into Chile. The pass through the Andes runs across the foothills of Mt Aconcagua. At just under 23,000ft, it is the highest mountain in the world outside the Himalayas. A week or so later, I flew from Santiago back to Buenos Aires for my last time before heading for the border with Brazil.

The Iguazu Falls are spectacular. They are 1km wider than Victoria Falls and when Elanor Roosevelt first saw them she said, "Poor Niagara!" She was right. Walking on duck boards across a vast tributary of rivers brings you rather dramatically to the edge of the falls. To think, before they built these platforms, tourists used to do it in canoes! Not a good time for your paddle to break. The spray rises about a mile into the sky and the roar of the water is deafening. In Buenos Aires, I had trouble getting a visa for Brazil with the

Christmas holidays, but I heard it could be possible at the border. When I got there, I was told it would take a few days. I showed my sadness, pulled out some money, he smiled and indicated to put it in the passport. I waited under a tree laden with avocados. Twenty minutes later I had a visa.

It was hard to get an idea of the scale of Iguazu, so I wanted to get up in a helicopter. The cheapest I could get was $500 which was a bit beyond my daily budget. I set about finding some passengers and luckily found three great Danes who would pay $400. Flying over La Garganta (the throat) was spectacular. We also flew upriver to a T-junction separating Argentina, Paraguay and Brazil and then flew on to see a massive hydroelectric scheme. Best of all, the pilot dropped me at the airport to save me getting a taxi and I flew to Rio.

Would I go back? Definitely. To see more of Patagonia, stay in Las Pampas, ride horses and drink fine wines on a better budget.

Australia

I was born and raised on the Mornington Peninsula, an arm of land that reaches out to the Southern Ocean south of Melbourne. Bay beaches on one side and ocean surf beaches on the other. It is stunning! But rather than share it with you through the eyes of a child, long summer days and camping holidays in the wilderness, I will start with my visits back as an adult.

On finishing university, I returned to Australia (always Oz to me) with my college friend Johnny. My parents had moved back so we had a base to explore from. At that time, in our 20s, the draw was mostly going up to town for parties. Melbourne, being the capital of the state of Victoria, must be one of the most Victorian cities in the world. It also has the second largest Greek population on the planet after Athens, along with Italians and an increasing Asian influence. It is a true melting pot, and the City is famed for its diversity of great restaurants.

We did manage some fun excursions upcountry too. We teamed up with some of my old childhood friends and weaved our way down the mighty Murray River that forms the border with New South Wales. We took in country horse races, parties in the wilderness and general mucking about on big farms. Driving through the spectacular forests of tall eucalyptus gums along the Maroondah Highway we headed for a three-day horse trek with friends in the foothills of the Snowy Mountains. The scale of the country hits you here. More snow falls on the Snowy than in all of Switzerland. As kids we skied here a few times. On this trip we would take a day to ride through dark forests of gums, gallop across adjoining lowlands and up into the hills again. A day's ride across the spurs and saddles of mountains would still take hours by car the long way round. We had a great time.

18 AUSTRALIA

My sister had her 21st birthday in my parents' garden and a few days later we embarked on a trip around Oz. First stop was Perth WA, pretty much a frontier city then with very few tall buildings. Perth is poised right on the edge of the Indian Ocean, with amazing beaches, and the 'Freemantle Doctor' wind blows in most afternoons. One of the highlights was a trip to Rottnest Island, a jewel lying out in the deep blue sea. Almost Mediterranean in feel, with the world's southernmost coral and home to the tiny wallaby-like marsupial, the quokka. Rotto was a dream.

Next stop was Alice Springs, where we headed to Uluru. Here we scaled the sacred site Ayers Rock, something you can no longer do. As you reach the summit of the largest monolith on the planet, this hot wind hits you and almost knocks you off your feet. A walk in the adjacent Olgas was almost as special. We were on a tight budget, so we slept in the car. It was so hot I remember climbing onto the roof and sleeping in the relative cool of the night under the bright stars. I would be woken by the occasional heavy rain drop and expect to be drenched soon after, but it never rained. In those

days you flew to Alice Springs to go and see the Rock. Little did we know it was nearly 500km away. Hardly next door, but in the outback that is nothing. On the way back to Alice we stopped about half-way there for fuel. We were confronted by a sign reading, 'Sorry No Petrol Today.' I was told, 'plenty of diesel mate, but no petrol'. So, we had to limp the next 200km at the fuel-efficient speed of 70km/h. Harder still, we needed to turn the aircon off to conserve fuel. The temperature was 41C and putting your hand out the window, there was a heating factor that was like putting it in a hot oven. We just made our flight. We were told it was was leaving from gate 2 which turned out to be a small wire swing gate next to the other gate onto the tarmac.

AUSTRALIA

We spent a day in Mt Isa, the hottest place I have ever been. It was 44C in the shade. Everyone headed for a long wander around the blissfully cool supermarket. Cairns was our next place, and up into the Daintree rainforest in the far north of Queensland. We stayed at Cape Tribulation, named by Captain Cook after HMS Endeavour scraped the reef here en route to Botany Bay in 1770. We trekked through the rainforest including once by night in the pitch-black dark. Here the rivers are crocodile-infested. You don't stand at the edge. They have a 0-20mph time of about a second. We couldn't swim in the sea here either thanks to box jellyfish, the world's most venomous marine creature, so we settled for the swimming pools in places we stayed, Jungle Lodge and Crocodylus. We flew over the Barrier Reef in a light aircraft and explored Magnetic Island. After this we headed down the coast to stay with family friends in Brisbane (Brisey). The last stop on our trip around Oz was Sydney. Despite being an Aussie, it was my first time there and it was great to see the iconic harbour bridge and opera house. We were there for Australia Day and it was the bicentenary celebrations. On the Manly ferry that night we stopped right under the spectacular fireworks.

Years later my sister, Molly lived in Sydney and I stayed a few times with her there. Each morning we would go down to swim lengths in the public seawater pool at Bronte. And there were trips down to Melbourne to see friends and family as well. These visits back to Oz were mostly about these two great cities and the places in between, like the 90-mile beach in Gippsland or Wilson's Promontory. I did go to Tasmania (Tassie) on a school trip back in the 1970s.

One year, with my parents and Molly, we chartered a yacht and sailed round the Whitsunday Islands off Queensland. My clearest memory of that charter was us all diving off the boat and swimming to the stunning Whitehaven beach. Once ashore, someone came along the beach and told us we should not swim there as it was shark-infested. I had to swim back to get the 'tinny', our aluminium dingy, tied off the back of the yacht. I might have broken my record time on that swim. Lunch that day was oysters prised from rocks lying in the shallows.

My last trip back, several years ago now, was probably my most memorable. We went up to the Western District where my mother grew up, and also spent a few days in Lorne on the Great Ocean Road, a place of childhood memories. But this trip to Oz was mostly about spending time where I grew up on the Mornington Peninsula. I might be biased, but with fabulous vineyards, bay beaches with crystal clear calm water and ocean beaches of champagne surf, it is still one of the best places in the world. I was lucky to grow up there. Australia is such a big country that you cannot see it all in one go. As is so often the case with travel, you are better to see a lot of a little than a little of a lot.

Would I go back? Always. To see friends and family, the far north, WA northern shores, the outback, maybe do a Sydney-Hobart race.

Austria

My trips to Austria have mostly been to ski, but I have visited Vienna a few times as well. My first trip to the capital was inter-railing in my college days and visiting a friend studying there. My impression of this historic city was of a place where East truly meets West. The bold baroque buildings had a hint of Imperial Russia about them. The city was at the heart of the dominant Habsburg Empire that ruled so much of Europe for centuries. You know immediately you are venturing into a place that has had global cultural influence. Famed for more classical composers than any other city, Vienna is home of waltzes, the art of Klimt, the power of the mind, Sigmund Freud, and the birth of 1920s Bauhaus Design. On that visit, I spent a few days as a culture vulture immersing myself in all I could take from Vienna.

A few things stuck with me from that trip. There was a slight disappointment that the River Danube does not run through the heart of the city. (I did visit the blue Danube a few miles away.) In the city I had to content myself with the Donau canal, though some great bars are concentrated around the canal to be fair. The main Saint Stephen's Cathedral has an unusual roof of patchwork tiles that looks like a tapestry. On my way to the majestic but serine Belvedere Palace, I was shocked to see a guard standing outside a bank armed with a machine gun. No big deal now but it was for me back then in the 1980s.

My subsequent trips to Vienna have been on business. I did spend a weekend in the lovely city of Linz, which is right on the Danube. I also spent a day focused on skiing the downhill course at Schladming the week after the World Cup was held there. I skied it about ten times. It was so steep in places I had to traverse it, especially into the finish area. Olympic skiers do it in under two minutes: I got my time down to around 20 minutes and quit while I was ahead.

But Austria for me has been primarily been about the Tyrol, most of the arm of the country that extends westward. I had some happy weeks skiing in the exclusive resort of Lech with a few days' skiing over the mountain to St Anton. Lech is the most picturesque Alpine village in which to spend Christmas. The food is as good as it gets in the Alps —especially if you like strudel. There's an array of amazing Austrian wines and the après ski borders on the outrageous. I have happy memories of drinking and singing in hilltop bars at the close of the day and skiing down the mountain in the dark with only the lights of the village below to guide us in.

Another fun weekend was a stag weekend in Ischgl. Here the theme was for the groom to ski down the mountain dressed as a fox with the rest of us chasing him, dressed in tweeds. Fairly treacherous at times but a laugh a minute. The next day we went white water rafting with two rafts. Given we were mostly competitive sailors, it was inevitable, to our instructors' horror, that we had acted like pirates boarding each other's vessels. It wasn't long before we were all in the river. Austria is a great place to have fun!

Would I go back? Yes. To explore Salzburg, learn more about the wines and do some cross-country ski touring in the Tyrol.

Barbados

I have been to Barbados a couple of times, once to visit a friend who lives there, and the second time to her wedding. The country is a relatively large island, the most south eastern in the Caribbean and a popular escape for Brits seeking winter sun. Away from the plush beach resorts, Barbados has a real charm.

The western, leeward side of the island is where you'll find the pristine beaches with calm blue sea. We spent a day at the polo and headed to the Barbados Yacht Club for cocktails. It felt very colonial a lot of the time. My favourite trips were to explore the interior and the windward coast of the east side of the island. This meant drives through fields of sugar cane dotted with brightly coloured shacks and the odd historic stone building. I paid homage at the high altar of rum at the Mount Gay distillery. Lunch at the Atlantis Hotel was followed by a walk on the beaches of the wilder Atlantic coast.

Night-time was mostly about sitting in smart restaurants right on the beach followed by more fun in the dive bars of Holetown and, best of all, Rasta karaoke.

Would I go back? Yes. To see friends or a pure working/beach holiday.

26 BARBADOS

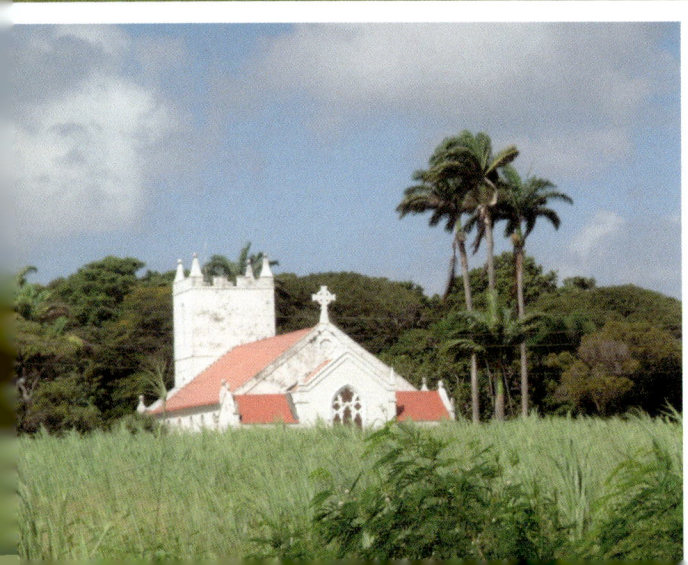

Belgium

There's an irony that Belgium is at the heart of the European Union but somehow lacks its own identity as a country. I have only one memory from my visit as a child with my parents, staying at the top of an old hotel in Gent that had no lift and a rickety staircase. Interrailing, I visited Bruges with its lovely canals and cobbled streets. It was probably here, on a tight budget, that I properly discovered moules-frites.

All my subsequent trips have been to Brussels on business. The Eurostar makes visiting a breeze and it really is a charming city. The centre is divided up into quarters (strangely nine of them), plus another one nicknamed the European Quarter as it holds most of the European Commission buildings. It is a great city to walk around. There are lots of bars with people drinking outside in the summer and some great restaurants. My favourite is La Quincaillerie. It means hardware store in French and this place really is set in an old hardware store with all the serving benches, wooden storage drawers, ladders and stairs. It is very atmospheric. Asking a taxi to take you there, you realise that Quincaillerie might just be the hardest French word to pronounce. Try it!

Would I go back? Probably. For work and to dine at La Quincaillerie.

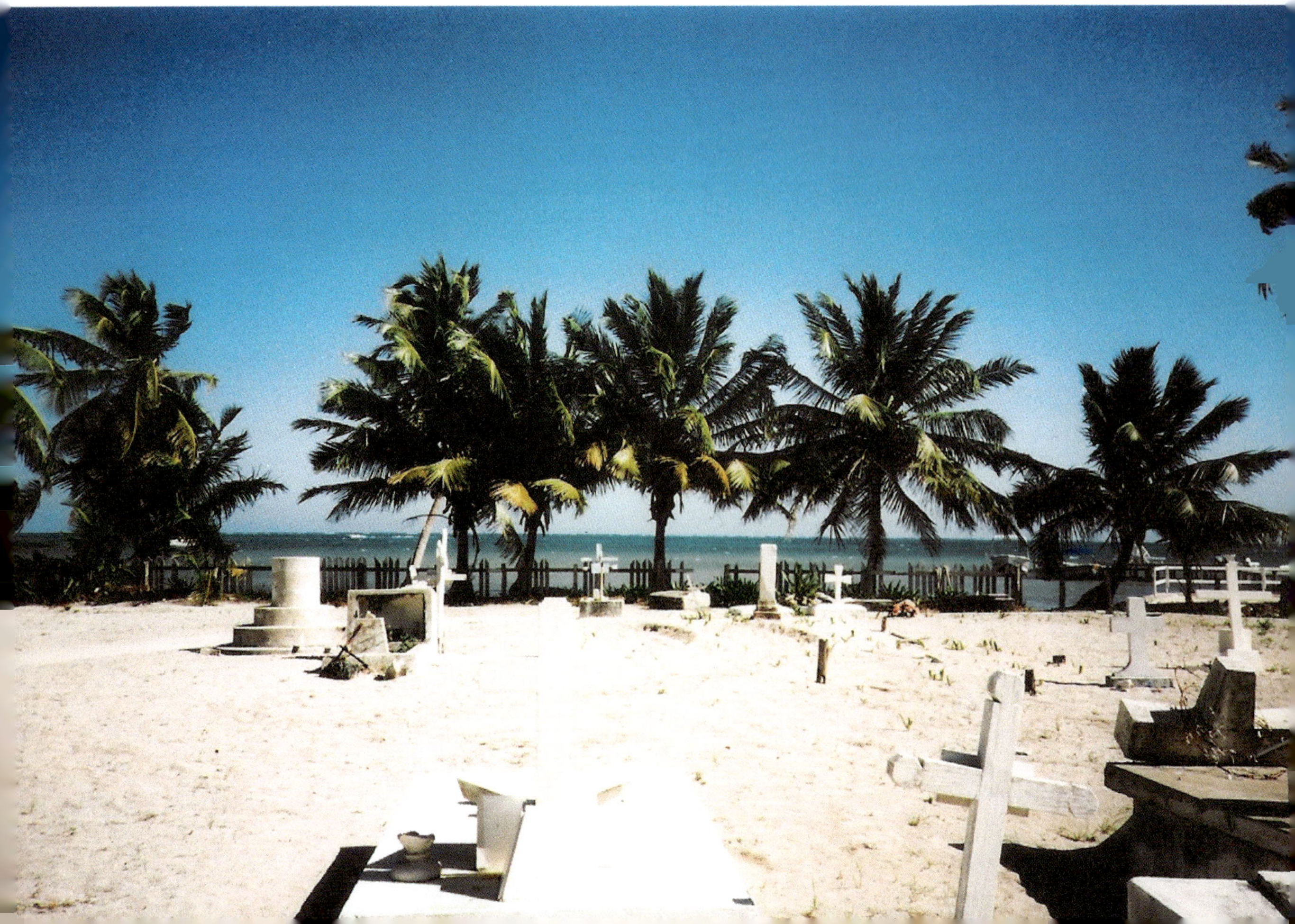

Belize

Around twenty years ago I was in Texas on business and decided to head to Central America for Christmas and New Year. The trip was mostly about seeing Guatemala with my girlfriend Ann Louise and an old friend Biggles and his partner Lou. Belize, formerly British Honduras, was next door and we needed a bit of beach time. To begin with we relaxed on the beaches of Caye Caulker and Ambergris Caye, but the draw of some deep-sea fishing beckoned. We hired a small boat with a local skipper. First stop was to the edge of the mangrove swamps to get bait. You look for the pelicans sitting up in the trees and follow their lead. Then you stand on the bow of the boat with a casting net and toss it wide on the water in front of you. The weights around the edge of the net sink and you pull a draw string which closes the bottom of the net and bingo you haul up a string bag full of small fish. Having watched the locals, I had to have a go. First go, no fish. Second go, I think I got one. I was getting better at it, but the crew were becoming inpatient. Casting net practice was not their idea of a day's fishing.

With a bucket full of bait, we headed out to sea. We were all quite hot at this stage and jumped in for a swim and a bit of snorkelling. Lots of small fish but nothing you would want to hang from the scales back at the jetty. When we got back to the boat there was a massive grouper, about the size of a small person, sitting almost motionless under the boat. We headed to 'the fishing spot' and caught several brightly coloured fish and kept the bigger ones that we were assured were not poisonous. Heading home into the sunset with our catch and a cold beer was great, until the boat started to splutter, and we ran out of fuel. As luck would have it a Rastafarian sailing an old boat with a ragged canvas sail diverted course after seeing the girls waving sarongs while we lay in the boat. He didn't want to sell us his fuel, but everyone has their price….and he knew what his was. The hotel restaurant cooked our fish for dinner. I remember the colourful trigger fish tasted peppery. The next day I bought a casting net and perfected my technique in the shallows. I still have it but have not used it since.

The next day we got a taxi inland to visit the Belize Zoo. It was a new concept; set in the middle of the rain forest. The project had been spearheaded by Gerald Durrell and David Attenborough only a few years earlier and was being held up as a model for zoos of the future. We had to see it. It was sort of like a game park in the jungle with much more space given over to the animals than the humans. The pens were vast areas with high wire fences and at times walking down the pathways between pens there was a feeling of role reversal, looking out at the animals from within our enclosed paths. There were the big cats of the forest, but the loudest residents were the howler monkeys swinging from tree to tree on their tails, something that monkeys outside the Americas don't do. I held a massive boa constrictor which, having wrapped itself around me, needed the zookeepers to prise us apart.

That night we stayed in Belize City, went out for dinner, and wandered round town. When we got back to our hotel, we were advised not to walk around at night due to the high murder rate. Phew. We had a few more days so we headed down the coast to Placencia. Fewer tourists made this trip and we were hoping to see manatees in the wild there. We had a hut on stilts right on the beach and at night you could hear the dolphins squeaking around 50ft away from where you lay in bed. The place felt reminiscent of Paul Theroux's 'Mosquito Coast', which was set just down the coast in neighbouring Honduras. We met an American couple who had settled there and built a house on the beach with a library big enough to read books for the rest of their days. It was like something out of a movie.

One night we were in a bar when a local fisherman came in pleading for help. On the way back to port he had turned too sharply on a big wave and his large, unsecured, outboard snapped off and went overboard. It was now lying somewhere on the bottom. We all stood up and suddenly we were part of the search party. We jumped on boats and headed to the spot where he thought it happened. I found myself donning a tank and getting ready for an underwater search. I didn't have a PADI qualification and this was clearly not a lesson, but apparently, I was OK to dive. There had been a storm that day and the water was murky in the dark. About six of us swam in a line along the sea floor with torches. We didn't find the engine, but the drinks were mostly free in that bar for the rest of our stay.

One thing that stumped me about Placencia was that very few cars, mostly Ford F100 trucks, had bonnets (hoods). The reason for this became apparent when we went out on a boat with some free divers. They use the bonnets as a type of lobster (what we would call crayfish) trap. The crays like to live at a depth of around 20-50ft, ideally somewhere sheltered. Enter the truck bonnet. The local free divers swim down to the bottom without any air tanks, lift the bonnet and grab as many crayfish as they can. They will try and hold a couple together in one hand and maybe put another under an arm before returning to the surface for breath.

Belize has the second longest barrier reef in the world after the Great Barrier Reef in Oz and is, therefore, a mecca for divers. Many come to the tourist resorts further north to dive the spectacular Great Blue Hole. After our willingness to dive for the outboard word got about that there were some serious foreign divers in town. Soon there were offers to take us out to the reef for a small fee. One hundred US dollars later we were headed to the most picturesque uninhabited island several miles offshore. We landed on the beach at the uninhabited Laughing Bird Caye. Shaped like a seagull in flight, it was only a couple of hundred metres long and maybe only twenty metres wide. It was straight out of Robinson Crusoe. We went and anchored off the island and submerged for my first proper dive experience. It was another world. We descended an underwater cliff face and I looked up at the glistening sunlight shinning on the seaweed and coral on the wall. When we got to around 100 ft the sea was blue black. It was disorientating. My diving credentials being below what had been assumed, I was running short of air before the others, so I made for the top remembering all the necessary safety protocols we had run through earlier as refresher. I didn't suffer the bends, but was quite shocked to see at the surface how far we had drifted from the boat at anchor. I followed the bubbles surfacing from the others, watching the boat increasingly becoming a spec in the distance. When they finally came up, we lay on our backs with our heavy tanks and flippered our way back. It was exhausting, but a great experience.

We never saw any manatees, but we did see lots of other sea life, including turtles. It was sad to see it on the menus in restaurants back then. We did eat conch quite a bit, the mollusc that lives in the big pink shell you would see blown as a horn in vintage movies. I confess it was delicious.

Would I go back? Yes. But next time I would get my PADI certificate first.

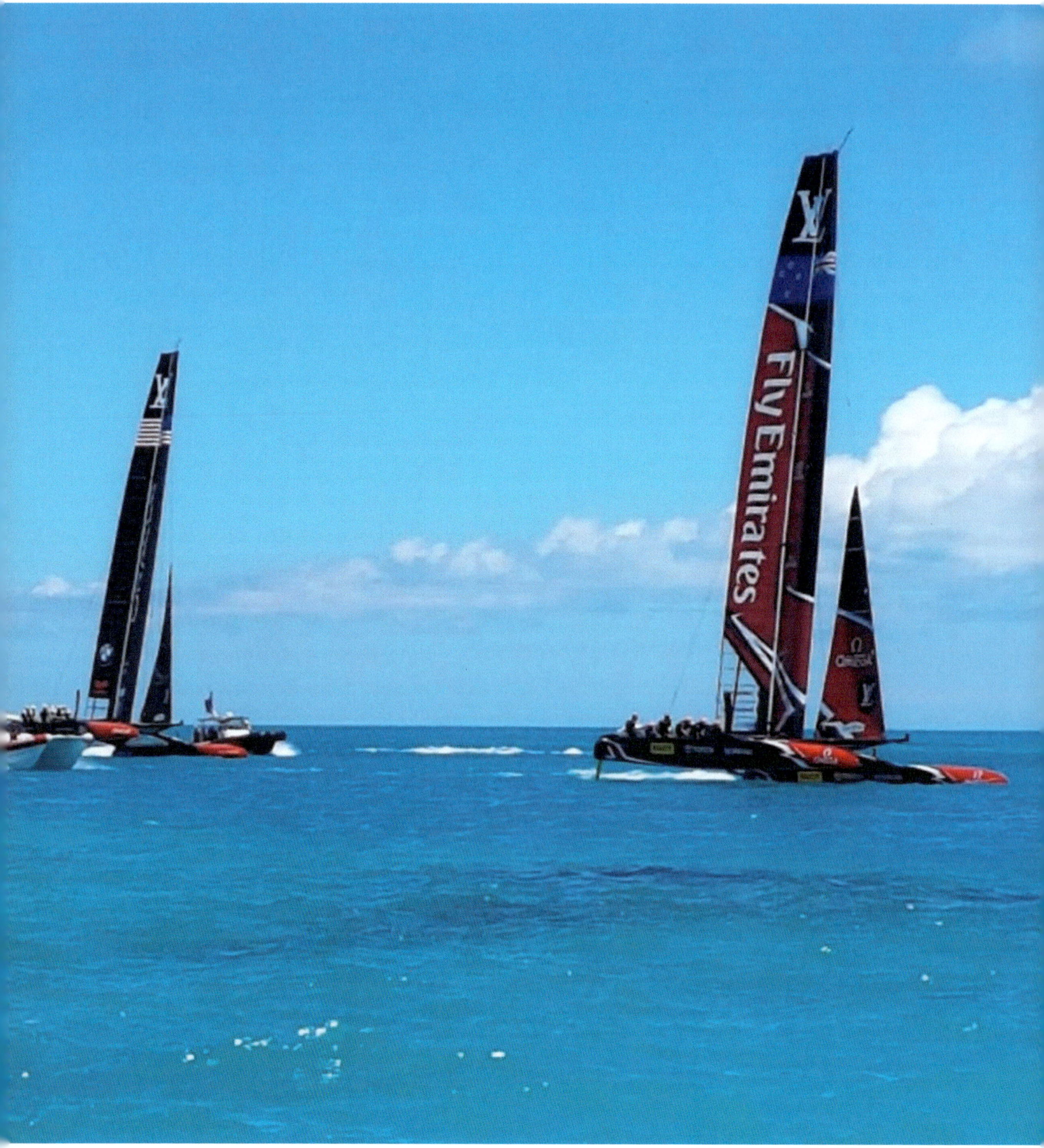
Fly Emirates

Bermuda

Bermuda is not a country. It is an Overseas British Territory in the north Atlantic Ocean. Therefore it doesn't count as one of my 80 countries, but as it is bigger and more significant than a few countries in this book so I have included it here.

In 2016, my mother casually mentioned that her godson had become port master in Bermuda. This was quite fortuitous because the America's Cup was being held there the following year, so we booked to go and stay with him and see the cup finals. He lived in a typical Bermudan house in the Somerset district and worked in Royal Naval Dockyard, right where the America's Cup Village was.

We spent several days watching the America's Cup finals between the USA and New Zealand. The steady breeze and bright blue water made Bermuda the perfect venue. We watched from hospitality tents, at anchor out on the course, and from the grandstand at the finish line on the final day. The boats were getting up to speeds of 60mph, which was breathtaking when they whizzed past us. The locals wanted America to win. They had vowed to return here, but NZ won and took the world's oldest sporting trophy home for the next battle to be held in Auckland.

The houses in Bermuda all have regulation white rippled roofs, designed to slow the pace of any infrequent deluge by directing the water down pipes into underground tanks. When a hurricane comes, residents push pineapples into the pipes on the roof to stop salty water whipped up from the sea contaminating their rainwater supply. They also throw the garden furniture into the pool to prevent chairs and tables turning into missiles, then invite their nearby friends to stay and party non-stop for a couple of days while barricaded in.

A friend Billy also made the trip from the UK and was staying with his friend at a great house on the harbour. We hired mopeds and explored the island. Great Sound has such a big diameter, that it is quicker to wheel your moped onto the fast cat from Dockyard to Hamilton than it is to bike round. Exploring the whole island by moped was great fun. We rode up to the top of the island to St George's, where the British first settled in 1612. My parents got the fast cat and joined us for lunch. We went out on a tug, visited the botanic gardens and I had lunch at a super beach restaurant with a newfound friend from the flight out. We visited people's amazing homes on the waterfront, had feasts on the beach as well as fine dining at restaurants with tables on the sand. Everywhere you looked there was white sand and blue, blue sea. Bermuda is beautiful.

Would I go back? Yes. Maybe for the Rugby World Classic or some big sea fishing.

Bosnia and Herzegovina

In 2011, I attended a conference being held in Sarajevo. We spent a few days in the city but, as is the way with a business event, you get little chance to explore a place. I did spend some early mornings and evenings walking around, however, and it was very atmospheric but not all in a good way. Many thousands of civilians had been killed during the Siege of Sarajevo, which lasted almost four years and was at the heart of the Balkans war (1991-2001). Sarajevo had hosted the Olympics in 1984, and the Olympic Stadium became the scene of many atrocities.

Wandering around the city, the war was still very much in evidence. You could see bullet marks and mortar holes all over buildings, testament to Serbian attacks from the surrounding mountains. Set in a valley, Sarajevo and its people were sitting ducks. Tower blocks had big chunks taken out of them high up and a fair amount was still to be rebuilt. A few significant modern buildings had been erected, but I sense it will be decades before the scars of the war will be gone. You do not imagine this happening in Europe in the 1990s. It did and it was chilling to see the aftermath.

Despite this, we did have some fun nights out, there were some buzzing places that felt like bazaars or Berber tents. Christianity meets Islam here. It must have been quite a place before the war. After the conference, all the delegates flew out. I went to the train station. I boarded a train to Mostar, the city where the famous arched bridge was bombed in the Balkans War and subsequently rebuilt. You could see it from the train station there. I didn't stop and headed for the Adriatic coast, where the country only has a few kilometres of shoreline. From Mostar, the train follows the Neretva River, weaving its way through the high mountains leaving the Herzegovina region for the last 10km to the port of Ploče just over the border in Croatia.

Would I go back? Interesting, but probably not.

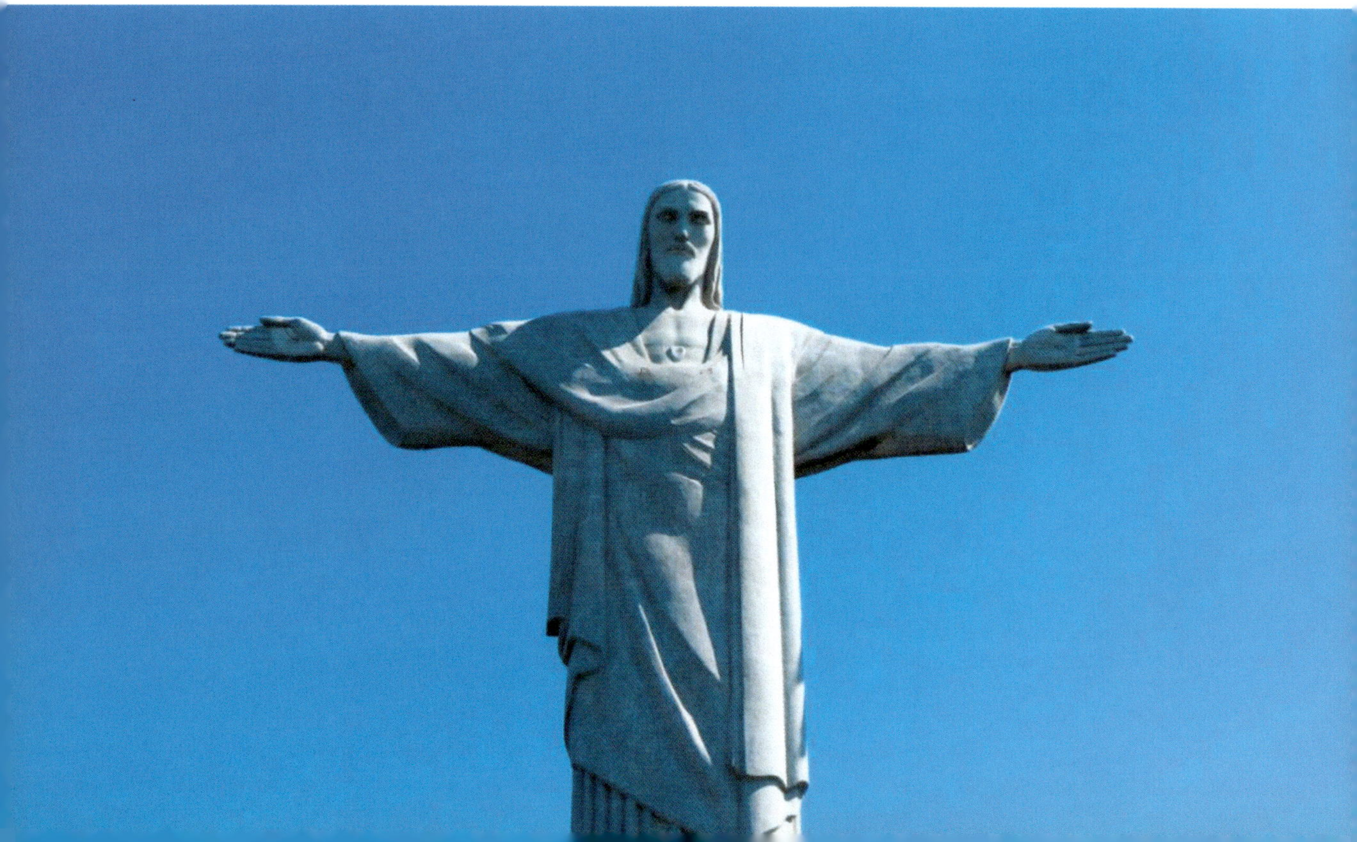

Brazil

I flew into Rio de Janeiro from Iguazu Falls in Argentina. I immediately felt the city was a wild place, if not a little dangerous. I stayed a few streets back from the Copacabana beach and wandered along to the Copacabana Hotel, a palatial white building right on the beach. That Barry Manilow tune kept playing annoyingly in my head. At the other end of the beach, you reach a small headland and, taking a right-hand short cut across it, you find yourself walking ninety degrees away from Copacabana. This is Ipanema beach and my internal music switched to a more agreeable Astrid Gilberto. These two famous beaches are distinguished by their own distinctive tiled promenades, just in case you forget which beach you are on after too many mojitos! Copacabana is a groovy wavey pattern and Ipanema is a retro spaceman-like theme out of the 70s.

I spent a couple of days seeing the sights. There was the obligatory trip on the cog train up to see Cristo Redentor, the 38m-tall concrete statue with his arms – each 14m long – stretched out wide. Here you get helicopter-like views across Rio to Sugar Loaf mountain.

I went to the then infamous Help nightclub. It had just been in the UK tabloids because of some premier league footballers' tour scandal. It was not hard to see why. It was very seedy, and it seemed everyone had escaped the crime-ridden Favelas for the night, probably hoping to fleece someone like me. Rio's famous beaches bounding the city are impressive but there is no way the waters are clean enough to swim in. The only peaceful place I found was the botanic gardens. I was starting to feel oppressed, so I jumped on a bus and headed a few hours up the coast to Búzios.

Búzios is the St Tropez of Brazil. Brigitte Bardot put it on the map in the 60s and the rich and famous have flocked there ever since. It was a breath of fresh air after Rio, with clear skies and crystal blue waters. There were smart restaurants with men fishing with nets right off the beach. I went out on boats and spent a couple of days on the beaches. There was no need to take food, everything was brought to you, as well as clothes from the hawkers plying their trade. It was the perfect end to my South American trip before heading back to Rio airport and returning to London.

Would I go back? Yes. To spend time in São Paulo, Florianópolis in the south, the modern capital Brasília, to see the tropical coast, Belém and go down the Amazon.

Cambodia

Cambodia is a must-see. Wedged between the more popular tourist destinations of Thailand and Vietnam, it is easily overlooked. Angkor Wat is the big draw, but even without this Cambodia and its people are beautiful. It's hard to believe that only a few decades ago the country was undergoing the ravages of war under Pol Pot and the Khmer Rouge.

I went with my sister, Molly. We arrived in the capital, Phnom Penh, where the French influence was still clearly visible. The corner cafés with the tables outside under sweeping awnings felt inspired by the grand Parisian cafes on boulevards of St Germain. Phnom Penh sits on the confluence of the Mekong and Tonle Sap rivers. During the rainy season, the floods of the larger Mekong force their way back upstream along the Tonle Sap in the City. So the river, uniquely, flows in either direction depending on the season. We met up with some friends at the Foreign Correspondents' Club, a truly colonial place, and had a great night out on the town.

We flew to Siem Reap, the town that is the gateway to the ruins of Angkor Wat. It has a sort of hippy trail feel about it where East meets western traveller, but it is no less of a place for it. We had fun nights out at some great restaurants and bars. It was true escapism.

The Angkor Buddhist temple complex is vast. Built in the 12th century during the Khmer Empire, it is the largest religious monument in the world, at 1.6km square. Each day we would go out in our moped-style tuk tuk and explore another area of the site. By the end of the day, we'd be a bit 'templed out', but by the following morning we were always ready for more. We spent three days there and it is still one of the best things I have ever seen.

We lazed away a few more days at Soukanville on the coast. On New Year's Eve, Molly's birthday, we had breakfast, lunch and dinner sitting on big bed-like structures right on the beach. Meals were interspersed with fresh mango dakaris, massages, manicures, pedicures, and all manner of other treatments available from local women walking along the beach. The evening ended with a cacophony of small fireworks that went on for hours all the way around the bay.

Would I go back? Probably. Just to do it all over again.

Canada

My first trip to Canada was to Vancouver with my then-girlfriend, Simone. We chartered a sailing boat and spent our entire trip, save shopping for provisions, on board. The good ship was called Paddington and was moored beneath a high railway bridge at Granville Island. The few ventures we did into Vancouver showed us that we were in the best spot in the city. There were great restaurants and a fabulous food market that offered pretty much all we needed for our voyage, including some great Canadian wines. Our plan was to sail through the Gulf Islands all the way to Victoria on the southern end of Vancouver Island and back. We pointed Paddington out of the harbour, and I handed Sims the wheel and told her she better learn how to sail in case I went over the side!

The backdrop in this part of the world is incredible, with forested wilderness right down to the water's edge and snow-capped mountains behind. By late afternoon we would anchor in still bays, grill the most amazing Pacific salmon steaks off the back of the boat and watch incredible sunsets. There was barely ever a need to go ashore. We saw dolphins but never orcas, and while we were disappointed, we were also slightly relieved as our boat wasn't much bigger than a killer whale. We meandered under sail through the chain of islands. On the last leg to Victoria, we were fighting a racing tide against us and after an hour of getting nowhere and the light fading, I took the counter-intuitive option of sailing straight for the lighthouse to calmer, shallower, but more hazardous water. We made it before dark.

Victoria is more Victorian than you would easily find in Britain. There are quaint tea rooms and Union Jacks flying everywhere. We mostly sat on the boat reading books, eating and drinking, and leaning over the side feeding harbour seals small fish from the bait shop on the dock. We bought a lot of bait. The morning we left Victoria for Vancouver, the thickest sea fog descended on us and we were suddenly vying with large ships on the sea border with US in the middle of the Haro Strait. You could barely see the bow and ships' horns would get louder as they got nearer. Massive dark shapes would emerge out of the mist.

This was before GPS was widely used, so our depth sounder and paper charts were our most reliable form of navigation. There was no zoom function or any chance of sighting a distinguishing mark on land or sea that would help determine our position. Canada has, by far, the longest coastline in the world and a lot of it is unmarked. It was a very challenging morning, but often it is the hardships you remember most vividly when travelling. After a few hours, the fog cleared, and we were greeted with a glorious sunny day. We made it back to port the next day, stayed our last night on board, and flew back to London.

It is normally your first trip to a country that you remember most. I went back to Canada several times, nearly always on business to Calgary with a ski trip tacked on. Other trips took me to Toronto and back to Vancouver, but it is the skiing in Banff, Sunshine and Lake Louise that I now mostly associate with Canada. It is the great northern frontier, and the people are incredibly friendly. If it were not so darned cold, I would spend more time there.

Would I go back? Yes. To Montreal, Halifax Nova Scotia, to ski Whistler and maybe to heli-ski.

Cayman Islands

The Cayman Islands are not counted in my 80 countries because, like Bermuda, they are a British Overseas Territory. But any sign of Britishness ends on the top left-hand quarter of the territory's flag. Once there, you would swear you were in a US holiday resort. I was here because it was the only viable way from the US to Cuba. Relations between the two countries had not fully thawed, so a neutral stopping point was needed. Seemingly deliberately, the flights did not line up, so you had to stay overnight. I decided to make the most of it and stay a couple of nights, hire a car, and explore the main island. I had hoped to ride horses in the sea and swim with rays, but the weather was too rough.

On departure, I arrived at the airport unusually early to find my flight was delayed by a couple of hours. Everyone was sitting inside on a cold concrete floor. I noticed the top of some yacht masts out the windows so went for a walk with my boarding pass, and arrived at a marina where I had a delicious lunch by the water at the George Town Yacht Club. A large yacht arrived into the port and I took their lines at the dock. It was an Australian couple who were sailing around the world and they invited me on board for a drink. I saw a plane fly in, looked at my phone to see I would be boarding in 30 minutes. I wandered back to the airport thinking some airport lounges are better than others.

Would I go back? Probably not.

MERCADO CENTRAL
MERCADO CENTRAL
MERCADO CENTRAL
MERCADO CENTRAL
MERCADO CENTRAL
550
495

Chile

Chile is that long thin country that stretches over 2,500 miles down the Pacific Ocean to Cape Horn and is the closest land mass to Antarctica. I travelled on a bus through a high pass from Argentina across the Andes and all the way to the atmospheric city of Valparaiso on the coast. It is a wonderful place with brightly coloured wooden buildings perched on the hillsides all around the bay. I stayed at a pension high up and looked over the port each morning eating breakfast. The terrain meant lots of climbing steps or using the fun rattly old funiculars servicing several of the neighbourhoods. Wandering around the old buildings was a delight. I spent a day at Viña del Mar, the coastal resort to the north with big beaches, and went to the amazing gardens there.

The bus trip to Santiago took me through mile after mile of vineyards. The capital sits in a valley where the wall of snow-capped Andes runs from as far as the eye can see to the north east, to the east and then disappears to the south. It's a stunning setting for what is a great city. The streets are alive. A highlight was visiting the Mercado Central. I had been told in Argentina to have the 'locos' there, considered a delegacy. It turned out they were abalone, which we used to dive for as kids, finding the large mother of pearl-like shells and cutting them off rocks underwater to sell to Chinese restaurants for $20 for a big bag. We thought we'd hit the jackpot and so did they. So here, several thousand miles across the Pacific, I found myself wondering what all the fuss was about. Chile was a relatively short and sweet trip, but worth it. I left to fly back to Buenos Aires.

Would I go Back? Probably. Patagonia and Tierra del Fuego in the far south.

46 CHINA

China

I went to mainland China in 1988 and spent several weeks there, mostly in the south west of the country. This was still very much a time of communist China, with no real signs of any wealth. The bulk of the population were peasant farmers even though there were over a hundred cities with populations greater than a million people. The country will now have changed beyond all recognition and I am glad I went when I did.

I flew to Hong Kong from Oz with my college friend Johnny, and we caught the train to the neighbouring city of Guangzhou (Canton). There was such a stark difference after the outwardly capitalist swanky Hong Kong. On our first night we ate in a snake restaurant. The locals took great joy in choosing the most tangled live snake among all the others in a big glass wall to ceiling vault in the restaurant. A member of staff would have to go and get it to take to the kitchen. Much to the neighbouring tables' disappointment, we just said we wanted to try snake. A little while later, some fried fritter-like pieces were brought to us. It tasted like chicken.

Chinese cities back then were drab grey places and we wanted to get to the interior. We got a boat up the Li river towards Guilin and stopped at Yangshou, a place that was just being discovered by travellers. It was freezing so we bought big Chinese communist coats. The food was limited but good. Duck and pineapple seemed to be the local dish with fresh mandarin juice or Tsingtao beer. The countryside from here to Guilin is the most spectacular geography I have ever seen. You pinch yourself at the shape of the mountains. A Swiss girl we met called Florence travelled with us for a while. We rode bikes everywhere and one day rode into a place to see a temple. There were dozens of tour buses and we heard someone shouting our names from across the street. It turned out to be a guy called Eddie Wong. He was a Hong Kong Chinese student from our university class at King's College in London on a tour from Hong Kong in jeans and a western waterproof jacket. He just could not believe it was us chewing on sticks of sugar cane in communist coats. Johnny had less time than me, so he headed north to Beijing while I headed deeper into the interior.

I took a long slow train from Guilin to the city of Kunming in Yunnan province. Getting a train ticket was always a challenge. There would be several thousand people on a train. My only advantage was I was tall and therefore a noticeably blond head above a crush of a sea of black. Occasionally the authorities would help me out. The scenery of mountains and multi-coloured crop fields passed us by from the train for a couple of days. Kunming was a dream place compared to where we had been. It had an almost Scandinavian feel. It was clean and heavily treed, unlike other Chinese cities. There were lovely parks and lakes and the people seemed less oppressed. It was teaming with children. I remember walking past a school breaking up for the day and shouting 'ni how' to a group of children staring at me. One shouted 'haylo' back and before I knew it I had a trail of children following me down the road on their way home, shouting a chorus of hellos. Every time I wheeled round to look at them there was an even bigger sea of faces with bright white teeth and black bowl haircuts, laughing as if they were being tickled. I was something different for them and they were a welcome change from the general Chinese conservatism for me.

I flew south to a place called Xishuangbanna. It was a small autonomous region bordered by Burma and Laos. Here one really felt a freedom and less under the watchful eye of the Chinese authorities. It was deep in the jungle on the banks of the Mekong River, and an hour-long flight saved me three days by road. Our plane was like an old DC3 and when I went to the airport a few days later to head back to Kunming, the flight was delayed due to engine trouble. The ground staff took the cover off and got a load of spanners out and started working on the engine on the tarmac in front of us. The day turned to night, I restarted reading the book I had just finished, and the following day, 28 hours after our scheduled departure, they got the engine going. It stalled a few times and then the staff pushed us to get on the plane quickly before it stalled again. We were tearing down the runway with the engine seemingly missing the odd beat but somehow, we managed to get airborne. I looked down the aisle and the door into the cockpit was left swinging open and shut to give a stroboscopic view of a high mountain range through the windscreen. We did a sharp bank, flew alongside the mountains until we gained enough height to fly over them. The woman in the window seat next to me had live chickens in her bag.

Having got a bit of a taste of adventure and a feeling I could slip under the radar of the Chinese authorities, I wanted to see if I could get into the disputed territory of Tibet, which was known on the traveller circuit to be very difficult but not impossible. There were stories of people who had done it. I got a bus to Dali on the edge of Erhai Lake. There were roadworks all the way there, with workers filling large potholes with rocks. Looking out the window of the bus on the high mountain roads you would see the wreckage of other buses lying at the bottom of deep ravines. We had already had one head-on collision, and everyone seemed to laugh when it happened.

Dali was a great place, inhabited by the minority Dai people. They dressed in bright colours, looked, and behaved so differently to the herd of Han Chinese that make up over 90% of the nation's population in the rest of the country. The town had three tall pagodas, amazing street markets and great food. There'd been little English spoken anywhere east of Guilin, but here it was non-existent. If I wanted to eat, I had to learn. One time I went out to the kitchen and pointed to all the baskets of green vegetables and did a mixing movement with my hands and pointed to a big bowl. A little while later at the table I got 6 big bowls each with a different vegetable. I found the children were the best teachers. They spoke more slowly, were more patient, and less weary of me. My Mandarin was getting better, but in this region the dialect would change dramatically from place to place. All you had learned the day before was unintelligible in the next town the day after.

I headed north on the long road towards my dream of seeing Lhasa, the capital of Tibet. I had several hundred miles ahead of me to get there. Lijian was the next place and already the buildings were beginning to take on a Tibetan feel. The next place was Shangri-La in the Diqing Tibetan Autonomous Prefecture. I was starting to struggle to find means of transport. The Chinese have a great word 'Mayo' – which seems to mean, 'I don't have, go away, sorry, I don't want, not here etc.' Increasingly no one wanted to help me, the military presence had increased, and the blond westerner was starting to stick out like a sore thumb. It was easy to forget that China had only opened to tourists a few years earlier and this part of China was not for tourists. Reluctantly, I gave up my quest and headed back to within range of the radar.

Chengdu is the capital of Sichuan province, famed for its cuisine. I went to the zoo, saw pandas, and visited some nearby temples. But being corralled here as a tourist was not really doing it for me and the draw of cruising down the Yangtse River beckoned. It was a bit out of my budget, but it would make up for not getting deeper into Tibet. I stretched to do it. I made my way to the city of Chongqing (Chungking), at that time a sprawling drab, grey place. Chiang Kai-Shek fled the communists to here. When I look at pictures of it now as a modern city, it is beyond belief. The Jialing River joins the Yangtse in the centre of Chongqing creating a peninsula of land where you can walk over a hill from one great river to another. The posts on the jetties in the fast-flowing river left wakes like those from large outboard engines.

We boarded a large river boat here and started our voyage down the Yangtse. The highlight was sailing through the Yangtse Gorges. One of the world's biggest hydro-electro projects was being planned then and has since been completed. It flooded the gorges, displacing millions of people in the process. We were lucky to see something that is now hundreds of feet under water. There were about six classes of accommodation on board but as westerners we had the run of the ship. We would sit in big leather armchairs in the old lounge up front near the bridge. It had metal framed windows and heavy curtains. Here, away from the crush of the hundreds of passengers, we could chat with Chinese generals, and politicians. I think they may have been the same thing. We would watch the life on the riverbanks glide by and occasionally step out onto the deck to get closer to it. I remember seeing chain gangs of prisoners quarrying rock and traders in tiny vessels taking their wares from one side of the fast flowing river to the other.

I made some good traveller friends on board, including John and Vita from Canada. We left the boat, walked up these massive stone steps to look for somewhere to stay. It was late at night and we could not find anywhere. Hotels were few and far between back then, it was mostly guest houses and of course there was no internet. We ended up staying in a wing of an old hospital there. And the name of this place was… Wuhan.

We trained up to Beijing, saw the Forbidden City and Tiananmen Square and the queue to see Chairman Mao Zedong's embalmed body. This was before the Tiananmen Square Massacre of uprising students. Back then Beijing was a city of mostly low-lying buildings with dimly lit streets at night. One night on the way back to our guest house after dinner, Canadian John and I jumped up on a sofa perched on a bicycle to be driven home in style. By day we rode bikes everywhere. The biggest problem was finding which bike was yours when you had parked it outside a shop.

My last thing to see was The Great Wall, apparently the only man-made object on earth that is visible with a naked eye from the moon. In the words of Chairman Mao himself, 'he who has not been to The Great Wall is not a true man.' I got the train back to Hong Kong. My trip around China was done.

Would I go back? Maybe. Shanghai and – as much as it pains me to say that it is part of China – Lhasa, Tibet.

Costa Rica

Most people go to Costa Rica to go on some eco-friendly kind of holiday. Not us. I needed to be out of both the UK and the US early one April for a week while moving back to the UK to live. I phoned up an old friend, Biggles, who has probably been to twice as many countries as me, and I asked him if he fancied a whistle stop tour through Central America. Like me, in those days, he was always en-route to somewhere and could normally take a detour. He flew to Houston, where I showed him the sights and we agreed we had just a week to get from Panama to San Salvador. We dubbed it, the 'throw-money-at-it' trip because of our need to cover a lot of ground in a short time. Also, we wanted to spend the most time in Nicaragua, the next country on from Costa Rica.

We flew into the Capital San Jose, had a night on the town and flew out the next day to Nicaragua. I would love to tell you I went on an amazing eco-friendly trip in the jungle, but I didn't. The best thing we saw on our night on the town was the street paintings, most of which were painted on corrugated tin fences.

Would I go back? Probably yes, on that eco-friendly holiday in the jungle and maybe to surf.

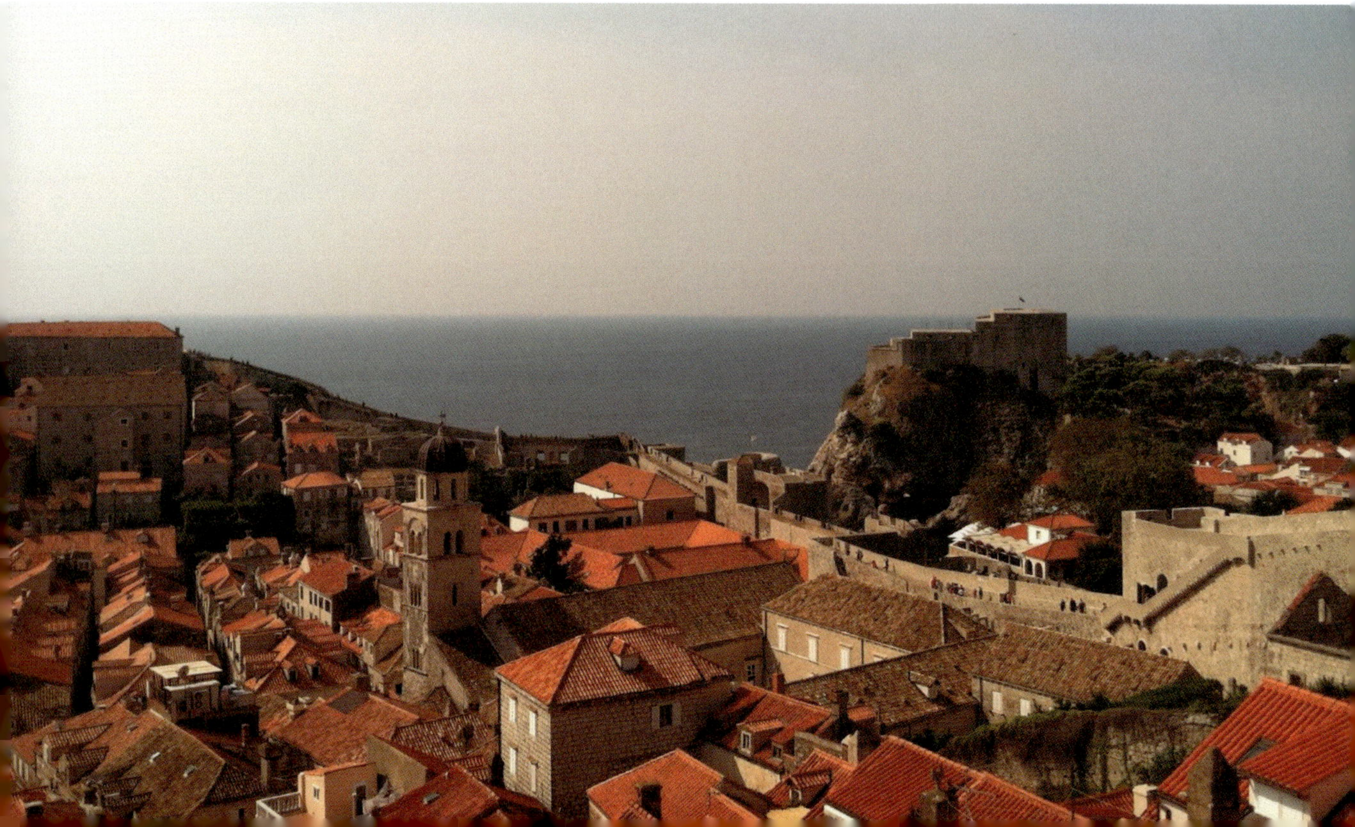

Croatia

I travelled by train across Croatia in the 1980s when it was part of Yugoslavia. The train stopped in Zagreb. I don't remember getting out, so for me that trip doesn't count.

My proper trip to Croatia was short and sweet. Having arrived by train in the port town of Ploče, from Bosnia and Herzegovina, I took a couple of connecting ferries to the Island of Korčula. The main town, Korčula, is a smaller version of Dubrovnik. It was a joy to stay there a couple of nights, wander round the town and sit outside in restaurants.

I caught the bus down to Dubrovnik and spent a couple of nights staying within the walls of the old city. It was late season, so the city was not over-run with tourists pouring off cruise ships, but it was still busy in the daytime. I wandered around the ramparts and found a gem of a bar, Buza, perched over the sea on the outside of the walls, and accessed through a hole in the wall. Despite it being touristy, the old walled city is really something. For me, Dubrovnik came alive at night. The tourists mostly cleared out and the stone walkways, polished by so many visitors, reflected a lovely light. That is the time to wander round the old city within the walls.

Would I go back? Definitely, to sail around the islands of the Dalmatian coast.

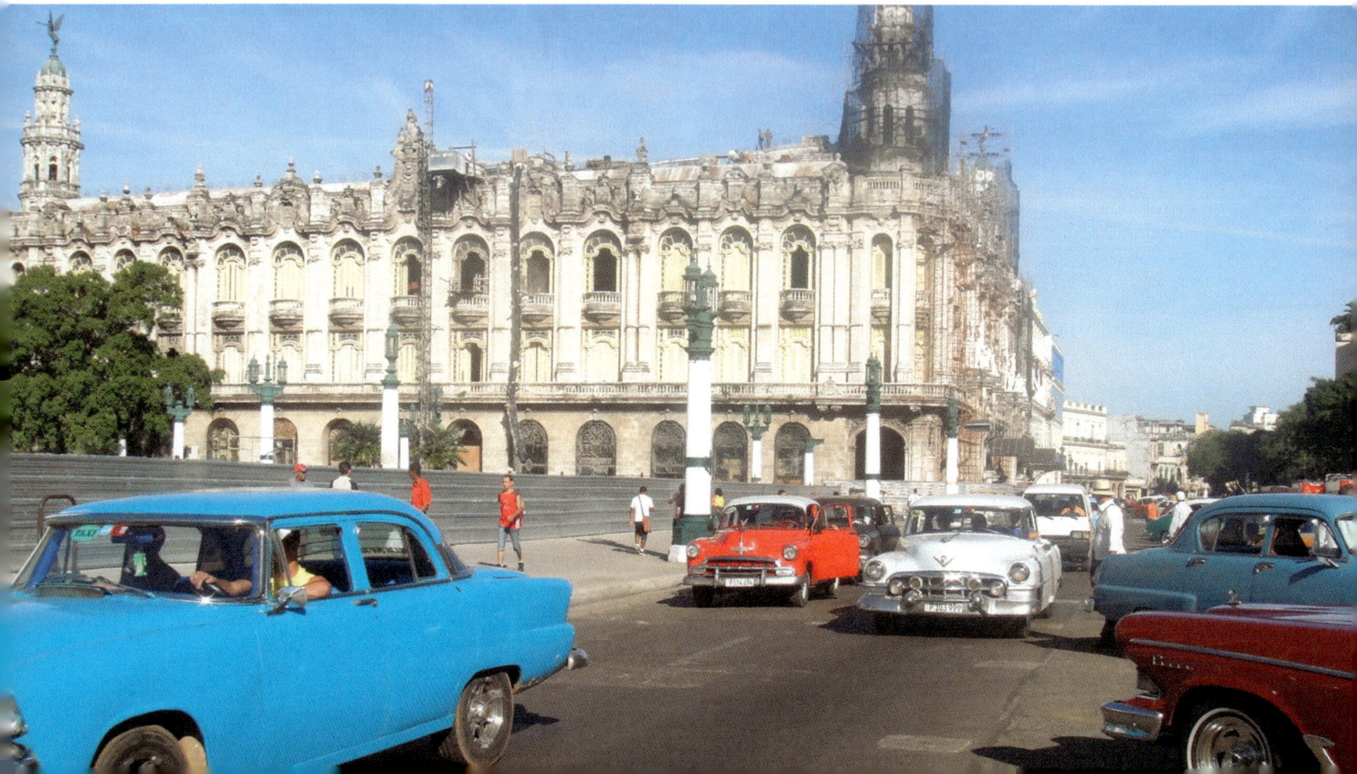

Cuba

I joined my friends Johnny and Sarah and their children, Poppy, Flo and Charlie in Cuba for a Christmas holiday. I fell in love with Havana from the moment I arrived. It started with the cars. The streets are filled with beautiful old American cars from yesteryear, many of them lovingly restored convertibles operating as taxis. You would hail these beauties just to go for a ride in one. The old buildings might have been crumbling but the streets were alive. My friends were down on the south coast in Cienfuegos, so I saved Havana for later and went down to meet them. The journey of a few hundred kilometres took us around the edge of the Bay of Pigs. It was here that an American invasion sponsored by John F. Kennedy failed in 1961. Cuba then ran to the USSR, which led to the Cuban Missile Crisis the following year. These events strengthened the Cuban people's love of Fidel Castro and their general distrust of America. Despite being only 90 miles from Key West in Florida, deep divisions remained between the two countries when I visited.

The few hotels that Cuba has are generally expensive so the way to go is to stay with people who have registered their homes with the government as 'casas particulares.' There aren't many restaurants either, so you usually eat in these homes. It is a great way to meet local people and they just ring a casa in the next place you're going to and it is booked for you. There was virtually no mobile phone signal, let alone internet, anywhere we travelled. There was just one hotel in Havana where you could buy internet access by the half hour. When it did work, it was very slow.

Cuba is a dichotomy in so many ways. The communist system has left it alienated from the western world. It is generally poor and there are real shortages of food. For us it varied from adequate to barely edible. But the people seem happy and the country has one of the highest levels of education and healthcare in the world. Despite the relative poverty, life expectancy is higher than in the US.

At Cienfuegos, we stayed on a small neck of land, Punta Gorda, jutting out into the bay. It was relaxed with some lovely art deco houses and a couple of reasonable restaurants. We moved on further down the coast to the historical colonial town of Trinidad. This place is a delight with its cobbled streets and beautiful neo-baroque buildings. There was music and dancing in the streets virtually everywhere you went. We hired an old blue Chevrolet station wagon and driver to take us to what turned out to be a dilapidated beach resort hotel for New Year's Eve. My eldest goddaughter, Poppy and I, sat up all night in an empty hotel bar drinking rum waiting to see in midnight. We played quiz games, like 'Name the ten countries in the world with only four letters.'

We headed back to the welcome liveliness of Havana, where we stayed in a great big house and had some fun nights out. We went to a restaurant that had great reviews called Porto Habana. It was in someone's apartment on the 11th floor of a residential block. We bumped into an old business colleague from London who was also dining there.

I had the last few days in Havana to myself and it was every bit as good as my first impression had led me to hope. I went to some great bars and cafes, saw live music at the Buena Vista Social Night. I went for drinks at the imposing Hotel Nacional where there were great old black and white pictures of Castro's meetings there, as well as the revolution's Che Guevara, whose image has since become a ubiquitous counter-culture symbol. I also paid homage to Ernest Hemingway, lunching on the roof of the hotel he had made his home. Go to Cuba before it changes greatly.

Would I go back? Probably not, I fear that if I return it will have lost a lot of its charm.

CZECH REPUBLIC

Czech Republic

Prague is my only experience of the Czech Republic. My first trip was a city break where I did a lot of walking. The few trips I have made since have all been for business.

It is a touristy place, so my favourite times to walk around were at night or very early in the morning. Having the medieval Charles Bridge, with its classical statues, all to yourself at dawn is a completely different experience to being there during the daytime when it is crawling with tourists. Similarly, the vista up the full length of Wenceslas Square to the Národní Museum is best appreciated at night. And there is no denying that sitting out in the Old Town Square in the evening, enjoying a Czech beer while looking at the spooky gothic towers and waiting for the next chiming of the astronomical clock is a good experience.

Would I go back? Probably, on business.

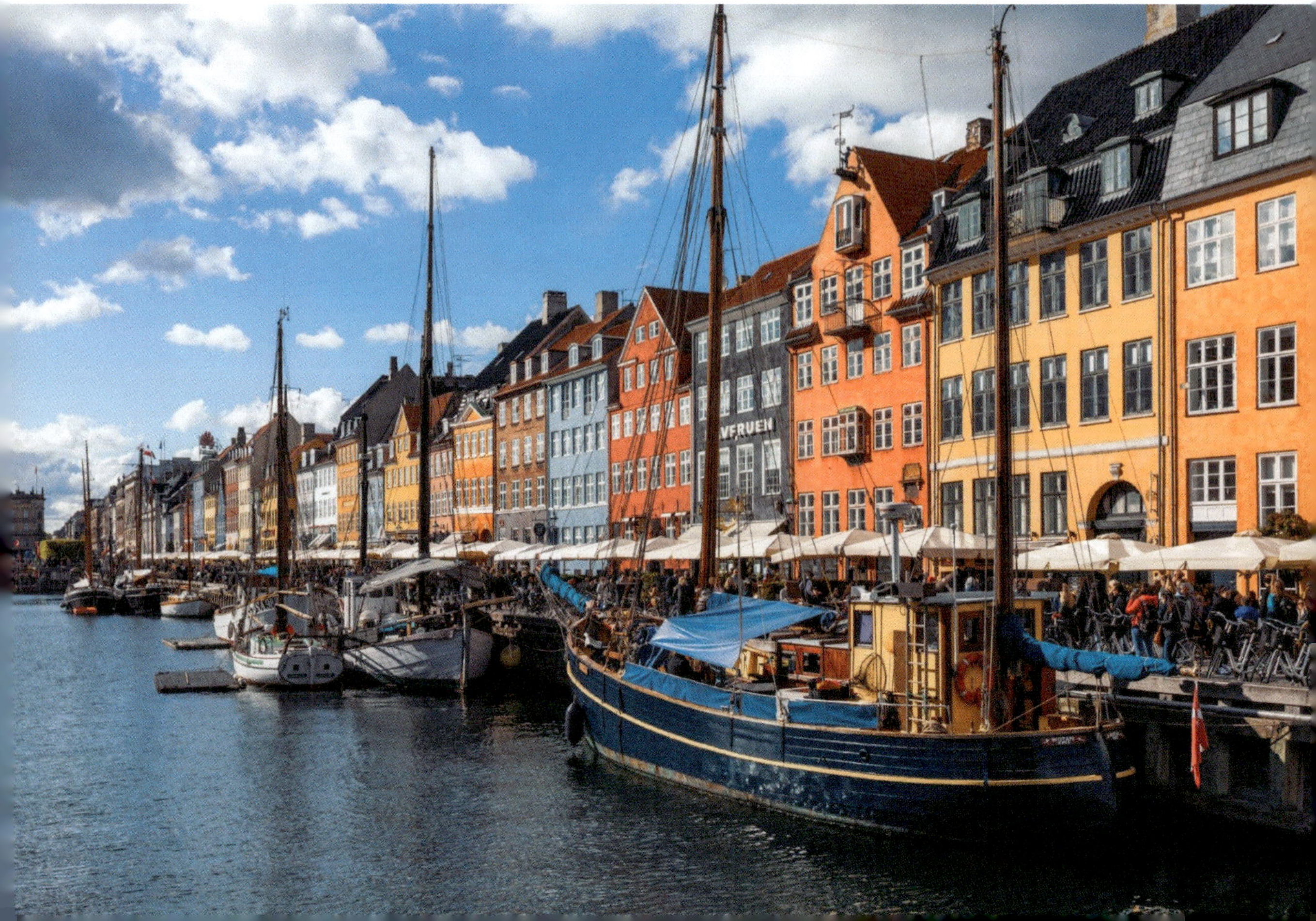
VFRUEN

Denmark

My first trip to Denmark was while inter-railing in the late eighties. I had an invite to visit. There is a model of the Greek Parthenon in the Metropolitan Museum of Art in New York, which stands on a plinth about four feet high, compelling you to stoop down and look through the columns into the inside. As I did this, there was a pair of sparkling eyes staring in from the other side. We stood up and laughed and got chatting. She was Danish and we ended up having lunch in the Met Café. I went to her American family in NY for dinner as well. We swapped a few postcards and I found myself staying with her family in Copenhagen some months later.

Having a local to show me around for a few days was brilliant. We walked and walked. I remember being disappointed with the tiny Little Mermaid statue but hugely impressed with the Gefion Fountain nearby. I am not sure how this dramatic statue of a tall goddess ploughing the sea with four huge oxen and water spraying everywhere lost out to a small girl sitting on a rock as the city's iconic statue. Also memorable was the old Copenhagen Stock Exchange: I admire the crocodiles with their tails so originally wrapped round the main spire every time I visit. It is such a green city, and many of the trees are cleverly shaped. We went to the canal at Nyhavn for drinks in the Scandinavian twilight and the amazing Tivoli. I boarded a train for Sweden. This was before the bridge across the Baltic, so the train rolled onto a ferry at Helsingør. The Kronborg castle stands here, immortalized as Elsinore in Shakespeare's Hamlet.

I have been back to Copenhagen several times since, mostly on business. On these trips, my socialising was typically with clients. A herring smorgasbord lunch sitting in the sun by the Nyhavn canal is a favourite. While your first trip to a country is often the most memorable, I do have fond memories of subsequent visits. One time I met friends and we spent a weekend cycling north from the City.

I also spent time in Arhus and Silkeborg on the mainland. More recently I sailed from Amsterdam to Copenhagen, skirting the sandy dunes in the Baltic sea to the south of the islands of Lolland and Zealand. There are lots of windfarms all the way up the coast which guided us into Copenhagen, where we docked, dined, wined and slept on board at The Royal Danish Yacht Club.

I love the Danes. They are straight talking, fun and funny and they enjoy life. It is no surprise that the concept of Hygge emanates from here. There is no word in English for 'encompassing a feeling of cosy contentment and well-being through enjoying the simple things in life'. But it perfectly sums up the Danes' contentment and their relaxed nature.

Would I go back? Yes. To the northern mainland tip at Skane and to ride bikes through the Danish Riviera in North Zealand.

Dominican Republic

I was at a conference in Chicago one November. It was freezing. I texted my friend Biggles who was at another conference in Miami. He said, 'come down here, the weather is great.' Miami is the airline gateway to the Caribbean, so we decided to escape to the Dominican Republic which makes up the eastern half of Hispaniola.

Santo Domingo, the capital, is where Christopher Columbus first hit the Americas in 1492. Being the first Spanish settlement in the new world, some buildings are very old. In contrast, the austere mausoleum-like monument which commemorates Columbus's landing is a modern monstrosity. After that we almost passed out on nicotine fumes in a cigar factory. We found a good restaurant and quite a few seedy bars and got fleeced in a casino. We were told it was dangerous to walk around at night, so we taxied. We asked one driver to take us to a fun bar and he drove us to a compound. The gates were shut behind us and there were guards armed with sub machine guns. Biggles felt we should see inside. I said, 'there's only one time to get out of here, and that time is now.' We did an about-turn and left what was either a brothel or a drug den. From then on, we found our own bars.

We headed for the beach along the coast to San Pedro de Macoris. It was a welcome break from the city and we stayed a few days before heading back to Miami and going our separate ways.

Would I go back? Probably not, though maybe as a route into the even more dangerous Haiti, which holds some interest for me.

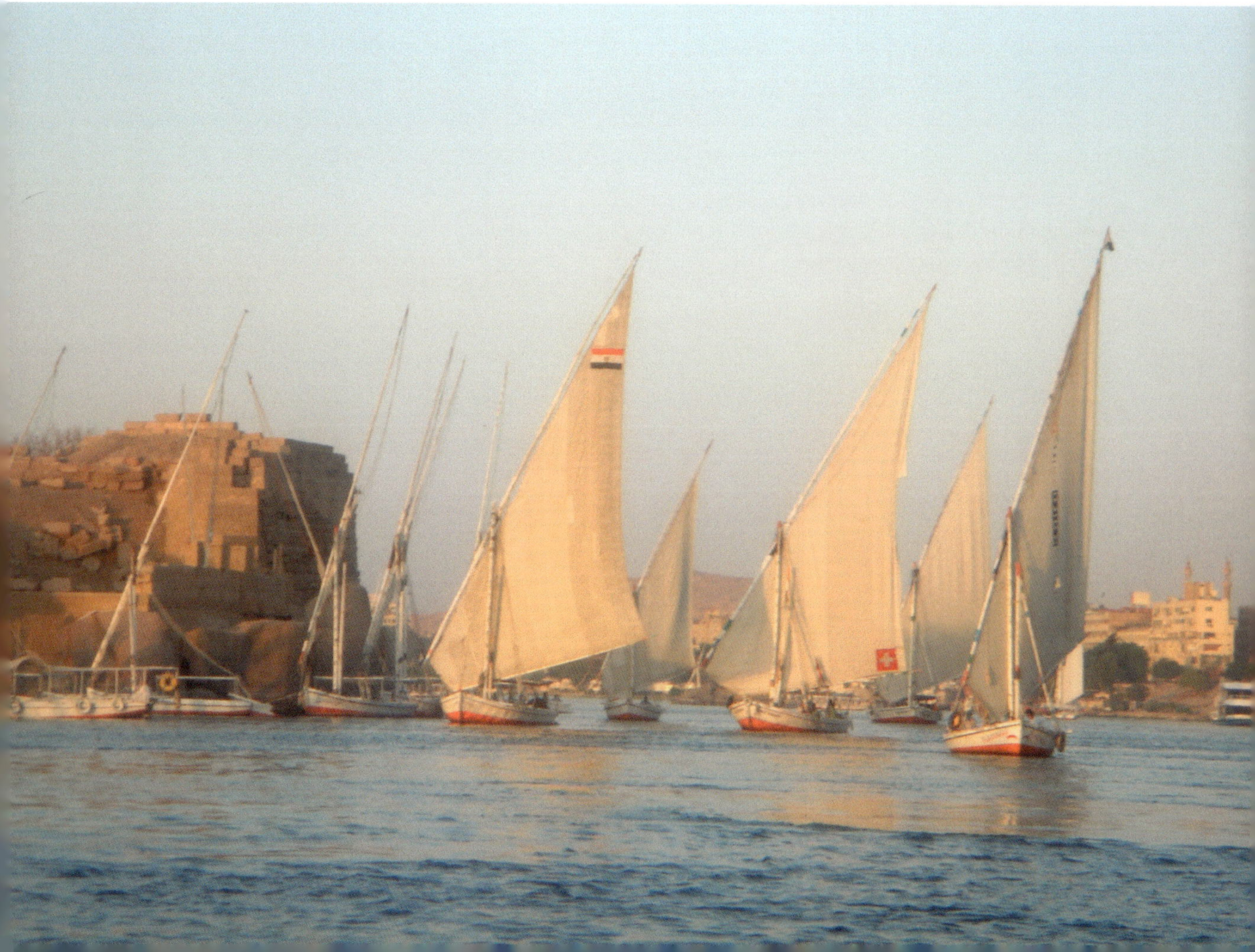

Egypt

One of my annual conferences was being held in Sharm El-Sheikh. I asked my parents if they would like to spend a couple of weeks in Egypt beforehand. We had talked about going down the Nile one day and this was our best opportunity. We landed in Cairo and caught a connecting flight to Aswan with the plan of a cruise down the Nile to Luxor. I had arranged for us to stay in the Old Cataract Hotel, where former guests included royalty and heads of state. Agatha Christie wrote and set much of Death on the Nile here. It is hard to think of a hotel balcony anywhere else in the world that beats this one. Perched on a strategic bend in the river, you watch feluccas waft by behind the palms, with large golden dunes on the opposite riverbank as a backdrop. As the colours deepen in the setting sun, you are forced to delay going to dinner and order more drinks.

On our first day we walked along the river to the dock where we chose our boat, a felucca called 'Aswan Moon.' In fact, we chose our crew. They were the least pushy and had big welcoming warm smiles. We agreed what seemed to be the going rate and they accepted my one condition; that I could helm the boat. Those cruises on the river were amazing. We couldn't get enough. We went every day. My mother kept asking them if they could sail us the 150 miles to Luxor in their old wooden boat with no cabin and just a bucket. They would have and I think she would have.

The other draw of Aswan was the trip a few hours south to Abu Simbel close to the Sudanese border. There had been terrorist incidents in Egypt targeting tourists, so we had to go in convoy. As the lead vehicle, we had an armed soldier in the front. Things can't have been that dangerous as he always seemed to leave his machine gun on the floor whenever he got out of the minibus. Abu Simbel encompasses two incredible feats of engineering. The first is the mere twenty years it took to build under Ramesses the Great in 1265 BC. The second was the four years in the 1960s during which they cut the temples up into 20-ton blocks, and then moved these 200m to a spot 65m higher in order to avoid the temples being engulfed by the flooding of Lake Nassar. The iconic four statues at the front of the main temple are each 20m high. You marvel at both the original construction of the temples over 3000 years ago and at how they managed to save them only 40 years ago.

Aswan also had some impressive temples. Any obelisk you have seen will almost certainly have come from the flawless stone found here. We were sad to leave Aswan, with its lovely people, good food and lots to see. We boarded a cross between a large ferry and a cruise ship and set sail for Luxor. The trip took a few days with the occasional stop. The temples at Edfu were stunning and a reminder that there is more to Egypt than The Pyramids and Luxor. The views along the Nile were timeless, the combination of fresh water and a hot climate providing a lush landscape all the way along its banks.

Luxor was much more touristy than Aswan, but it was still great. The temples of Karnak are on a huge scale. You wander through colonnades in awe of what must be the most enormous stone pillars on the planet. We went to the Luxor Hotel for tea and there was more chartering of feluccas. We found a crew who were keen to do some racing against other tourists. Such fun.

We made a couple of trips to The Valley of the Kings. The tomb of Ramesses VI was a complete surprise. You walk down a long hall into the tomb and enter brightly painted stone walls and ceilings. It is like it was painted yesterday, not 2,500 years ago. On our last day in the valley, there was quite a commotion with officials and TV crews at Tutankhamun's tomb, which was closed as Tut's mummy was being moved for the tomb's refurbishment. I found the man in charge of operations and explained that we were from Australia and had come a hell of long way specially to see it. He wasn't that sympathetic but a note from my wallet helped him understand our plight and we had the temple all to ourselves for a peaceful ten minutes before arriving back outside to a media frenzy.

We took the train to Cairo and checked into the El Gezirah Hotel, set on an island in the middle of the Nile. The infinity pool illusion didn't quite work with the dramatic difference in colour to the river, but it was a lovely spot to escape the hustle and bustle of the city. We went to the Pyramids at Giza of course. I climbed up into the tomb of the Great Pyramid and we went to the Sphinx. A visit to the National Museum makes you realise that every Tutankhamun travelling exhibition you have seen is just a fraction of what was buried with him in his tomb. Room after room of it tells you that the treasures found in his tomb are nearly all here.

My parents headed to Alexandria and I went on to my conference in Sharm el Sheikh on the Sinai Peninsula, which was a blast. There I did a bit of snorkelling in the Red Sea and we had some fun dinners. We met up again at Cairo Airport and flew home. It was a really great trip.

Would I go back? Maybe, to go diving in the Red Sea.

El Salvador

El Salvador was the last country on my whistle-stop tour through Central America with my friend Biggles. We left the bus in Honduras and crossed the border. There were no onward transport options, so we walked into town and had lunch. After about an hour we saw a hand-painted yellow car pull up, which looked like an attempt at being a taxi. The driver expected we wanted a taxi to take us to the border: when we said we wanted to go to the capital San Salvador, about 5hrs away, he struggled to compute a price. Fuel was his main concern so we said we would pay for the fuel and from memory we offered $100. His smile suggested that was a good price…for him. He was shy but a good driver, the most important attribute on the pothole-riven main highway.

We had no idea where we were going in the capitol but the Marriot sign high up on a building guided us in. We had our last night out on the town but didn't want to push our luck. San Salvador has one of the highest crime rates in Latin America, and that is saying something. Gang violence between rival gangs and towards the police and the military is an overhang of the civil war that raged from the late 70s to the early 90s.

I left for the airport in the morning driving along roads through dense, lush vegetation. Panama to here in a week had been a bit of a rush, but a very fun trip.

Would I go back? Not really.

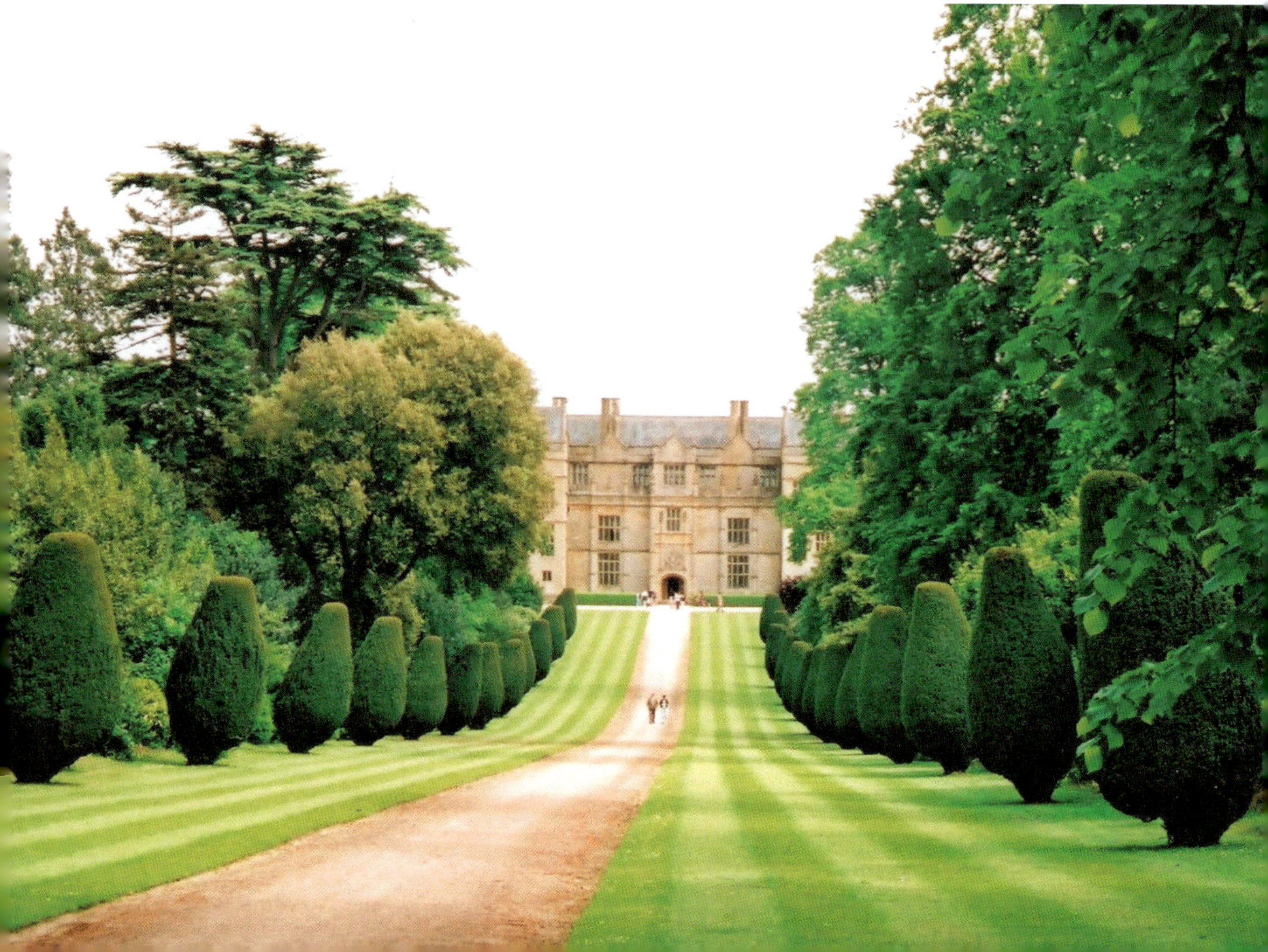

England

England is the country where I have spent most of my life. This almost makes it the hardest country to be objective about in terms of travelling. My first trip here was as a tourist, aged thirteen, with my parents as part of our trip around Europe for six months. It was 1976, the year of the drought, and I was starting to wonder about England being a cold wet place.

We arrived in London and stayed near Baker Street. We walked and walked and walked. I remember vividly seeing all the things that I had seen in books and on TV back home. Things like Big Ben, Trafalgar Square, Buckingham Palace, and St Pauls cathedral. Best of all was the Post Office Tower, the building the big cat climbed up in the kids' TV comedy, the Goodies. London is a great place for a holiday when you're a child. There were double decker buses you could jump on and off while they were moving. (I still go for the front seat upstairs.) There were black taxis where you could sit facing backwards on the folding dickie seat, and pedalos you could ride on the lakes in the parks.

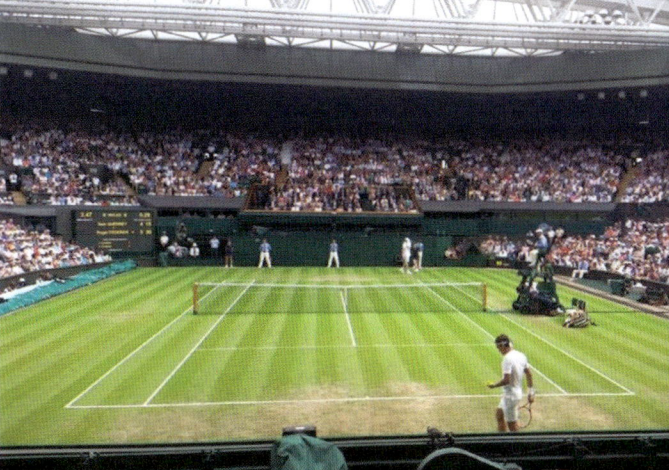

We also went to Hamleys, the massive toy store. London is, and always will be, a truly great city.

We bought a second-hand car from a garage in Hammersmith to drive round Europe – and sold it back to them for £200 less six months later. I recognised the place when I was walking past it over thirty years later. We drove out of London in our blue Hillman Hunter into the depths of the English countryside. The landscape was very parched from the drought. We spent a lot of time in the south east of England. Mum and dad were on a mission to buy oak furniture to take back to Oz, so we spent a lot of time sitting outside antique shops. These shops fill me with dread even now.

We took the car ferry to the Isle of Wight and visited the model village at Godshill, followed by a trip to Cowes to see the Royal Yacht Squadron. The sailing shops in the high street sold us some gifts to take to our sailing friends back home. This bit of the trip was fortuitous: although the four of us ended up living on different sides of the world in the following forty years, we now all live near to each other in Cowes.

We drove north to York and on to Scotland, hoping to see the Loch Ness monster, and then back down through the lakes before getting the car ferry across the channel to the continent, where we travelled for a few months. It was winter when we returned to England. The illusions of it being a hot country were shattered. We drove down to a wet and cold Cornwall for a few days before flying home to Melbourne.

My next trip to England was three years later to join my parents who had sold up in Oz to buy an English Pub in the Cotswolds. It's a picture postcard countryside there, but for me it was dead of any life and about as far as you can get from the sea in England. I missed the beach and mucking about on the water. So I escaped and went up to the bright lights and big city as soon as I could. I studied engineering at Kings College London and ended up living and working in probably the world's greatest city for over thirty years.

There were lots of holidays and weekends away seeing England. But most of them involved being near the sea. This meant all the coastal counties and mostly out to the south west, Hampshire, Dorset, Devon and Cornwall. We would do annual camping trips to the wilder shores of north Cornwall. I holidayed in the Scilly Islands a couple of times, where the sea is almost the blue of the Caribbean. There were visits to – and some stays in – stately homes with amazing gardens. All the things you would expect in England's green and pleasant land.

A big part of my time out of London was spent sailing. We had a 25ft boat in my twenties and I had a more serious 38ft racing boat in my forties. I sailed those boats around the Solent countless times and down to the West Country many times for cruising holidays and regattas over the years. The Solent is the body of water that lies between the English mainland and the Isle of Wight. There is a sandbank in the middle of it and once a year, when it is at its most prominent, a cricket match is held there. This would only happen in England.

Living in London provided so many fun times and experiences. It is hard to think of another city anywhere that offers so much. The theatre, concerts, museums, art galleries, top restaurants, swanky bars, and great pubs.

London is also a green city with many great parks and gardens. And there is a surprising amount of outdoor living and al fresco dining on long summer evenings. I had countless dinner parties in my own roof garden there.

Samuel Johnston famously said, 'When a man is tired of London, he is tired of life,' and I always imagined I would never tire of it. But after a year living in a high-rise apartment in New York City, I found on my return to London that I was hankering for more open space and the sea. I bought a house in Cowes, on the Isle of Wight, and after a few years here, I am convinced that it is the best place to live in England. It has the best climate too. The Island is England in miniature, but it also has quite a different feel from the mainland. Come and see for yourself.

Would I go back? It's where I live

Estonia

There was a conference in Helsinki and I decided to fly to Tallinn for the weekend beforehand and get the fast ferry across the Baltic Sea to Finland. It was a fleeting trip, but I enjoyed walking around the cobblestoned old town. I was surprised at how many medieval buildings there were and enjoyed walking round and taking in the atmosphere. A few years later I went back to see a client with a work colleague, Kerli, who was from Tallinn, and it was great to see the place from a local's perspective. We went to some good restaurants serving delicious local fish. The hotel I stayed in had the sauna in a windowed turret on the top floor, looking right over the city. It was a fun place to sit and take the in view.

Would I go back? Probably only for work.

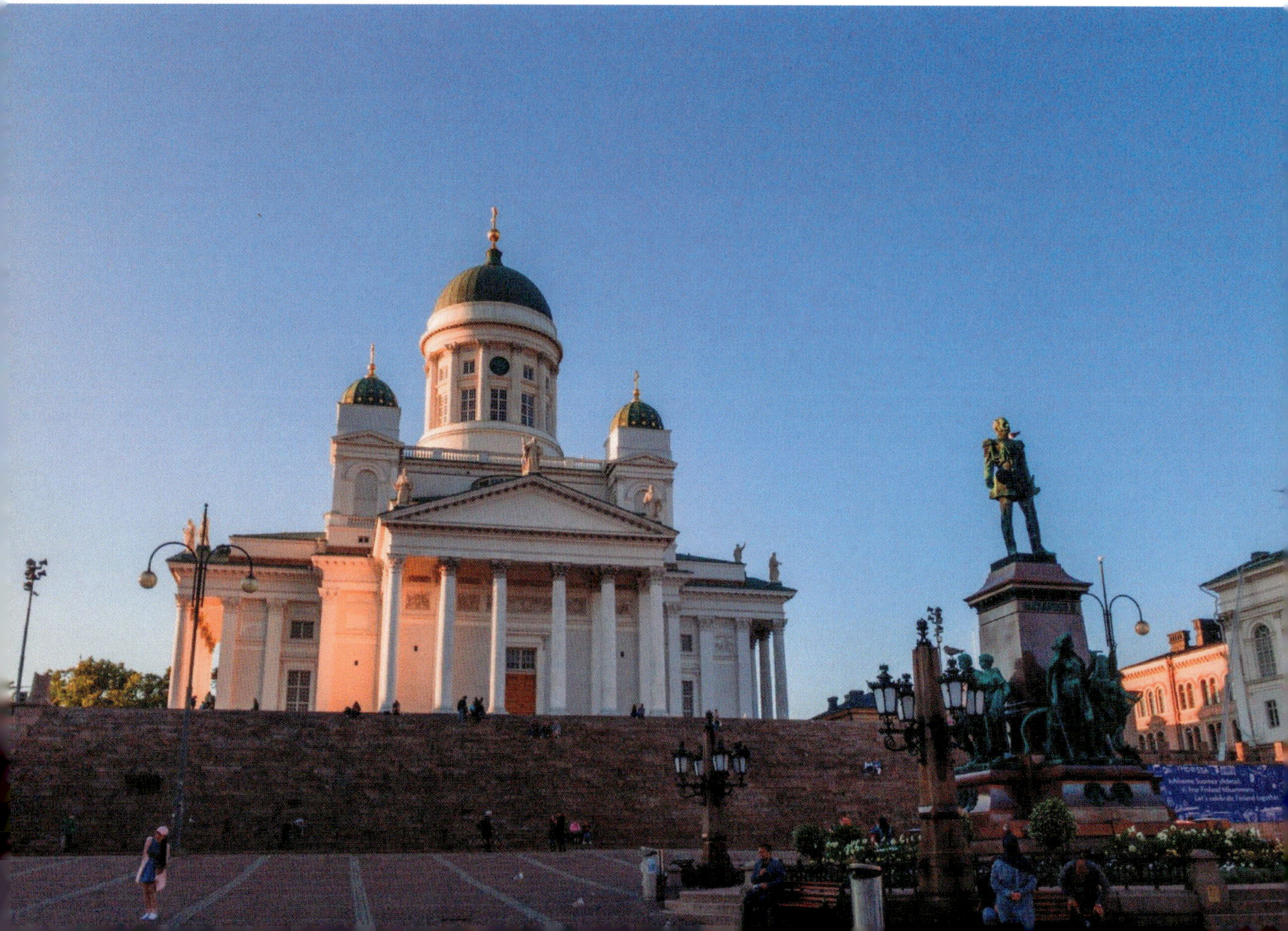

Finland

I have been to Helsinki a few times for conferences and to see clients. It is an impressive place to arrive in by boat. The skyline is dominated by the cathedral with its tall dark-green dome surrounded by four smaller ones. The city is a series of islands and inlets, where the sea freezes in winter. The cobles are large with deep gaps. (It was a struggle with my wheely case, I remember.) I would go running in the mornings and did some long walks along the various sea fronts. One time I stayed in hotel where my room had its own sauna with views over the harbour. My favourite bar there is Ateljee Sky Bar on top of the Hotel Torni; a great place for drinks at sunset. We also went to some fun conference parties at Teatern theatre restaurant and bar, at the top of Esplanadi Gardens. The slow roasted meat there was to die for. The highlight of one business trip was a networking cruise around Helsinki. I found the Fins were quite reserved to begin with but after a few drinks they really, really let their hair down. Not a place to be tea total.

Would I go back? Yes, to sail.

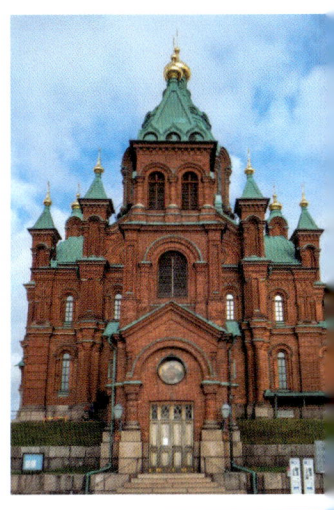

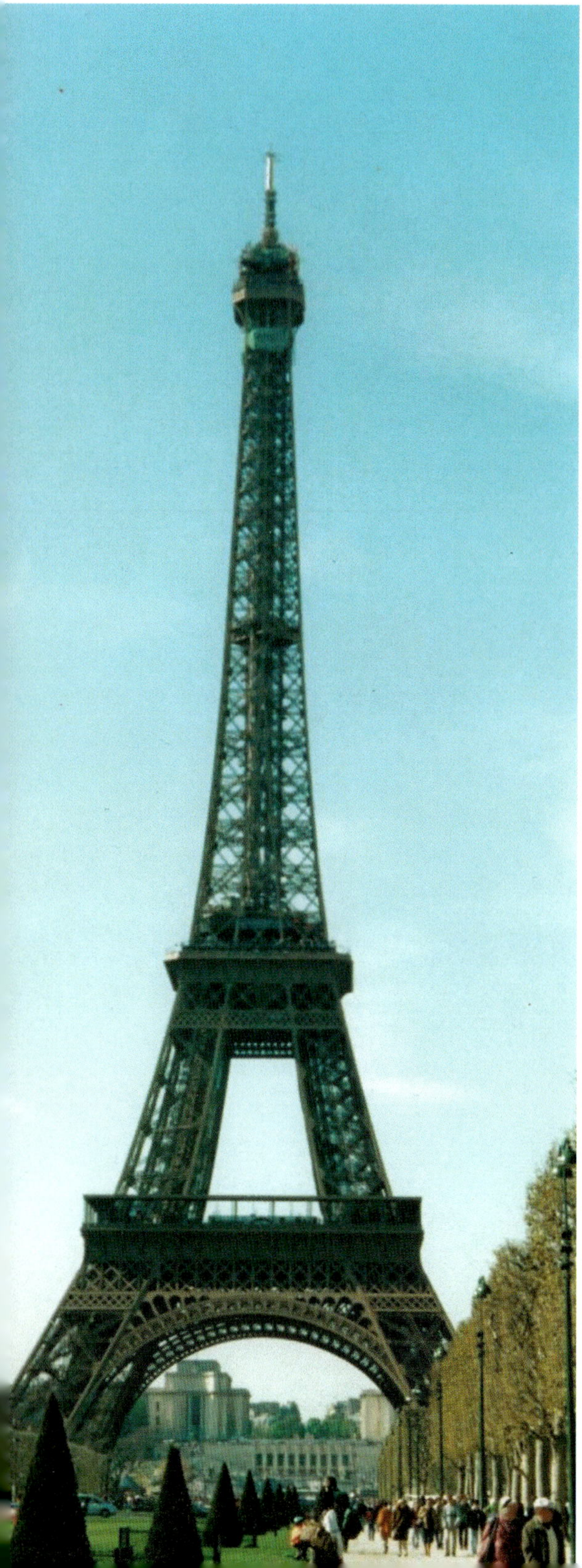

France

France is the country I have visited the most. I have been dozens of times, mostly for pleasure. My parents lived there for several years and it is just a train ride from London or a ferry across the channel. The country is so diverse and has so much to offer that it is little wonder that so many French people don't go abroad for holidays. While there are many exotic long-haul destinations to be explored, I still long for holidays in France.

My first time was with my parents on our trip around Europe. When I moved to England, there were weekends in Paris in the school holidays. In my last year at university, I studied French renaissance architecture which gave me an excuse to nip off to Paris for 'my studies'. So, I could bore you to death with the architectural history and details of many old buildings in the City. Years later, a dear French friend, who lived in London, declared, 'Paris is a museum.' Being French, she could say that. I won't disagree. It is still mostly old buildings and really is like a step back in time.

For most tourists it starts with the iconic Eiffel Tower. Strangely, with so many visits, I only ever admired it from the ground. It is especially beautiful from Trocadero across the River Seine. I think the price and the long queues had put me off. And then the opportunity arose to avoid both. My company was sponsoring a conference in Paris and I was keen to host a client party up the Eiffel Tower. So, we got the corporate treatment and made some reconnaissance trips up and down the tower in the staff lift. I think we might have been their toughest booking ever, but we had a great party looking over Paris at night. My parents and some friends came too. At that same event we were lucky to have a private evening tour of the Louvre. It was amazing having it all to ourselves with the guide showing just a few of us the Mona Lisa up close.

My favourite spot in Paris is Musée Rodin. The house and gardens are stunning, and both are packed with some of Rodin's greatest works. The glittering gilded dome of Les Invalides towers over the garden and glistens in the sun against a blue sky. Other favourite spots include Musée d'Orsay, for its vast impressionist collection, and Sacre Coeur on top of Montmartre, for splendid views over the city. The stained glass at St Chappelle is the best in the world. Favourite spots to stay are Ile St Louis and the Rive Gauche, but I have many happy memories of the Marais on my early trips. There are too many restaurants to mention, but Chartier is a classic cheap French brasserie for a great atmosphere, Boffinger is top drawer French, and I always get a later train to allow time for a full set menu dinner at Café Gard du Nord. Versailles was a day trip I could easily do again.

Journeys to the French countryside from Paris often involved the TGV and I drove south from Normandy quite a few times in my thirties with my girlfriend Katherine. With the freedom a car gives, you are faced with a choice of going left towards Burgundy and the Alps or right, down the coast in the direction of Bordeaux. A hard call for any wine lover to make. Taking the right fork means heading for Brittany, one of the most spectacular parts of France. The gateway is Mont St Michele, worth the stop just for the Restaurant La Mere Poulard, the best omelette restaurant in the world. It is worth driving the whole coast of Brittany from here, visiting the lovely Ile de Bréhat, an island surrounded by rocky waters, then onto the wild Cap Finistère and the along the rugged south coast before taking in the Gulf of Morbihan. We took a trip to beautiful Belle Isle and rode bikes. I would go back for a week's holiday in Brittany in a heartbeat.

Inland are the spectacular chateaux of the Loire, and then further south along the coast is the beautiful port city of La Rochelle. My parents lived nearby in rural Vendee close to the Venice Vert. We would make many day trips to Ile de Re. If you like oysters, this is the place. I also sailed from La Rochelle to Portsmouth once.

Further south takes you through Bordeaux. I drove down this coast making my way to San Sebastian in northern Spain once. It was September and the last towns of Biarritz and Saint-Jean-de-Luz were all shut up. Cross the border and the streets were packed with people out late at night. France feels quite reserved in that way. The Pyrenees demarking France and Spain have lovely scenery all the way to the Mediterranean. Toulouse is a fun student city and once you are near the Med you have medieval Carcassonne, en route to Languedoc and the Camargue. I sailed out of Sète on a friend's new boat on one trip. A family friend from Oz has lived in the walled city of Aigues-Morte for many years and we stayed there often.

Further round the coast takes you to rustic Provence and the chic Cote d'Azur. It is a treat to stay with friends in this part of the world. Some English sailing friends have a boat in St Maxime.

Doing the famous Voiles de Saint Tropez regatta with them was a dream. It might be touristy and expensive, but St Tropez is stunningly beautiful.

There's a lot in the middle of France which I drove through many times, but two other areas I've spent a lot of time in are the Alps and Burgundy. In my twenties I had a French girlfriend, Rosaline, who was from the Alps and we visited her family there a few times. They had a chalet as well as a house by Lac Annecy. It is a dream place for hiking. One weekend we climbed the Tournette on the other side of the lake, standing nearly 8,000ft high. The views were incredible. I have also skied in several French resorts including Val d'Isère, Courcheval, Chamonix, and Megève. Burgundy is my favourite wine, so any opportunity to visit this part of France is very welcome. And opportunities have presented themselves in spades.

My parents got chatting to some people on a barge on the canal in Aigues-Mortes, and before long were holidaying with them on the French canals. They were hooked. So, when a barge owned by some Aussies pulled in one evening, mum and dad ended up buying it. They restored her lovingly, renaming her Pastis and travelling all over France, including through the heart of Paris. I visited them many times and we had great fun travelling around the canal system from Burgundy into the heart of France. It was a very special time in our lives.

Would I go back? Oui, Oui, Oui. Toujours! A long wine tour of Bordeaux is next on my list.

Germany

We drove down the Rhine as a family in the seventies. My next time in Germany was inter-railing. I stopped in Cologne where the cathedral towers over the railway station. It's amazing to think it was left standing while virtually everything around it was destroyed in WWII. I was heading north to Scandinavia, so I went on to Hamburg, home to the bright lights of the Reeperbahn where the Beatles spent two years playing day and night. It is said that to master something takes 10,000 hours of practice and a big chunk of that for the band was done here. John Lennon later said, "I might have been born in Liverpool, but I grew up in Hamburg."

Nearly all my trips to Germany after that were on business, and there were dozens of them. Berlin has grown to become the capital and the biggest city since reunification, but before then Bonn in West Germany, scarcely a city, was the heart of government. Unlike England or France, where the capitals are clearly the biggest cities, Germany is made up of federated states, or Länder, and the capitals of these are also the great cities, all of which I have visited for a conference or business meeting at one time or another.

My first trip to Berlin was off the back of a vast computer exhibition in Hannover. It was just a few years after the wall came down and the eastern sector of the city still had a communist feel about it. The Brandenburg gate and the Checkpoint Charlie museum were memorable for the stories of escape from east to west. The Gate of Babylon in the Pergamon Museum was also amazing. It was excavated at the beginning of the 20th century in what is now Iraq and reconstructed here. I have been back to Berlin a few times since. The transformation since reunification has made it a great world city.

I spent quite a lot of time in Frankfurt, the financial centre. Stuttgart in Baden Wattenberg, home of Mercedes Benz, is a lovely city and Munich, BMW's home, is also great, especially in summer. I went to the Oktoberfest with clients a few times. It was gruelling. One weekend trip from here was to the fairy tale Neuschwanstein castle, commissioned by King Ludwig II in honour of Richard Wagner, nearly bankrupting the state of Bavaria in the process.

Leipzig, in what was East Germany, has the largest railway station in Europe and was also one of my business destinations. More recently, Dusseldorf is the city I have spent the most time in, with various business meetings and events in the Ruhr region. It's a great place for a beer after work by the massive River Rhine that wraps itself around the city. Huge barges go up and down river for hours on end. My favourite restaurant there is Zim Schlieffen in the Altstadt, where the pig's knuckle is a must-have.

The place I've visited the most, though, is the beautiful university city of Wurzburg on the River Main. I worked with a company there for several years and got to know this baroque city and the surrounding countryside. This is the top of the Romantic Road in Upper Bavaria. The white Franconia wines from this region are stunning and we would sit on long trestle tables between the vines in vineyards looking over the city lying in the Main Valley. It was during my time in this place that Germany and its kind people really grew on me.

My last trip was pure pleasure (well, except for the night of fog and rain in the German Bight sea area and the Hamburg shipping lanes). We were sailing from Amsterdam to Denmark which took us through the 100km-long Kiel Canal that links the North Sea to Baltic across the thin neck of Jutland. We stayed the night in Rendsburg in a small tributary off the canal. The following morning, we packed into the locks by the big ships at Kiel before sailing off into the Baltic.

Would I go back? Yes.

Greece

Greece was also part of our family trip in the seventies. We arrived by ferry from Italy and camped our first night in a camping ground. Some Greek friends back home in Oz were lending us their villa on the Island of Kythira off the south eastern tip of the Peloponnese. The camping ground was on the edge of the Corinth Gulf and we sat in the café at the water's edge. We got chatting to an Austrian man sitting at the next table. Ted was a professor in Ancient Greek History who spent his summers travelling around Greece. He told us all about the places we should see and was surprised we were headed to an island few tourists visited. He was on his way to Athens and offered to be our guide there. He showed us right round the Acropolis and the Greek history museum. Greek history had been his life's work and his insights were fascinating.

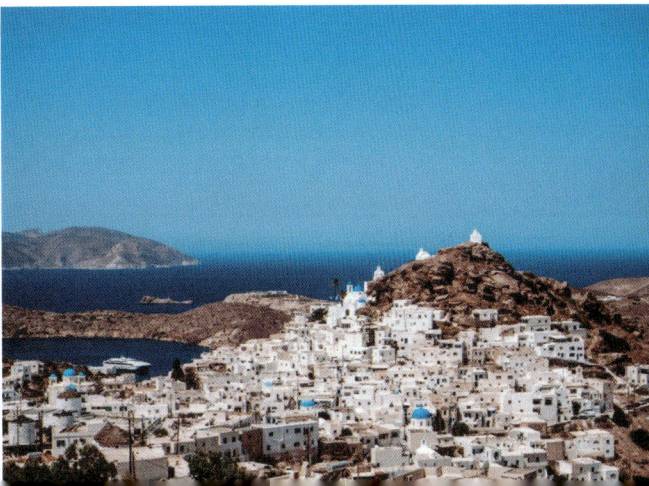

He had not been to Kythera for years, so we asked him if he would like to come with us. He was our guide again for some sites along the way. We went to the impressive amphitheatre at Epidaurus and spent the night in the seaside fishing port of Plaka, further down the coast. We got the ferry across to the island and spent a couple of weeks relaxing, learning Greek and meeting all the locals. It was basic living, but enormous fun. We drove on to see the ruins at Olympia and then to Patras to catch the ferry to Italy.

My next trip to Greece was inter-railing: I got off at Athens and met up with some fellow travellers and we all slept in our sleeping bags in a park right by the ferry port in Pireas. Staying there saved money and meant we were less likely to miss the boat leaving at dawn. I left the boat at the island of Ios in the Cyclades. I remember all the whitewashed buildings on the brown barren landscape. I climbed the streets high up in town until I found a guest house with an amazing view over the harbour. Ios was a party island attracting young people from all over Europe. The tiny square down in the town would get so packed that it would take about half an hour to get across it, though you would do it under 30 seconds in the morning. The drinks were cheap and locals would sell these amazing kebabs from their windows. It was all very carefree. After a week of lying on the beach and eating and drinking late into the night, it was time to leave. From Athens I caught the train north to Thessaloniki and across the border into, what was then, Yugoslavia.

My last trip to Greece was many years later in my thirties. With my girlfriend Katherine and an old friend Sophie, we chartered a boat for a week to sail around the Ionian islands. It was heavenly. We sailed to seven islands on that trip. We anchored off the uninhabited island of Kalamos and then to Castos. We tied up in Vathy on the island of Ithaka for a couple of days. Ithaka, famous in Greek mythology, was the home of the hero Odysseus as described in Homer's Odyssey and the Illiad. Sophie had been working as a chef on the island that season so we instantly knew all the locals. Our last sail was to seaside village of Fiskardo on Cephalonia. It was like something out of a film set. We spent lots of time swimming in the beautiful blue water off these islands. A boating holiday in the Greek Islands is as good as it gets.

Would I go back? Yes, more sailing round islands and to see Delphi.

Guatemala

In the mid-nineties, my girlfriend Ann-Louise and I met up with our friends Biggles and Lou in Guatemala City. On our first night we went out for a nice dinner and Biggles suggested a stroll after dinner. The girls said, 'you boys go,' and that was our pink ticket. It was dark in all the streets with no streetlights. We found a bar and then another bar and ended up in nightclub. All the stools were bolted to the floor. There was a pump action shotgun above the bottles on the wall behind the bar. A fight broke out, the police arrived, and in the kerfuffle, we ended up crawling out through a sea of legs on our hands and knees. Our navigation home was not too hot, and we arrived back at the hotel to our respective dressing downs. This sparked what became known as the 'stroll manoeuvre,' whereby you put your hand behind your head and stretch your arm out suggesting you need to walk dinner off with a gentle stroll. Thereafter, the mood needed to be carefully judged to suggest it.

We hired a four-wheel drive and headed to the old Spanish capital of Antigua. Here the wide cobbled streets lead into a large central square. Everywhere you look there is a volcano as a backdrop; the town seems surrounded by them. It is an atmospheric place with colonial buildings in faded yellows and reds. The square at night comes alive, much the way it would if you were in Spain.

From here we made for Panajachel, a town in the Guatemalan Highlands on the shore of Lake Atitlán. We had been told to stick to the main road due to the possible presence of bandits on the smaller roads.

It was a long trip and we were not going to make until late that night, so halfway there we took a short cut that would save us a couple of hours. It was already getting dark and we were all tired, so we agreed to go for it. The road got narrower and narrower, turning into a dirt track with bushes scraping both side of the jeep. In the headlights we could see a couple of men in the distance on the road ahead, one with a gold tooth sparkling in the light. There was a bit of a panic, but we decided to maintain our speed at the risk of running them over. They stepped aside. One of them had a riffle slung over his shoulder. They were probably local hunters, but we didn't stop to find out. We were rather relieved when the track widened and opened out to tarmac on our descent into Panajachel that night.

When we ventured out the next morning, we saw that Panajachel was a gem of a place. The lake was cobalt blue, cradled by three enormous volcanoes. We took boat trips on the lake and bought the local cowboy hats and wore them everywhere. The children here were beautiful. We went to a small local bar for New Year's Eve with a few other travellers. It was great. We drove to a colourful market in the hilltop town of Quetzaltenango, pronounced something like 'Way way Chenango.'

We dropped the car back in Guatemala City and flew to Flores on the edge of Lake Peten Itza. We stayed right on the lake, where we had amazing sunsets from our terrace.

The main objective from here was to head into the jungle to see the lost ancient Mayan city of Tikal. Right up until the 1960s, Tikal was covered in jungle. Some of it still is. Seeing these stone pyramids rising out of the undergrowth and partially covered in vines is quite something. We stayed at a lodge right in the jungle, inside the National Park near the ruins. Apparently there had been a wild jaguar in the grounds a few days before us. We would walk through the dark dense flora before dawn to climb the pyramids and watch the sun rise, and go again at sunset, walking back through the bushes in the dark. It was teaming with wildlife and the noise was deafening at dawn and dusk. The wildlife was as impressive as the ruins, and we saw many monkeys swinging in the trees and beautiful toucans. We left Tikal for Belize. I have since been to every other country in central America, but Guatemala was my first, and for that it is the most memorable.

Would I go back? Yes, to see the Pacific coast.

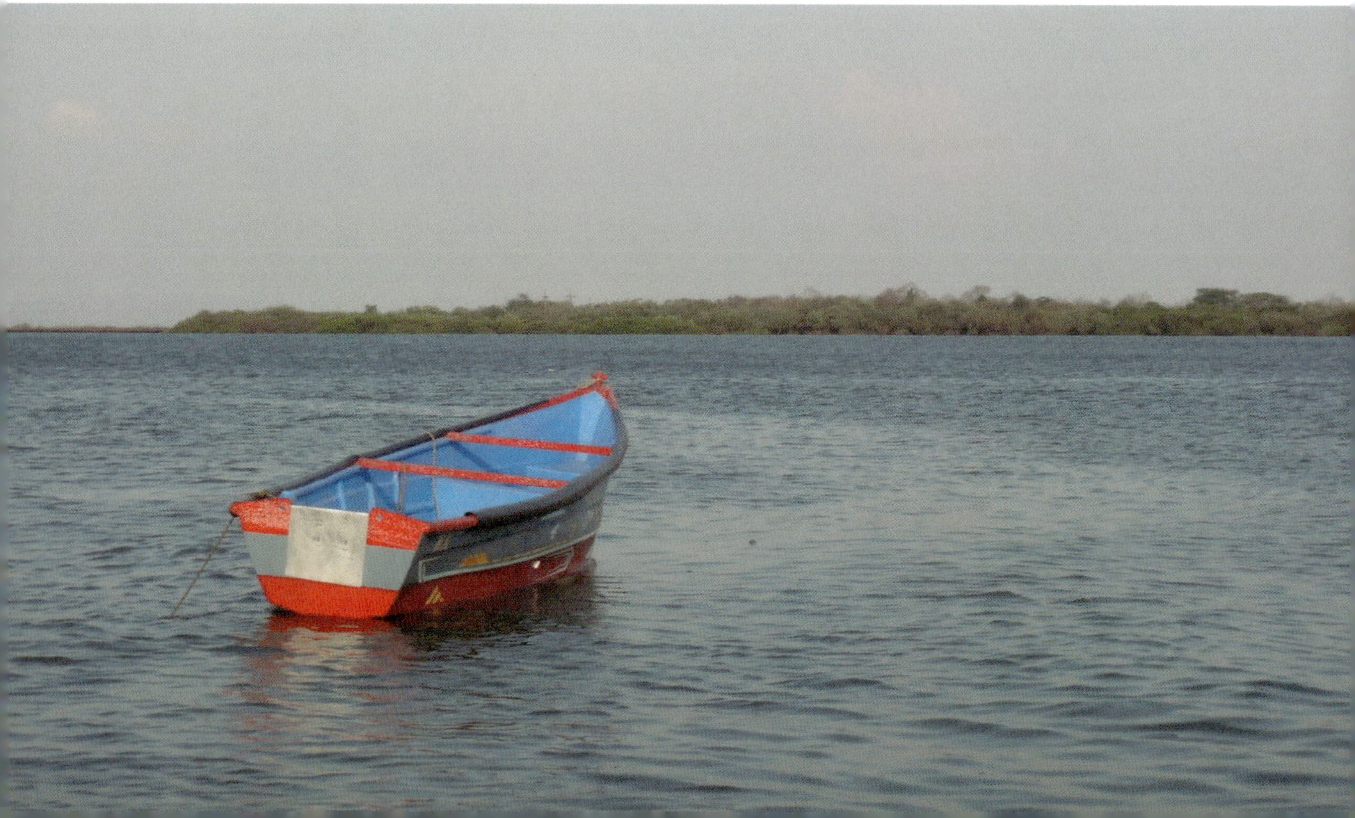

Honduras

It was over twenty years after my trip to Guatemala that I visited neighbouring Honduras. This trip was also with my friend Biggles. We were on our whistle-stop tour from Panama to El Salvador and every country in between. Because our time was limited, we had dubbed this the 'throw money at it' trip and we were now on an even tighter schedule having dawdled in Nicaragua. When we got to the border, a tuk tuk driver insisted on driving us across the bridge over the river. We arrived at the other end to the eager money changers holding huge wads of tatty bills like piano accordions. We got ripped off by them and were pleased to find a bus waiting. It was a few dollars to the next big town, so we jumped on board. After waiting a while we asked the driver when the bus was leaving and he said in Spanish, 'when it's full'. So, we counted the empty seats, paid for them and he closed the doors, started the engine, and pulled away.

I started reading the guidebook and looking for where we would stay the night. The towns along the way were not sounding very inviting so I chanced on a passage and read it out loud over the noise of the bus engine to Biggles, 'hey how about this place? Isla del Tigre is a majestic volcano rising up out of the sea.' We were literally driving past the road junction to it and saw a taxi sitting there. We shouted to the driver to stop and he did as if there was some sort of emergency. And we jumped off the bus that we had for paid for all seats twenty minutes earlier. The other passengers looked at us in disbelief. One minute we were in a hurry to get on and now we were in a hurry to get off.

The taxi saw us coming, but we didn't care. It was that kind of trip. We got to the port which was teeming with students all waiting for boats. It turned out it was Tegucigalpa Spring Break. Tegucigalpa is the capital of Honduras and the murder capital of the world. The queue for the boats was massive and it was taking forever to load and launch each one. A local fixer came up to us, grabbed our bags and walked us to the first boat, told us how much we had to pay the driver and him and we put to sea immediately. The faces of the few students on board with us beamed as if they had just been upgraded to first class. The limited accommodation on the island was first come first served. Luckily, there wasn't much competition in our price range. As we approached Isla del Tigre, it was indeed a perfect volcano rising out of the sea.

That night we had fish and chips. The smallest fish they had was twice as long as the diameter of our plates. It was delicious, battered and deep fried whole. We walked up to the main square heaving with students drinking, singing and dancing. It was a beautiful warm moonlit night, and we took in the ambience. The next morning, we debated hiring a boat to take us directly across the bay to El Salvador, but came to the conclusion that the authorities might prefer us to arrive via border control. So, we got the boat back the way we came and waved goodbye to the fun big mound in the sea and headed for the El Salvador border.

Would I go back? I might steer clear of Tegucigalpa, but I wouldn't mind seeing the Caribbean coast and Mayan ruins at Copan.

Hong Kong

Hong Kong is not a country and therefore not one of my 80, but it is a significant place for me. It pains me to write about it as part of China. It wasn't during my visits there in the late eighties. In those days the main airport was Kai Tak, with its runway jutting out into the harbour. When flying, I would often ask if I could see the cockpit. Once up there, chatting to the captain, I would ask if I could do 'a landing', signalling to the jump seat behind him. I got called before our final approach, got in the jump seat with the headphones on to air traffic control. The plane would approach the runway flying through a slot calved out of the high-rise buildings. As a passenger, you could look along the wing and see people seated at their dinner tables looking at you. Seeing this runway approach head on from the cockpit was even more surreal.

On arrival I made my way, to meet Johnny, already staying in Cheung King Mansions in Kowloon. This was a well known warren of small hotels and rooms to rent set in a high-rise building. We had bunks and the door would open just wide enough to be able to squeeze into the room. Some rooms had windows, but this was a disadvantage with the pollution rising in the air-well, only a few feet wide. We called an old London friend, who thankfully said 'don't stay there, come and stay with us.'

Our friend's place in the Mid-Levels, above Central on Hong Kong Island, was luxurious, with great views over the harbour. There was a maid who cooked and did our washing. It was quite an upgrade from where we were in Kowloon. Their place was in Old Peak Road, which was a bit of a climb up lots of steps. Getting into a taxi from the Star Ferry at Central and asking to go to 'Old Peak Road' the driver would look at you quite blankly. Saying it again a little bit louder….nothing….then 'Ole Pleak Loa' and he would reply 'Ahhh Ole Pleak Loa' and we would be on our way.

On this first trip, the new HSBC building designed by Norman Foster had just been completed and was receiving accolades from around the world. The China Bank was under construction and set to be much taller. We went to Aberdeen on the south side of Hong Kong Island, then the most densely populated place on the planet, and had lunch at the floating Jumbo restaurant. Afterwards we saw all the live fish in underwater cages. The pollution levels here were said to be thirty times the EU acceptable level. I felt less good about our lunch. We went up to the peak for walks and drove in sports cars with roofs down at night over to Stanley, on the other side of Hong Kong Island. We went to the Portuguese colony of Macau on the fast ferry, with the shutters going up and the locals starting gambling as soon as we left Hong Kong.

I came back to Hong Kong after visiting China. The switch from communism to extreme capitalism was stark. We went to the expat tennis club for lunch and then on to the islands by boat from the Hong Kong Yacht Club. The China Bank building was pretty much completed in the weeks I had been away. I ran into some travelling friends I'd met in Queensland in a bar in Wan Chai. There on the wall was a picture of a kangaroo drinking up at the bar. The barman in the photo was on old family friend of ours, Doug. He owned the pub at Gipsy Point in Oz and found Joey in the pouch of a mother hit on the road and taught him to drink from a beer mug and play pool. Joey became a bit of a celerity in Oz, and I'd played with him for hours as a kid. One day he got bored of me, put his font legs round my neck as if to dance with me. He stood on his tail, lifted his back legs up against my stomach and knocked me for six. I was shaken but not stirred and he just leapt over a six-foot fence and disappeared. I told my friend in the bar this story. It was too tall to be believable. I never imagined I would see a picture of Doug and Joey in a back street bar in Hong Kong.

I have been back a few times since on business. I got involved in importing kitchenware from there to the UK and many years later had banking clients there. I stayed in the Marriot in Central on my last visit, which might just qualify for the best buffet breakfast in the world.

Would I go back? Probably.

Hungary

A business conference was being held in Budapest, so, being somewhere new, I went. I loved the city immediately. Unlike Vienna, the mighty river Danube flows right through the middle of the city. I had seen black and white pictures of the gothic revival buildings lining the river in old books as a child and it was great to see them for real. The river divides the city in two, the hilly Budu on one side and the flatter Pest on the other. The old buildings are slightly run down in places, but it gives the city a certain charm.

I was only there for a few days and was mostly working, but I did manage to stay on after the conference finished. There are some great restaurants around District V in Pest where you can sit out on a warm summer's evening. The highlight on my last day was a visit to the Széchenyi baths, where I whiled away a few hours in the palatial baroque building that housed them.

Would I go back? Yes.

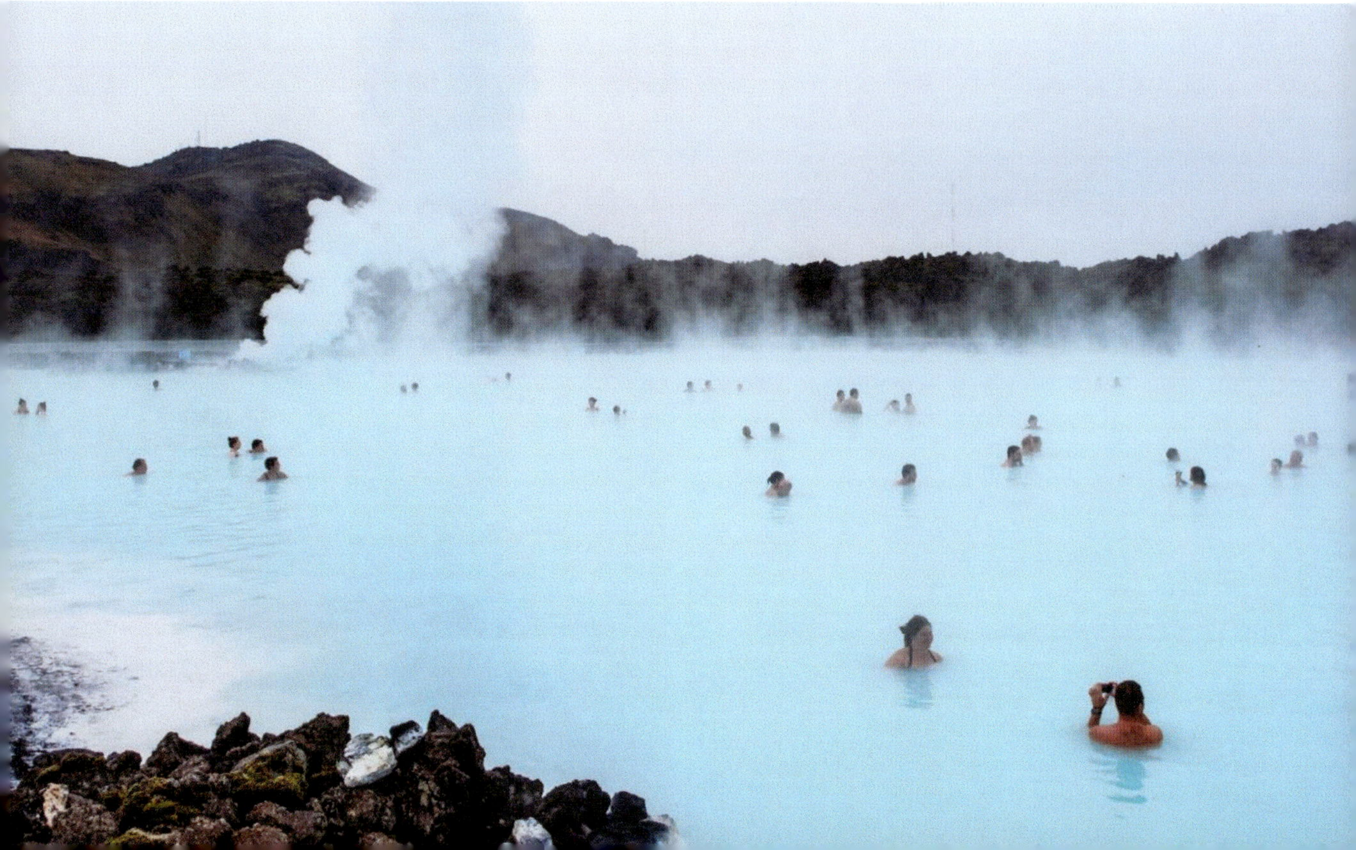

Iceland

I have been to Iceland a few times. The first time was as a stopover between New York and London, a break from the bi-weekly full transatlantic flight. The bus took me from the airport into Reykjavik across the barren rocky landscape. I had a fun weekend walking around and doing a boat trip. There were masses of puffins and the occasional whale out to sea. It is a small place, cold at night, but the main street is packed with friendly locals out until the small hours.

The Blue Lagoon near the airport was a must-see and I spent a few hours in the geothermal saltwater baths there. The salt is like cream and you can apply it to your face and arms as if it was moisturiser. It was quite surreal wandering and wallowing round the bright light blue pools with their brilliant white salt edges against the jet-black volcanic rock, with steam rising everywhere off the water. Feeling refreshed, I caught the airport bus at the entrance to Blue Lagoon and boarded my flight to London. On my trip back to New York from London, with a few hours to kill between flights, I left the airport armed with my boarding pass and wallowed some more at Blue Lagoon. A much cheaper option than a transatlantic business class flight and quite a bit more rejuvenating.

My last trip was on a friend's stag weekend. It was in the middle of winter and we went quad biking in deep snow in some isolated hills near the city. Our instructors told us to maintain single file. We got over the brow of the hill and to their horror it was suddenly a racetrack. Getting a group of people who regularly yacht race each other to follow one another was never going to happen. It was like something out of the US TV show, Banana Splits. There were all the usual challenges like paintballing and some unusual ones like the local custom of eating raw fermented shark meat with vodka shots. We did find some great restaurants though and we went to Blue Lagoon on our last day. While it wasn't the most cultural trip, it was fun to revisit.

Would I go back? Yes. To see blue whales in the north.

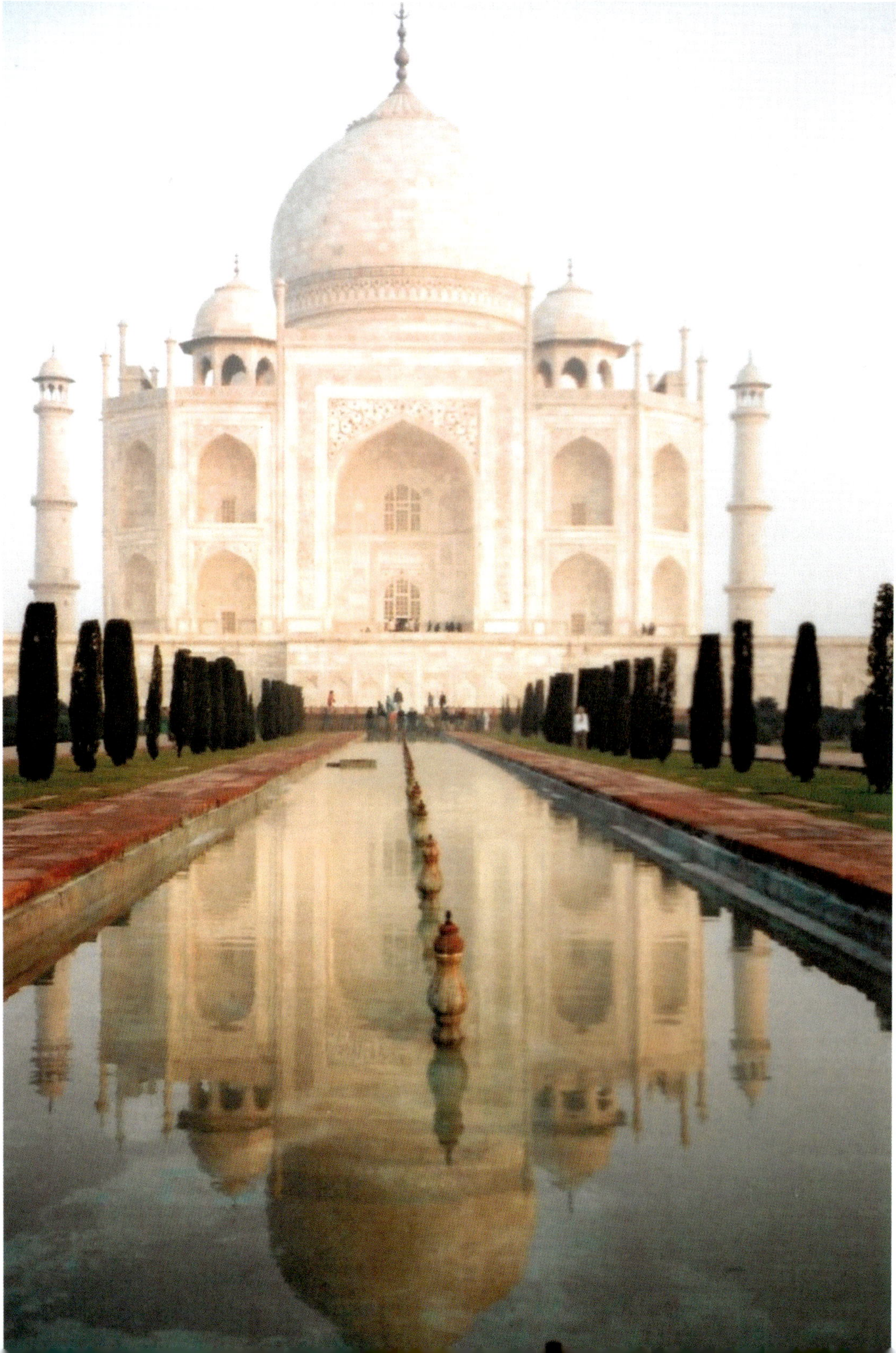

India

People always ask me, 'which country is your favourite to travel in?' It is a difficult question, but if I had to choose one country to go to every year for the rest of my life, I would probably choose India. It is hard to put my finger on it exactly. It is the combination of the warmth of the people, the food, the colours, the sounds, the smells, the sights and so much more. You feel alive, nearly always safe, and welcome. There's extreme poverty but the chasm between rich and poor almost feels less apparent than in the west. People with virtually nothing will nearly always muster up a smile. Most of all, India is spiritual. It grabs you and takes you by surprise over and over.

My first trip was quite touristy. I went with my girlfriend Katherine on a package holiday to meet some friends in Goa. As the plane touched down the runway was lined with hundreds of sticks and reflective silver streamers fluttering in the wind forming the landing lights. We ditched our package hotel accommodation and stayed in an old Portuguese guesthouse in Candolim, just north of Panaji, the Goan capital. We were right by the sea and the beach shack restaurants would lay a narrow red carpet down the beach to save your feet from the hot sand, adding a touch of class in the process. These places would create the most delicious fish curries from seemingly nothing. One night we had tandoori crayfish. An oil tanker had run aground on the beach, and the sight of it was a little shocking at first but we kind of grew used to it.

We hired mopeds and rode everywhere with no helmets. The biggest danger was cows. They, being sacred, had the run of the place. We even saw one get on a bus. We went to the bustling markets in the capital and ventured further north, crossing rivers on packed car ferries. A highlight was Anjuna market where the array of coloured fabrics, silver and other handmade goods was astounding. At night we would sit up on the rocks and look down at life on the beach. It was like a south Asian Bruegel painting. As a first holiday experience in India, Goa was great.

My next trip was on business to Mumbai (Bombay in the days of British Raj). Driving in from the airport you would see mile after mile of barefoot children playing cricket with a piece of wood and a ball. I holed up at the Taj Mahal Palace with a room looking over the Gateway of India. It was such a beautiful hotel with the most amazing old world stone swimming pool in a beautiful garden. Sadly, it was the scene of a terrorist siege in 2008, killing 174 people.

I was speaking at a conference and went to various business lunches and had some fun nights out. I did a television interview and after that for days people would show up at the hotel wanting to talk to me about their business idea. Some flew in from Delhi on spec. You have to admire the get-up-and-go of so many Indian businesspeople. And not all men. At a Chamber of Commerce lunch at the top of the Oberoi, I sat next to a woman in a sari who ran a pharmaceutical company with thousands of staff. I learned that it paid not to assume anything on that trip.

My main contact there, Arjan, would send a driver to pick me up and at the end of a busy day I would be sitting stifled in the back of this smart car stuck in traffic jams. There would be beggars knocking on the window, some of them were children, and I would tell the driver I needed to walk. He would protest that it was not safe but more for fear of what his employers would say for allowing me to get out of the car. I would reassure him that I would say he tried to stop me and then do a runner. Those walks back to the hotel were the best part of my day. Mumbai was fun at night too and I would enjoy the walk home. The streets were dark, and people would be lying everywhere just sleeping on the cold concrete. Women with young children curled up beside them, this was their home. Somehow it felt peaceful. One day I did venture part of the way into a slum. It was quite shocking, but I didn't feel unsafe at any point.

My third trip to India was taking my parents around Rajasthan for a few weeks. It was at the turn of the millennium that I asked my mother what was the one thing left she'd most like to do in her life. She said there were two: one to fly on Concorde to New York, the other to see the Taj Mahal. I booked the plane tickets to NY the next morning. When Concorde stopped flying a few years later, it felt like a sign that we'd better fulfil mum's second wish while we could. I had said from the outset that the Taj Mahal was likely to be a bit disappointing, so I planned a trip to take in the great palaces of Rajasthan. It is easy to forget that the Indian subcontinent's wealth (GDP) was greater than that of the whole of Europe by the tail end of the renaissance in the 17th century. The scale of the impressive palaces of Rajasthan serves as a reminder.

We flew to Delhi, visited the Red Fort and after a day of tussling with various con artists got the train to Agra. We got up in the small hours of the morning to get to the Taj Mahal before sunrise. Watching the iconic shape of the dome emerge from the darkness and gradually coming into view is a true sight to behold. As the daylight unfolds the surrounding gardens become a throng of birds and monkeys. The big surprise as you walk up to this soft white marble mausoleum is that the exterior is encrusted in gemstones. This is what gives the appearance of a soft sparkly silvery white from a distance.

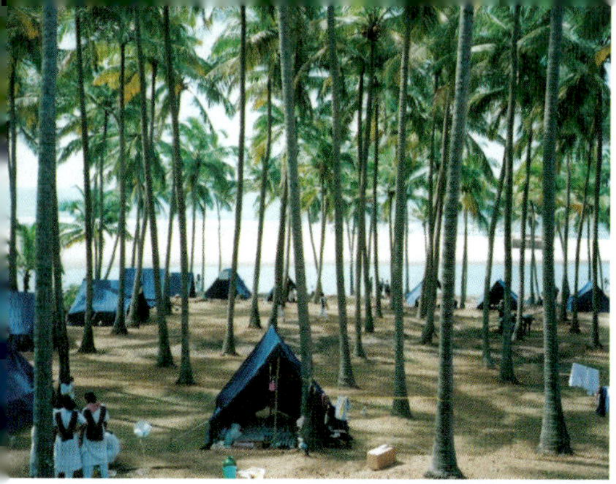
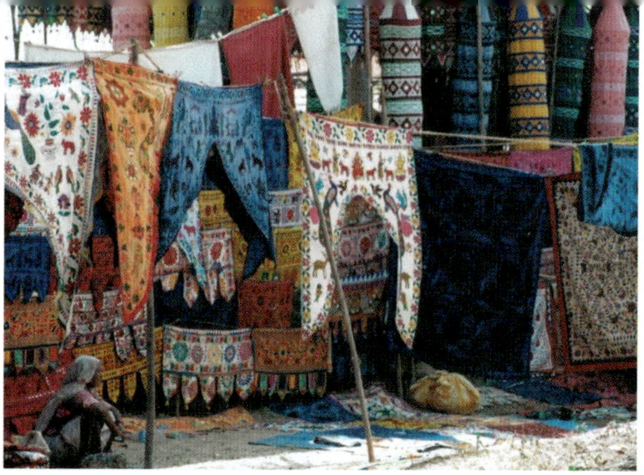
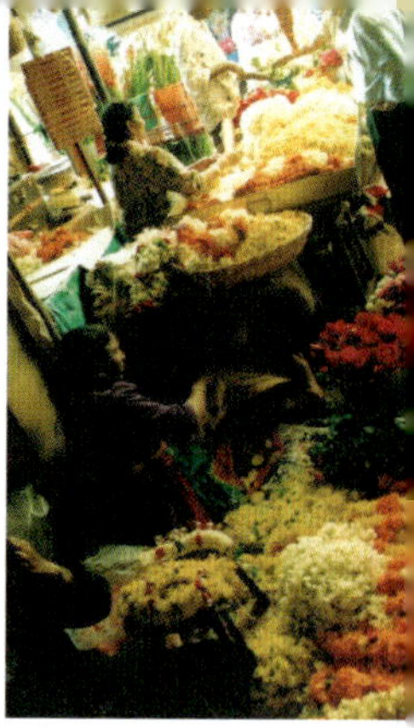
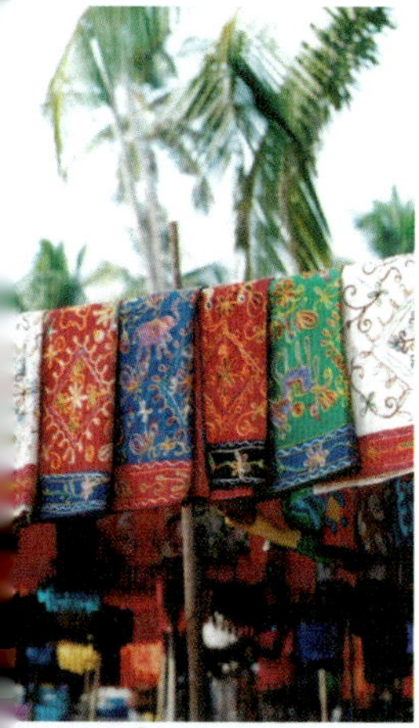
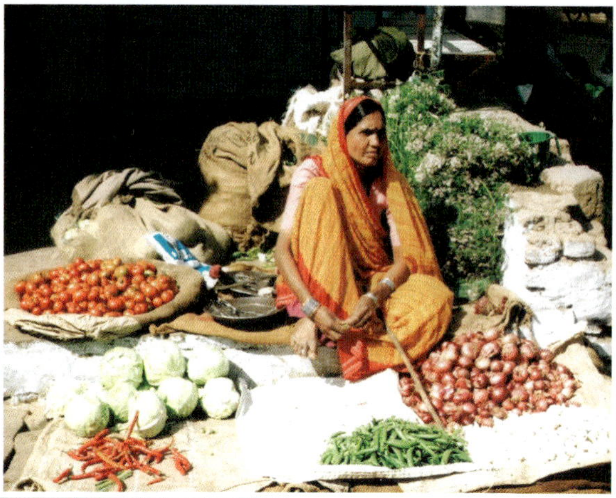
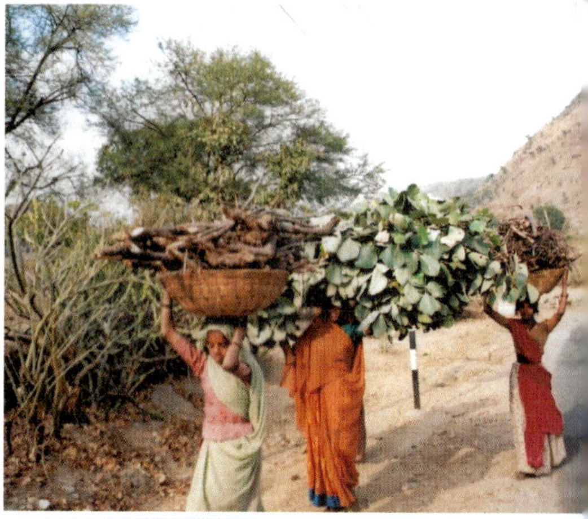
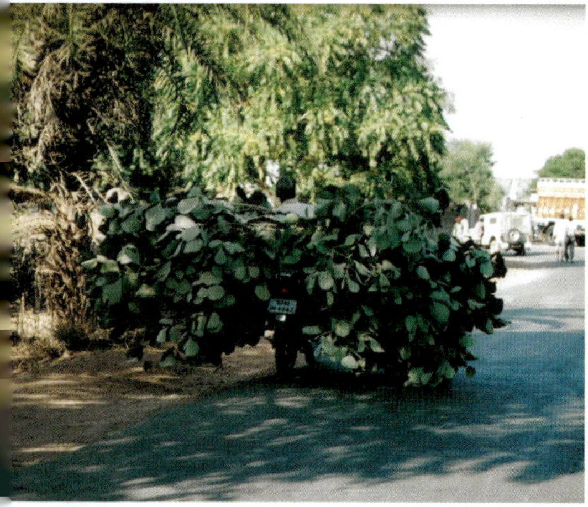
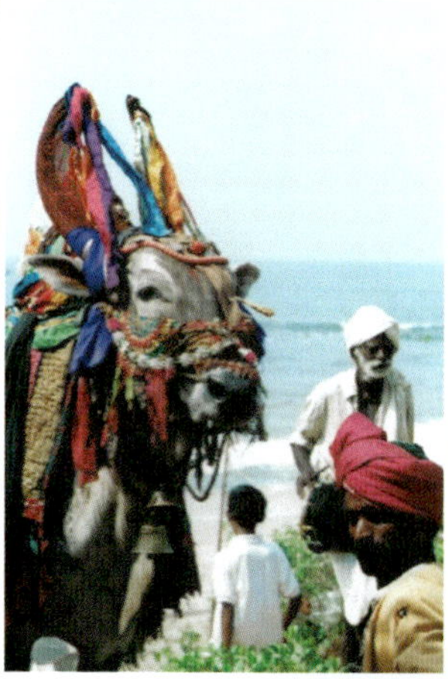
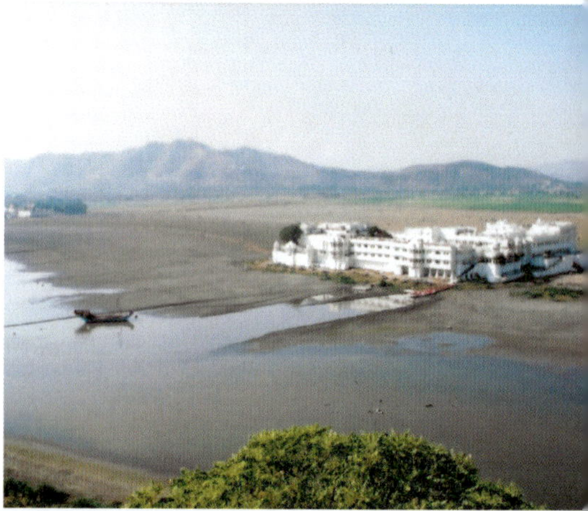
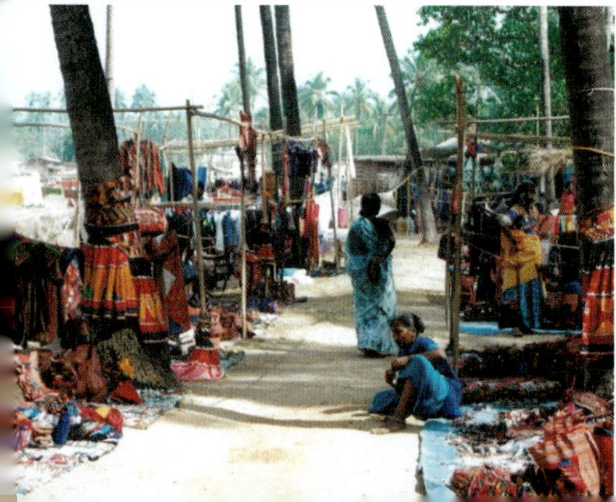
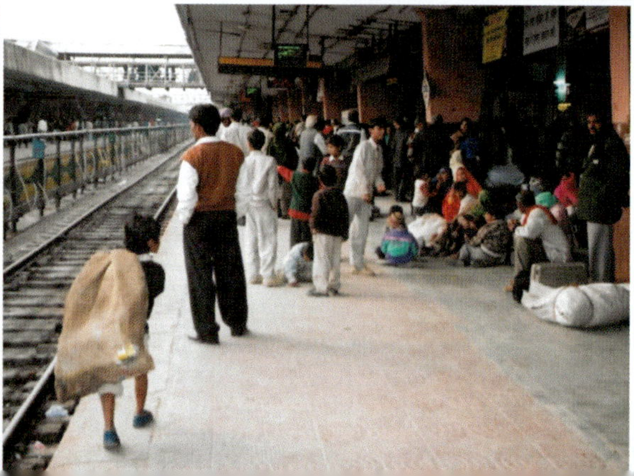
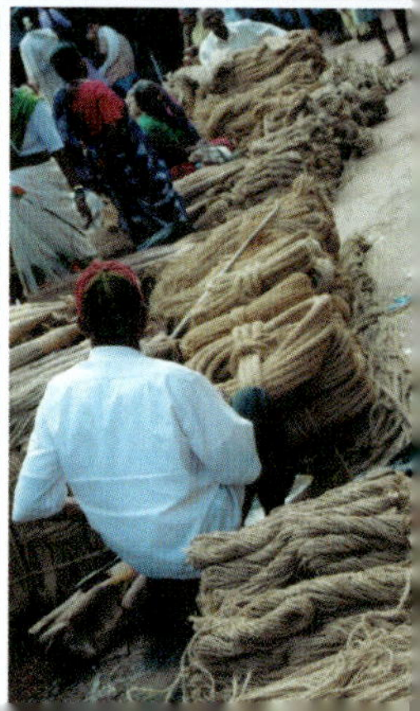

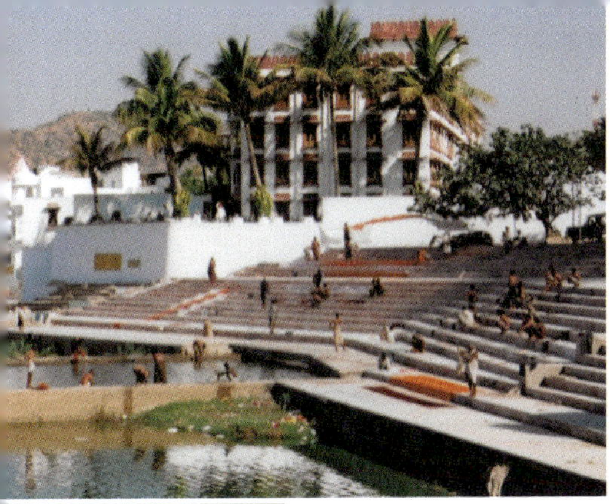
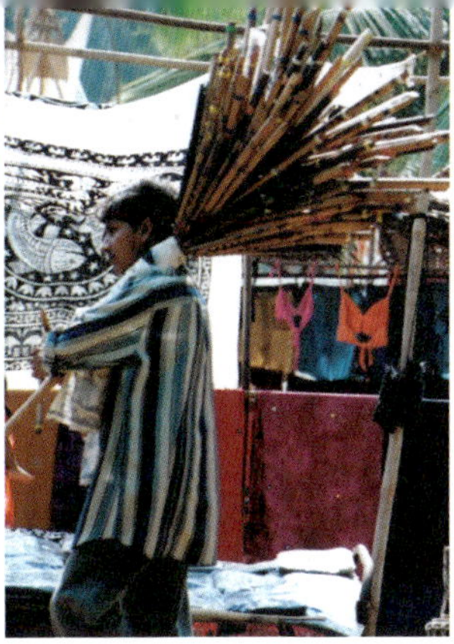
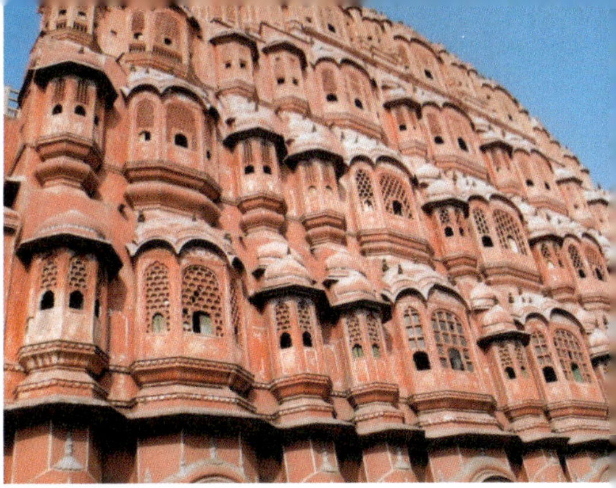
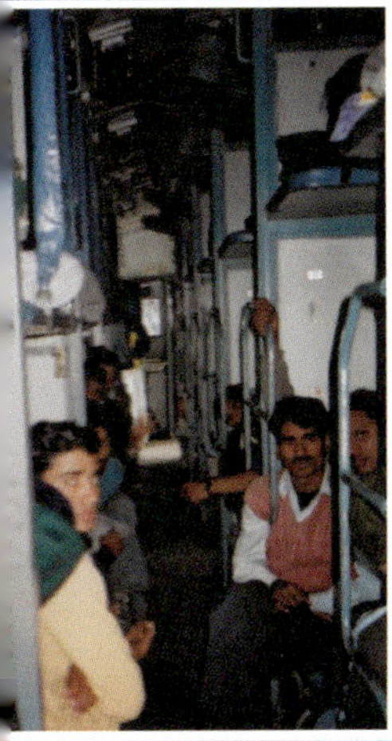
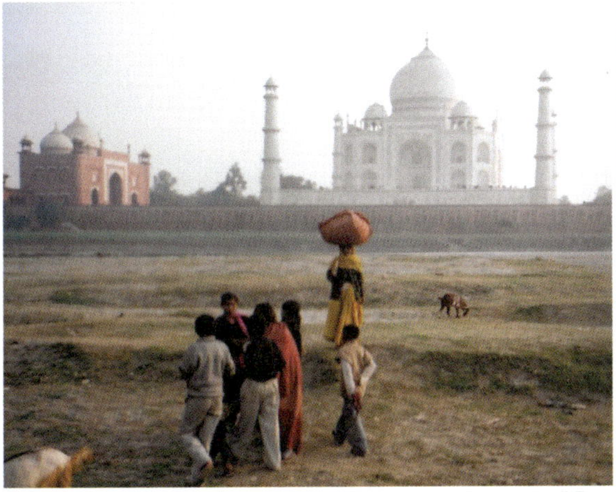
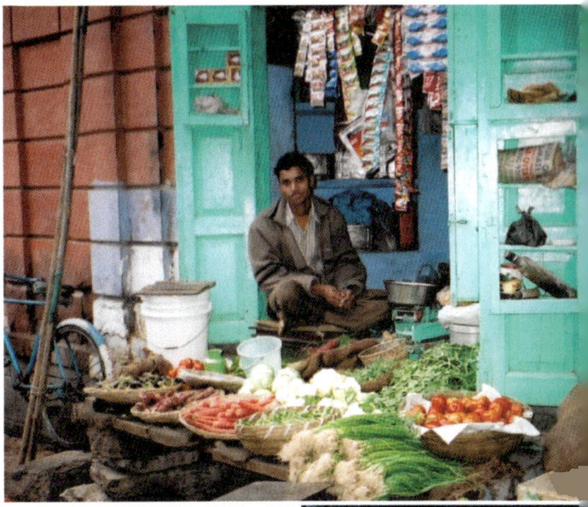
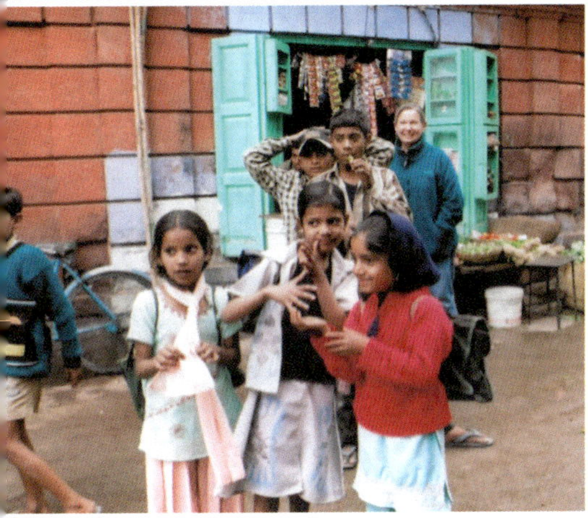
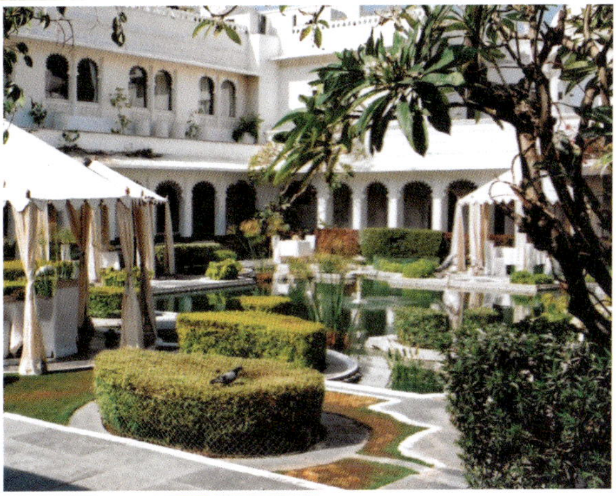
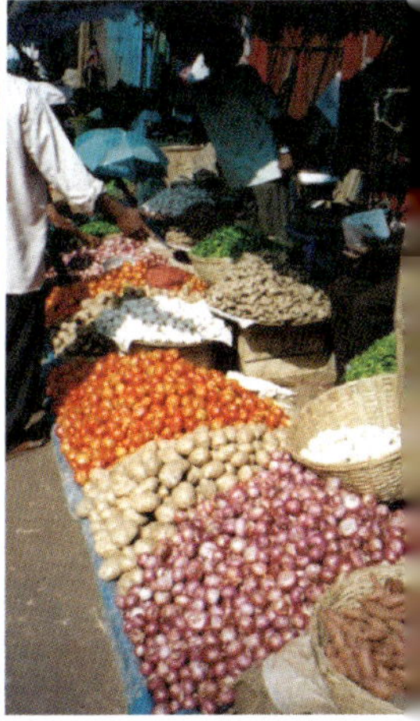
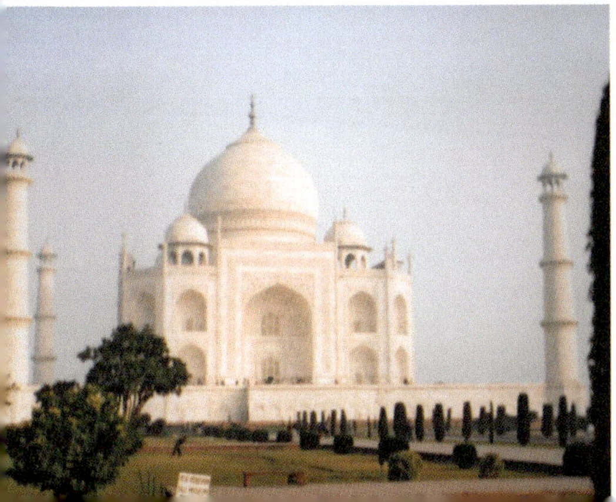
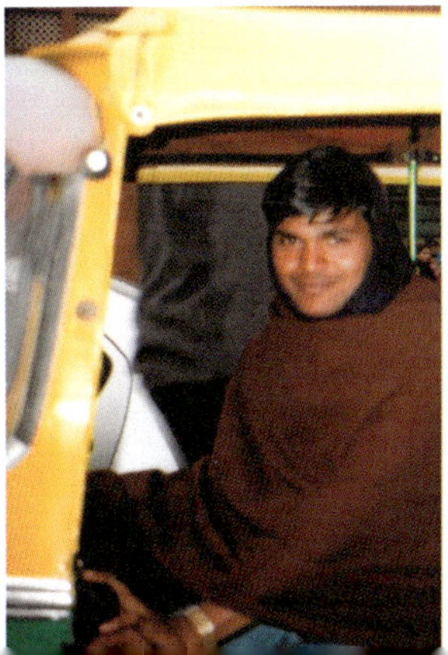
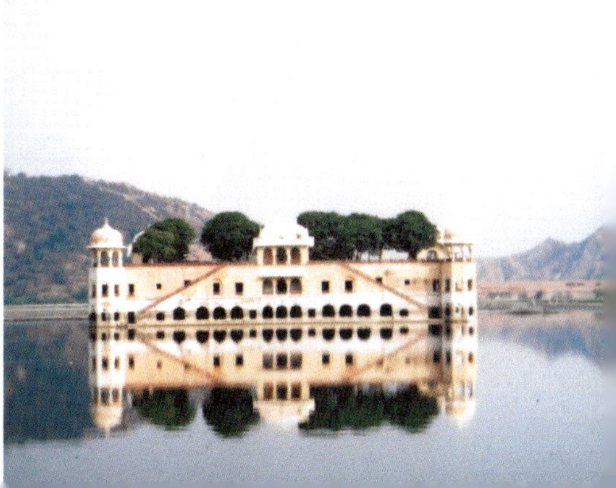

We spent hours there taking in the atmosphere as the day progressed. We went inside where the acoustics magnify the slightest whisper. And my parents posed for the classic Princess Diana shot with the Taj in the background. Later that day we went in a tuk tuk to see the Taj Mahal from across the river at sunset. Few tourists bother to do this, and it was a magical time with local children running around everywhere on the riverbank.

The next day we went to Agra Fort and it is from here that the love story behind the Taj Mahal is most poignant. The Taj was built by the Mughal emperor Shah Jahan in the 17th century as a mausoleum to his beloved young wife who died in childbirth. Its construction nearly bankrupted the state, and his plan was to build a black matching mausoleum for himself mirroring the Taj on the other side of the river. His third son usurped his throne, and imprisoned him under house arrest in a section of Agra Fort. From his rooms, we looked down the winding river in the haze to the Taj Mahal in the distance, just as he would have done hundreds of years earlier. His coffin next to hers is the only thing breaking the symmetry inside the tomb. The Taj is far from disappointing. It is almost overwhelming. My mother was right, it was worth going to India just to see it.

The rest of our trip was to be dedicated to seeing Rajasthan. We got a train to the capital, Jaipur, known as the Pink City for the colour of its buildings. From here we went to see the Amber (Amer) Palace just outside the city, passing the Jal Mahal palace mirrored in the lake. We hired a great driver, Sohan, from Jaipur who drove us cross country to Jodhpur in his old, but immaculate, Morris Oxford. It was great to see some of rural India, to be able to stop whenever we saw something. He took us to some great places for lunch and all the guesthouses and hotels we stayed in put him up in the drivers' quarters for free. That was the deal. We asked Sohan to join us for most meals. He was quite shy, but he knew India well for years of driving round. We felt lucky to have found him.

We headed to Pushkar, set on the sacred Lake Puskar. Here a walk around town meant a walk around the lake at its heart. No alcohol allowed, though we did smuggle some brandy in. We stayed in the Pushkar Palace Hotel for a couple of nights with its fabulous terrace restaurant overlooking the lake. Next stop was the town of Bundi. There were no tourists here and we could wander into old palaces that were abandoned. After a night here, we went to Chittorgarh and on to Udaipur, home to the fabulous Lake Palace. Unfortunately, the lake was mostly dry, but we did have a lovely lunch at the Lake Palace Hotel. There was shopping for silver and prescription spectacles as well.

We did our last leg with Sohan to Jodhpur, with its towering Mehrangarh Fort. We walked up the hill to it through cobbled streets chatting to locals along the way. Nearly all the buildings are painted in a cobalt blue paint to deter termites. The fort has a timeless feel. It looked ancient and futuristic all at once. It was almost like something out of Batman. We booked train tickets for the long journey to Jaisalmer and were told to ring the station on 2535 before getting up the next morning. The train was due to depart at 6am so I called every hour from an old rotary dial phone beside my bed to be told 'train is coming in two hours.' By late morning we went to the station to wait a few more hours for the train to arrive. It was a long old journey through the dusty Thar desert on a rattly train. The choice was to close windows and overheat with no air, or open them with air full of dust and sand.

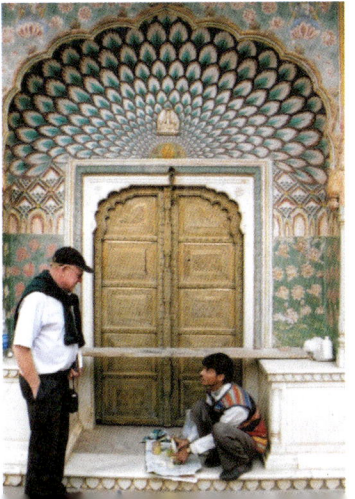

Nothing quite prepares you for your first view of Jaisalmer. It is a walled city, a great golden sandcastle in the desert. As you wind your way up the ramp through massive wooden gates with spikes at elephant head height, you pinch yourself as you feel like you are entering something out of a fairy tale. Our hotel room was part of the walls and we would sit looking out at men hammers and chisels carrying out maintenance on the fort. Jaisalmer is a series of paths, no cars or tuk tuks, but cows have free reign. We sat in some great rooftop restaurants high up on this ancient mound, looking out to the desert horizon. Jaisalmer is in the western tip of India where Pakistan wraps 180 degrees around it. Fighter jets flying up and down the border were a daily occurrence.

Mum wanted to go camel riding, so we booked a trip out to camp, in a sort of luxury tent, in the Thar Desert right on the border. Our favourite tuk tuk driver with his stereo blasting out distorted Indian tracks weaved us through the back streets of the lower suburbs to meet with a land rover to take us out to the middle of nowhere. We were the only people there with a few tribesmen to cook basic Indian food for us. We sat round a big fire under a starlight sky. The next morning, we rode camels through the desert as planned. It was more comedy than a serious camel trek. We spent most of the time in hysterics. We dismounted and returned to the relative civilisation of Jaisalmer. With no airport and a whole day's journey to get there, few make the effort to visit. It is one of the most incredible places I've been. We all agreed that 'Jaisalmer was the gem' on that trip to India.

Food often plays a big part in how much you enjoy a place and India provides a culinary experience in spades. It is nearly all veg, meat is for tourists and often this is what leads to 'Delhi Belly.' My father talked of how much he was dreading weeks of curry before the trip, but by the end of it he was addicted. The tiniest, most spartan kitchens, with seemingly few resources, would somehow turn out meals that were beyond belief. After days of constant surprises, we would invariably ask if we could watch them cook our meals. They weren't coy and were in fact proud and flattered that we would take an interest. Their main secret was fresh local vegetables and spices cooked on high heat. Nearly all dishes had an onion and garlic sludgy paste prepared earlier as their base, giving dishes a great consistency. In some kitchens they would show you ingredients and make your curry to order. The love that these smiley happy people put into making food is something to behold.

Would I go back? In a heartbeat. Still to see: Srinagar, Kashmir, Shimla, Ganges at Varanasi, the Himalayan foothills, Assam, Calcutta, Houseboats in Kerala and anywhere in between.

Indonesia

My visit to the world's most populous Muslim country was really a long weekend break from Singapore. Rather predictably, I went to Bali. But get away from the cheap, package tourist spots like Kuta Beach, and Bali can be very chic. I would like to have got further inland and to the wilder coasts, but I was just having a few relaxing days by the beach. I stayed in the far end of Seminyak further up the coast from Kuta in a great family-run hotel with a long beach frontage. It was a quiet spot where I could sit on the lawn reading books with a beer watching volleyball on the beach at sundown. There was even a pool bar and I had the place pretty much to myself.

I would go for long walks on the beach each day and chat to friendly local families along the way. I stopped at the very swanky W Hotel for lunch one day and enjoyed some cocktails at the lively bars of Potato Head and Ku De Ta. But most of all I relaxed in a lovely local hotel with a great garden.

Would I go back? Yes, to Bali and some of the other 13,000 islands and the jungles of Borneo.

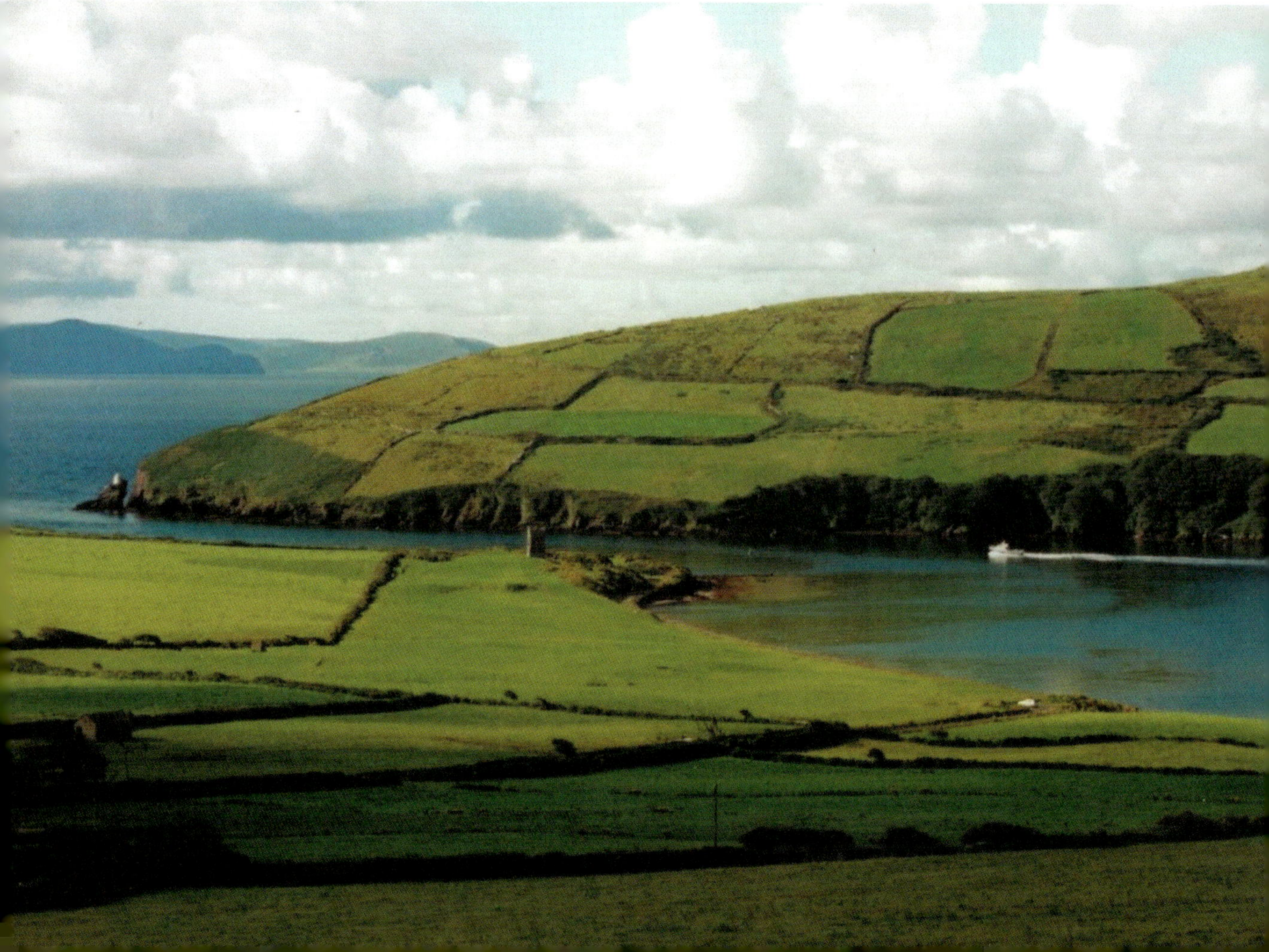

Ireland

The Emerald Isle really is a land of the colour green, thanks to its relatively high rainfall. I have been several times and am always happy to go back. My biggest trip there was with my girlfriend Katherine in the 1990s. We went for the start of the Tour de France. Yes, it often starts in a different country. And after the Dublin parties we headed off on a tour around the country. We went to Kilkenny and onto Cashel for a couple of nights and stayed in a beautiful country house B&B, with lots of land. The black Labrador of the house became our guide around all the surrounding fields. I loved Cashel. It's in the heart of Ireland. It had a pagan feel about it and the people in the pubs were friendly and great fun. We tripped to Tipperary, where my grandmother's parents came from.

Dingle on the far west coast was our destination and here the scenery is breathtaking. A place where the velvet green landscape meets the deep blue sea. Ryan's Daughter was filmed here and the landlady in our B&B went on for hours on end with her stories about Tom Cruise and Nicole Kidman. But the biggest draw was the resident dolphin, Fungi. I walked through thick kelp into the sea near where he was swimming in the evenings, but he would play tricks with me, disappearing for ages before coming up for air in a different place. I never really got to swim with him, but I felt we connected.

The south west coast of Ireland is like a hand, with twenty-mile-long fingers protruding out into the Atlantic Ocean. It makes driving

round the coast long and slow. It seems to go on forever. Stopping at every lookout for views across bays or out to sea to the Fastnet Rock makes for a long, slow, but very scenic, road trip. The provenance of the food in Ireland means you rarely have a bad meal: nearly everything on your plate comes from less than ten miles away and the people are very proud of it. We stayed in foodie Kinsale for a couple of days. Oysters and Guinness were normally the order of the day here.

We headed onto Cork, a lovely city. The covered market there was a great place for lunch. Cobh, pronounced Cove, is the seaport from which nearly half the Irish population left to emigrate to America. It was the final port of call for the ill-fated Titanic. The yacht club here is also the oldest in the world. From Cork we went to Blaney Castle where I lay on my back at the top of the tower to 'kiss the Blaney stone', in order to be endowed with the gift of the gab for ever more. This was the last stop before catching the ferry from Rosslare to Wales. I don't remember being very chatty on the long drive home to London.

My other trips to Dublin were on business, but we always had great nights out. Great craic/crack as they say. We would end up in the bars late at night in Leeson Street followed by breakfast in cafes which served Blue Nun wine in teapots. My last few trips have been to Kinsale where I stayed in a house with commanding views over the harbour. We would walk down the hill to the bright orange-painted Bulman Pub for pints of Guinness and stagger back up for dinner. We also did some great sailing around the coast here.

Would I go back? Yes. Further north up the west coast, Galway, and Waterford.

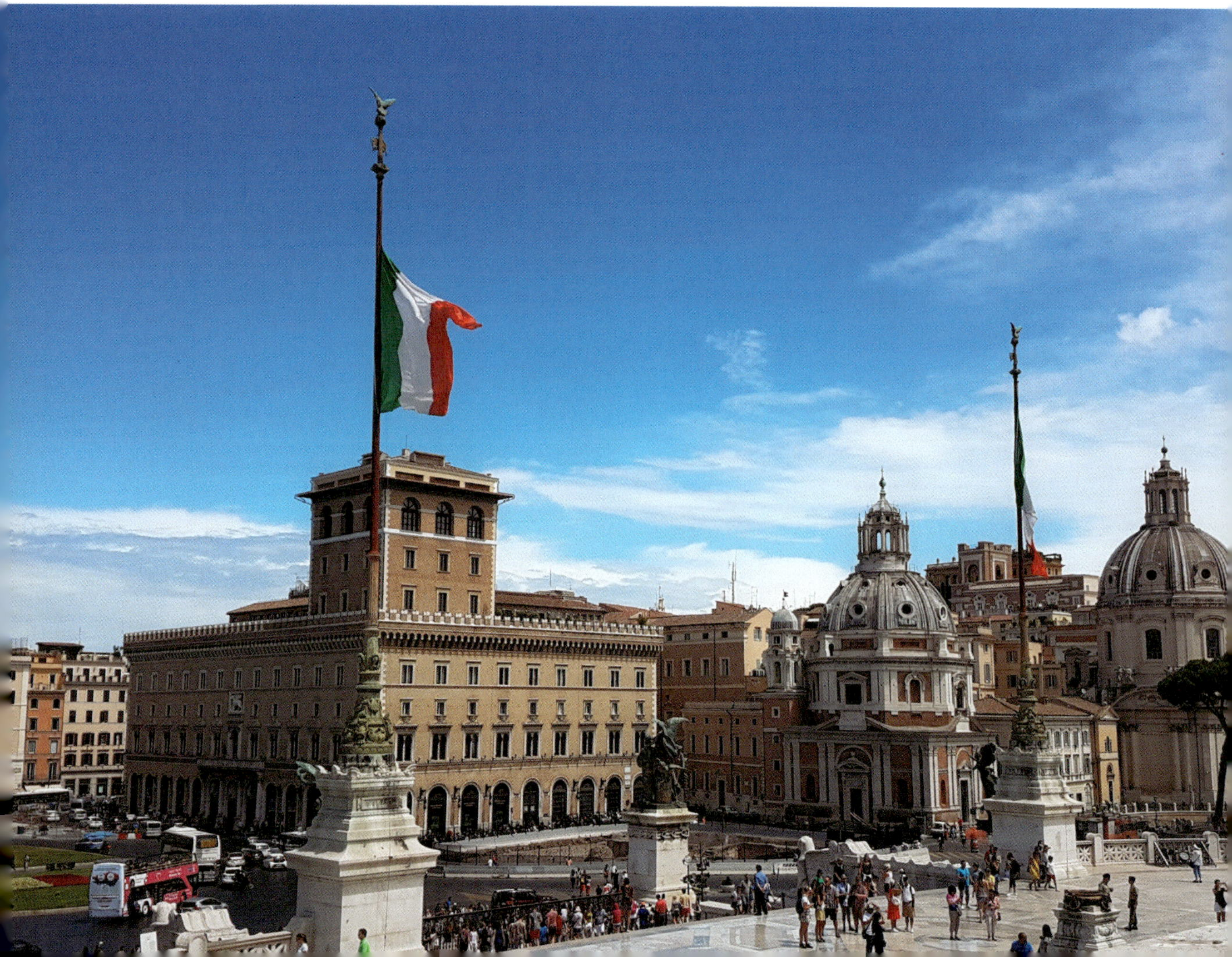

Italy

Every Grand Tour of Europe must take in Italy and our family trip there in 1976 did just that. We drove through the Alps to Venice and then down the Adriatic coast to Brindisi to get the ferry to Greece. Once back from Greece, we drove round the heel of Italy to stay with some relatives of friends in Taormina at the foot of Mt Etna in Sicily. After that we went up the coast to Sorento and Capri, and on to Rome. We stayed with some more friends in the lovely hilltop town of Cortona, then went on to Florence and Pisa and on to the Riviera. It was actually a trip around Italy seeing the sights while eating a lot of pizza, pasta and gelati.

My next trip was a ski trip to the Dolomites and then inter-railing through Italy en route to Greece. I stopped for a walk around Bologna, home to Europe's oldest university and most famous pasta sauce. But the most memorable trip in the eighties was when Johnny and I drove down through

France to Umbria to meet friends we'd taken a villa with. It was up in the hills above Lake Trasimeno in a hamlet called Castel Rigone. By pure coincidence, it was next door to the house our Australian friends had lived in when we tried to find them over a decade earlier. It took me a few days to work out I had been there as a child. This was a cultural holiday with day trips to Florence, Siena, San Gimignano, Perugia, Assisi and Cortona. At night we had Italian cooking competitions in the villa. We piled into the car and headed to Rome. We stopped to see the papal gardens of Tivoli, famed for their fountains, but there was a sign in Italian suggesting the fountains were not working. As we were about to pay for our tickets we asked 'Fontana?' and were told 'Fontana Si! Aqua No!' So, we gave the gardens a miss. In Rome we did all the touristy things; the Vatican, Colosseum and more. Our friends flew back, and we hit the road for the long drive back to London. Getting out of Rome was proving to be a challenge. We were going round in circles. Every time we stopped near someone and shouted out the window 'direzione Milano' we were either given a shrug of the shoulders or a long unintelligible list of directions in rapid fire Italian. It would be like asking for directions to Edinburgh in south London, I guess. When we did eventually find the main road north out of Rome we had street vendors banging on our windows at every set of traffic lights wanting us to buy things. We drove non-stop and made it out of Italy through the Mt Blanc Tunnel to Chamonix in the French Alps by morning. We shook off the tiredness of the long drive from the Italian capital by seeing how far we could climb up Mont Blanc in just a pair of trainers. We made it to the glacier. I have been to Milan and Rome many times since on business and love them both as well as conferences in Genoa and Rimini. I once rode around Rome on a moped staying with friends who lived by the Vatican. That was mayhem. I did a wonderful trip one year to the Italian lakes from Milan staying in beautiful Bellagio. There was a staff away weekend to Sardinia. But my four most recent trips have been most memorable because they were all about some great sailing.

On the first of these trips, I was invited to join friends sailing around the Amalfi coast on their beautiful classic yacht called Manitou. It was once John F Kennedy's private yacht, and it was immaculately restored. There were pictures of him on board and a bathtub under the floorboards where he was said to have wooed Marilyn Munroe. That trip was like something out of the film, 'The Talented Mr Ripley' and we were in many of the places where it was filmed. Our trip had started in Rome where we had dinner on a friend's rooftop balcony looking over the city. We saw some sites and headed to Naples, the home of pizza. I had to visit Sarita, said to serve the best pizza in the world and immortalised by Sofia Loren in L'Ora di Napoli. Very good but not 'my' best in the world.

We sailed out of the old-world Naples Yacht Club, visiting some lovely ports for our week of cruising. Highlights were Positano and Amalfi. We walked up to Ravello for lunch

lunch and sailed down to Agropoli and visited the ancient Greek city of Paestum with its three, spectacular acropolises. We sailed to Capri, through the gap in the big rocks and then on to the glorious islands of Ischia and Procida. It was an amazing trip. I think the Amalfi Coast beats the Riviera. But my next trip to Italy was to compete in a Classics regatta at Imperia on the Italian Riviera aboard the very same Manitou. It is such a lovely town and being lined up with dozens of other classics and competing made for an amazing atmosphere. Straight after that I drove to Genoa to get the car ferry to Sardinia to compete in the Swan World Championships in Porto Cervo. Very different from racing the classics, but the most idyllic location for racing and great fun as well.

The last sailing trip was with a group of friends where we chartered two 50ft yachts to sail the island of Giglio, which had recently become famous for the sinking of the Costa Concordia. One of the guys in our group had an aunt who lived on Giglio. She'd won a trip there in a beauty contest decades ago, and met and married the now-major of the island. We all squeezed into their apartment with their extended family for food and drinks. Classic Italian hospitality. It was the annual festival in the hilltop town and we did more partying than sailing, but it was great fun.

Would I go back? Always. To see Venice again, opera at Verona, the market in Turin, ski touring, Sicily, Puglia, Stromboli and more! And those sailing trips all over again.

Japan

I have been to Tokyo a couple of times on business. The first time was to meet some clients and research a book I was writing on a Japanese analysis technique. The second time was to speak on that technique at a conference. Tokyo is an amazing city. The central district of Ginza is bright white light at night. It almost feels like the middle of the day. On the first trip, I went out with Japanese clients and contacts who were hell-bent on showing me a good time. We went to some amazing traditional Japanese restaurants and I was guided through the ceremony and customs of a traditional Japanese meal. I could barely walk after kneeling for so long through dinner. We went to karaoke bars where it was obligatory to sing 'My Way.' I heard it so many times, I had to try hard not to sing it with a Japanese accent when it was my turn. Sometimes you would look up at a building and see all the bright coloured neon booths with groups of people performing. It was a lot of fun. After that we went to see the nightlife of Roppongi. We went to a nightclub where they had lockers for your coats, jackets, scarves, hats. These normally reserved people would suddenly turn into party animals.

My number one thing to see was the Tokyo fish market, the world's largest, and one of the locals with us on our night out agreed to take me. She insisted we needed to be there by 5am before everything winds down. And most of all to see the tuna auction. A full-size tuna weighting 200kg can sell for tens of thousands of dollars ($1.8m is the latest record) and the bidding frenzy is fascinating to watch. The scale of the place and the variety of seafood is quite something. There were lots of fish species I had never seen and an abundance of it. I saw oysters in shells a foot long. The finale here is to go to one of the many sushi restaurants that surround the market. They are tiny booths that seat maybe a dozen people up at a counter, with queues outside. The sushi there is the best I have eaten.

Tokyo is challenging but exciting. A map of the underground is like a picture of a pile of noodles with kanji characters on top. It was great fun going round supermarkets and department stores trying to work things out. The Big Camera electronics superstore was my favourite. It was fascinating to play with so many gadgets I had never seen.

The second trip was a bit more luxurious. I ended up being upgraded to a suite on the top floor of The Peninsula Hotel. It had great views over the city. At night the light of Ginza was so bright below that at bedtime you had to close the blackout blinds by pushing one of the many buttons on a console beside a bed big enough to play tennis on. I walked a lot on that trip, taking in some of the parks and other districts. The busy Shibuya 6-way pedestrian crossing was mayhem.

Would I go back? Yes. Bullet train, Mt Fuji, spring blossom, Osaka, powder skiing.

Jordan

A few years ago I spent a week in Jordan as a stopover on my way back to England from Thailand. I arrived late at night, hired a small car and headed off into the night to the ancient town of Madaba. The roads were badly lit, with speed bumps in random places. You were meant to know where they were. I stayed in a tumbledown hotel by the mosque and woke to the loud call to prayer at dawn. There was an impressive 6th century mosaic map of the Holy Land to see here and then I headed south towards Petra.

Rather than taking the main highway from the airport to Petra full of tour buses, I opted for the winding road through the mountains to Kerak. There is an imposing fort here and I drove to the top of the town and found somewhere to park at the back. I couldn't find the main entrance to buy a ticket but there was a big hole in the fence so I entered there in the hope that I would find my way around. I spent about an hour walking the grounds of the fort. The views out were incredible. The place was deserted. I found the entrance and exited here. It was unmanned. It was located at the end of a short street with shops either side with shopkeepers standing in doorways. It felt a bit eerie and I suddenly felt unsafe. I walked to the car and left. Less than an hour later there was a terrorist siege there with western hostages held. Thirteen Jordanians and one Canadian tourist died in the subsequent shootout. I had driven on to Petra unaware, but it was all over the news – including the western channels – that night. I sat up at the bar for dinner with a good bottle of Jordanian red, feeling very lucky and reassuring friends and family I was OK. I had planned to visit some known hotspots in the north near the Syrian border on this trip, but began to re-evaluate.

I was up before dawn and took the long walk into the ancient city of Petra. As you weave your way through the narrow high walled passage for around twenty minutes, nothing quite prepares you for your first glimpse, through the tall chasm in the rock, of The Treasury. And as you step out into the clearing there it is, right in front of you, Petra's most famous image. A cathedral-like façade carved out of the rock. It is awesome but it is only the beginning of the ancient city of Petra. The main valley contains dozens of tombs and temples carved out of the pink sandstone cliffs. I climbed up high to the sacrificial altar to get a perspective of the valley. There, an old local woman pointed to a path signalling there was another valley this way and she made a quiet roar like a lion. I was a bit confused and sceptical. There was nothing in the guidebook about a second valley, but I was curious to see what she was on about. So, I descended the path for several minutes to find a big lion carved in the rock. Ah, the roar. I looked down the path and sure enough it opened out to another valley, not as impressive, but completely deserted. I had it to myself for the hour it took to explore the small temples down the sides. At the bottom it met up with the other valley and the tourists. From here there's a path that takes around an hour to climb. In a clearing at the top is The Cathedral, a larger scale version of The Treasury. The views out over the mountains towards the Dead Sea are stunning. I sat here for a while taking it all in with a freshly squeezed pomegranate juice. I walked back up the main valley again and left ancient Petra at sunset after walking all day. I had a drink in the cavernous bar carved into the rock at the entrance and headed back to my hotel. An amazing day.

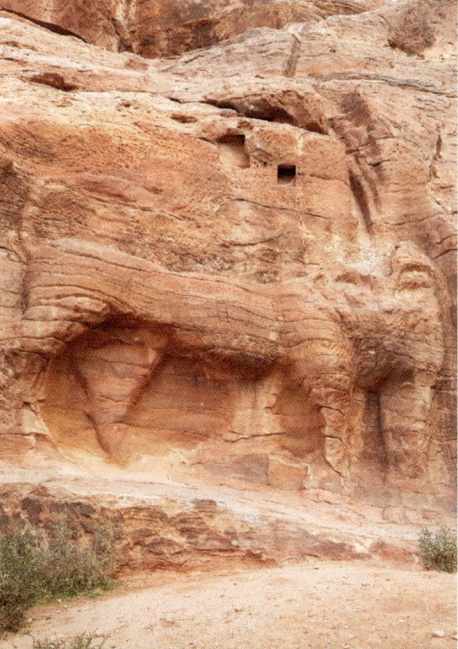

Jordan held a bit of the Lawrence of Arabia for me, with memories of Peter O'Toole shouting out 'to Wadi Rum' and 'we take Aqaba.' I wanted to see these places almost as much as Petra. Wadi Rum was a true desert landscape. T.E. Lawrence's Seven Pillars of Wisdom, also the title of his autobiography, rise out of the sand there. And then I went onto the port of Aqaba at the top of the righthand narrow gulf of the Red Sea. Jordan swapped 6,000 sq km with the Saudis in the sixties to double the length of coastline here to 20km. I drove down to the Saudi border and swam in the turquoise water off sandy beaches there. I walked all around Aqaba, saw the fort and was taken by the gardens growing all the local produce right by the sea. In the evenings I took a drink in the Aqaba Yacht Club looking across to Eilat in Israel. I met Israelis on the flight to Jordan who would fly to Thailand from here connecting in Amman to save the extra several hours flying time that flights from Tel Aviv must take down the Red Sea over the Indian Ocean below the Arabian Peninsula.

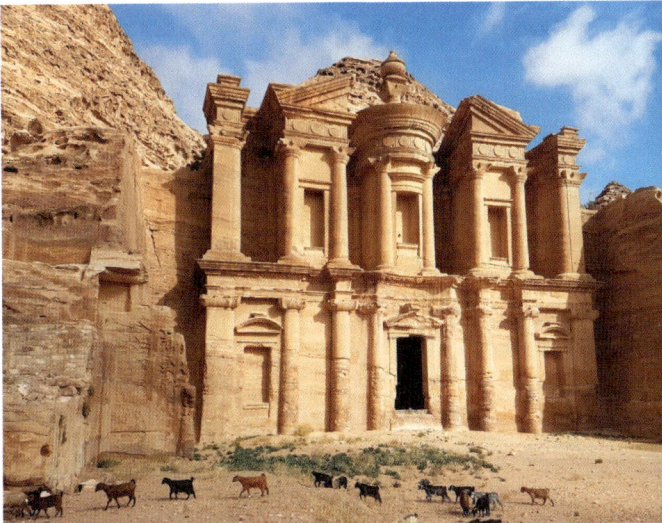

From here I drove up the fenced border with Israel to the Dead Sea, which has the border running right down the middle of it. At 1,400ft below sea level, it is the lowest place on the planet. The sea is a brine so salty that nothing can live in it. The mud is good for your skin and you cover yourself with it. The buoyancy of the salty water is so great that you cannot swim on your front. Your body wants to bend upwards in the middle forcing your face under. Not good for the sensitive eyes, lips, and nose. It burns basically. So, you must lie on your back and wallow round with no fear whatsoever of sinking. You cannot even stand once at chest height. Your legs just pop up from under you. A group of American GIs came into the water and terrorist paranoia had me thinking they would be a target. On the last night I sat with a drink looking across the sea to the lights of Jerusalem, 4,000 ft higher at the top of the West Bank.

Would I go back? Probably not a second time, but highly recommend a first visit.

Kenya

I had been wanting to go to East Africa for years. There is a romanticism about the trading ports on this side of the Indian ocean. A friend Jina, who worked with me years ago, grew up there and her parents still lived up by Lake Naivasha a few hours north of Nairobi. 'Come to Kenya for Christmas' she said. I told her I would come and find them in the New Year. I touched down in Nairobi, stayed the night in the airport hotel before flying to Tanzania for the first part of my East African trip. My first real Kenyan experience was arriving in Mombasa a week later. I got a taxi through the city to Nyali Beach. Driving down Links Road here with the old white signposts with black stripes and black lettering was a reminder that the British had colonised Kenya. The hotel was empty and right on the edge of a white sandy beach. It was great to be swimming in the sea in December.

The Swahili island of Lamu was my next stop. It might just be the only commercial airport in the world where you walk out the front door to hail a boat to take you to town. There was a sense of intrigue boarding on an old bright blue wooden boat and watching the main town on the island opposite draw closer. For several days I holed up in Lamu House, a lovely boutique hotel, and soaked in the amazing atmosphere of the place. In many ways it was like stepping back a hundred years. I felt sorry for the donkeys, each carrying more sand, cement and concrete blocks than several men could.

There was a thriving boat community here and I would spend hours just sitting in the hotel restaurant watching the world go by. It was the perfect mix of an old-world place and relaxation.

Jina was staying with her aunt and uncle at Kazingo at the other end of Lamu Island, an eco-friendly resort they had built up over many years. I had planned to walk the circa 5 miles along the beach to see them, but the hotel advised against it. We were close to the Somali border and there had been kidnappings, one of the reasons why tourism on Lamu had recently been in decline. So, I jumped on the back of moped taxi and we battled through deep sand and sank in mud on the approaching beaches. They were all quite surprised to see I had made it that way and we had lunch in the big open barn-like main building. We had sent my moped rider back on his own and I got a fast boat back to Lamu town which was a more pleasurable journey.

On my last day, I went to the village of Shela just along the shore from Lamu Town and wandered the atmospheric streets. I met Jina and her sisters for lunch at the stylish Peponi Hotel where Jina's family knew the owners. We sat in our own cool dining area looking out to sea. After lunch we walked down the beach and hailed a boat to take us to the airport to fly to Nairobi. We stayed at their friends' fabulous house up in the district of Karen. Their garden extended into bushland. The next day we drove a few hours north to Jina's parents' place by Lake Naivasha.

The old straight road to the lake passes by the dormant Longonot volcano. We turned off to the left to skirt the southern shores with mile after mile of rose-growing farms. If you have bought a bunch of roses in the UK with Produce of Kenya on the label they will have come from here. Forty percent of roses sold in Europe do. Take a look next time you buy them. Not what you expect around a hundred miles from the equator, but this gives away the lake's secret. You are at an altitude of 7,000ft. The days are hot, and nights are cool and the lake, at around ten miles in diameter, provides an almost abundant water supply for produce growers. The Carnelley family have run Fisherman's Camp on the edge of the lake forever. The family home is up the hill looking over the lake.

There are times when you travel when you land on your feet. This was one of those times. I felt part of the family immediately. Nigel and Sarah, pleased to have their three daughters at home, were on brilliant form. The girls would say 'Daddy can we do this?' and Nigel would say 'Sure, let's do that tomorrow.' I stayed in a cottage near the house. It so reminded me of holiday homes where I grew up in Oz with the same colonial influences a world away. The view over the deep blue waters of Lake Naivasha through the huge Euphorbia Candelabra cactus trees was stunning. On some days, large bright green carpets of water hyacinth would drift into view. In the evening we would go for walks up behind the house to see giraffe and zebra everywhere.

Lake Naivasha is a playground for wildlife. It is surrounded by fever trees and teeming with more species of bird than you can count. Large animals come to the water's edge to drink and it is full of hippos wallowing in the shallows. We had a great day fishing catching black bream on a boat in front of the Naivasha Yacht Club. The locals who took us weaved through the brown mounds in the water. Pointing at the hippos, they would say, 'that one is okay…..that one over there, he's definitely not okay.' These powerful animals can launch their 3,000kg of body weight right out of the water and be in your boat in seconds. People are killed here every year, so

I was happy not to go any closer to the one 'that was definitely not okay!' The fish that night was delicious.

The girls wanted to go on safari, so Nigel phoned up Lord Delamere and asked if we could drive up to his estate for a bit of game spotting. To see the wildlife at sunrise and sunset we needed to stay the night, so a couple of old stone outhouses were put at our disposal. Going on safari can cost hundreds, even thousands of dollars, with vans full of tourists connected by walkie-talkie all descending on the latest sighting. Lord Delamere said he would be grateful if we could get him a bottle of scotch on our way.

Delamere's Soysambu 48,000-acre conservancy sits on the edge of Lake Elmenteita in Kenya's Great Rift Valley. This is Happy Valley of White Mischief fame. Notable guests include Winston Churchill, Evelyn Waugh, Theodore Roosevelt and us. Most of the big game you would expect are here which is helped by the abundance of food. There are 6,000 zebra and you see quite a few with claw wounds running perpendicular to the stripes on their hind legs. I would get out of the jeep and walk into a sea of zebra, which would part leaving me surrounded with a ring of them all looking at me. There were herds of buffalo, which I didn't walk into. Nigel and Sarah had a wealth of knowledge and experience and had some great stories. We all wanted to see a leopard. They are so well hidden in the trees. Sarah said our most likely encounter would be if they came to where we were sleeping in the middle of the night. Their favourite trick was to steal the family pet and take it up a tree. The door on my hut didn't close very well, but luckily I had drunk enough beer to not lie awake in the middle of the night thinking of snakes or leopards.

The next morning before dawn we headed out in the jeep looking for a kill. We would look up in the sky for the signs of vultures circling. We saw hyena ravaging leftovers but no big cats. We visited a raptor centre and saw massive eagles with legs as thick as your arms. The guy living there had loads of videos of leopards breaking into his house at night. I was glad I saw that after my night in the hut rather than before it. One of his eagles had been captured and imprisoned here, apparently as punishment for carrying off a small child. The highlight of this safari was seeing the enormous Rothschild giraffes, which are much bigger than normal giraffes, with darker spots. We approached two males fighting, a young one taking on the patriarch. They were launching their necks at one another and you could hear the hollow-sounding bangs a mile away. I got out of the jeep and walked towards them. They stopped fighting and the old boy just stood there for a moment looking down at me. He was so majestic. I don't think I have ever been more in awe of another creature. Having got my measure, he slowly wandered to get back to the business of defending his territory. It was such a powerful moment that I sat in the jeep almost speechless as we left the estate.

We took the gravel and dirt roads around the

back of Lake Naivasha home. Nigel, bilingual with Swahili, would stop to chat to every local Kenyan. Lots of British had lived up here over the years, but few had stayed. There were lakeside properties with sprawling lawns down to the lake as evidence of a bygone era. Everyone for miles around knew Nigel and he was completely at one with the place. He would sometimes stop and point out the flowers. The girls weren't paying attention and he would say, 'admire the flowers, it's not all about the big five (cats) you know.' It reminded me to just take it all in and enjoy every moment. We got a puncture and then the spare got a puncture. Nigel would make a call, word would get out and a spare would turn up ten minutes later on the back of a moped. The locals here were lovely people with big white smiles.

On my last night sitting out on the terrace with the family, Sarah asked me what I had enjoyed most about my stay. I was a bit stumped. Was it the fishing trip? Walking into herds of zebra? The big giraffe? At this altitude, the stars were hanging in the air like bright jewels: you could make out the silhouette of the mountains against the blue-black sky across the silvery lake. The crickets occasionally broke the silence, and you could smell the garden in the cool night air. Taking it all in, I turned to Nigel and Sarah and said, 'The thing I have enjoyed the most is the feeling of feeling truly alive.' I am eternally grateful to them and Jina for my time there.

We headed back to Nairobi. Before coming to Kenya, I re-watched the film Out of Africa. So, I wanted to go and see Karen Blixen's house.

Touristy I know, but it was worth seeing the setting. I took Jina and her sister for lunch next door in return for humouring me for being a tourist. Then we went to see the giraffes at Giraffe Manor. Again, touristy but fun getting up close to them. Very close in fact. You put a pellet in your mouth, and they will bend down and kiss you taking it between their lips. When I stood before the big giraffe in the wild a few days earlier, I had no idea I would be kissing one. I said my goodbyes and checked into Ole Sereni hotel on the edge of the Nairobi National Park close to the airport. On my last day, I did a short safari from the hotel, mostly to see rhino, before flying out for London.

Would I go back? Yes, to do it all over again!

Laos

Laos was the last country in south east Asia for me to visit, save the Philippines, and there was only one place I really wanted to see: Luang Prabang. I flew in from Thailand and checked into a typical guest house. This ancient city lies on a neck of land formed by the Nam Khan River joining the larger Mekong River which flows in from the part of southern China I had been to decades earlier. It is more the size of a town, with a perimeter only a few miles around. With all the shuttered buildings in the streets the French colonial influence is obvious. There are many fine gilded temples as well, which accounts for the hundreds of monks you see, dressed in bright orange robes. At dawn they form a long queue as part of the silent Buddhist alms-giving ceremony to receive offerings of food from the devoted locals. You could hear a pin drop in the silence.

The food was good pretty much everywhere you went in Luang Prabang. I loved the fresh juice bars set up on the side of the road. The street markets sprawled into a labyrinth of back allies which were fun to visit at night. One morning, I bought a bird in a little bamboo cage and climbed the hill that dominates the skyline and released it. I learned later they are trained to fly back to their keeper, but even so, there was something fulfilling, almost spiritual, about releasing the little creature that had chirped away at me on the walk up. This was a place for walking, and I think I must have walked every street many times over by the end of my stay. Watching the way they constructed buildings was interesting, with nearly everything being fabricated onsite. You could cross the Nam Kam River on bamboo foot bridges, lit by fairy lights at night. For the mighty, fast flowing Mekong, you had to cross by boat. My time in this quiet unspoilt part of Asia was relaxing and well worthwhile.

Would I go back? No, it's done.

Latvia

My trip to Riga was a fleeting stopover. I had flights changing there so decided to get the same connecting flight the next day. The city, on the edge of the Baltic sea, is a curious mix of wooden and art deco buildings in a pedestrianised medieval old town. The roofs are mostly red tiled and the 400ft spire on the town hall dominates the old town. At night the main Livu Square becomes lively with restaurants and nightclubs. An increasing number of British stag and hen weekends are finding their way here. The beer is good and cheap and progressing to vodka shots for an all-nighter wouldn't break the bank. I was there in winter, but I could imagine a weekend there with long summer nights could be fun.

Would I go back? Maybe in summer.

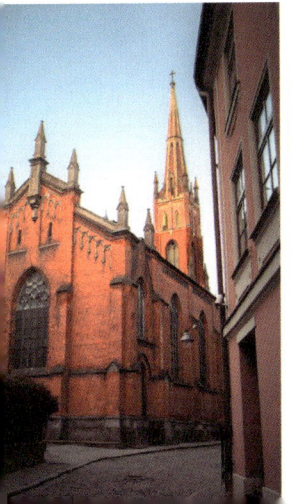

LITHUANIA

10 LIETUVOS BANKAS

AI9728144 2001

10

LIETUVOS BANKO
VALDYBOS PIRMININKAS

S. DARIUS   S. GIRĖNAS

10 DEŠIMT LITŲ

Lithuania

A Lithuanian friend in London invited me to her birthday weekend and I thought why not? At that time, I had never visited the Baltic states and was curious to see what they were like. A travel experience where your friends are locals is completely different than going somewhere on your own. The destination was Klaipeda, a port city on the Baltic. I landed in Vilnius and drove the 200km into the night to reach the coast. It would have been quicker to drive to Minsk in Belarus, and I confess I was tempted to visit Europe's largest landlocked country. Arriving in the dark, I miraculously found the party. Later we went on to a nightclub. It was mostly full of skinny blonde women and overweight men. The women danced and the men stood at the bar consuming vast quantities of vodka. By the end of the night the women were left standing and the men were legless, quite literally collapsing in heaps on the floor. Luckily, I avoided most challenges to shots.

The next day we had brunch in the main square and then caught a ferry a few hundred metres across the lagoon to the Curonian Spit. This narrow spit of sand dunes between the lagoon and the Baltic is 100km long and emanates from the Russian enclave of Kaliningrad, originally Konigsberg, prised from the Germans at the end of WWII. A long walk in the dunes in the bracing Baltic wind was a good way to blow out the cobwebs.

I drove back to Vilnius and spent the day walking around both the capital with its baroque buildings and another medieval old town. On my way to the airport, I got caught speeding and was pulled over. I handed them my Australian passport, which normally confuses matters. Their English wasn't great, but it was better than my Russian. They maintained stern faces. I took the risk and pulled out my wallet and sensed we had a deal. I bought my passport back for the last couple of large notes I had. As we made the exchange, I noticed the picture of the officers on the money looked just like them.

Would I go back? Not especially.

Malaysia

My trip to Malaysia was brief. I was already in southern Thailand when I decided to head south across the border to the island of Penang. I was curious to see George Town and the colonial influences there. It was a major trading port for the East India Company and the British influence remained more untouched here than places like Hong Kong or Singapore. The city was low-rise buildings with an eclectic mix of Chinese shophouses, bold British colonial and mosques. Given the history, a drink at the Eastern and Oriental Hotel was obligatory. I sat with my beer on the terrace looking over the sea towards Butterworth. The staff all wore white gloves. I spent a few days by the beach at the south of the island before heading back to George Town for breakfast. There, on a whim, I went and changed my flight and left that day for Sri Lanka via Bangkok.

Would I go back? Yes, KL, Langkawi, Tioman, Sarawak.

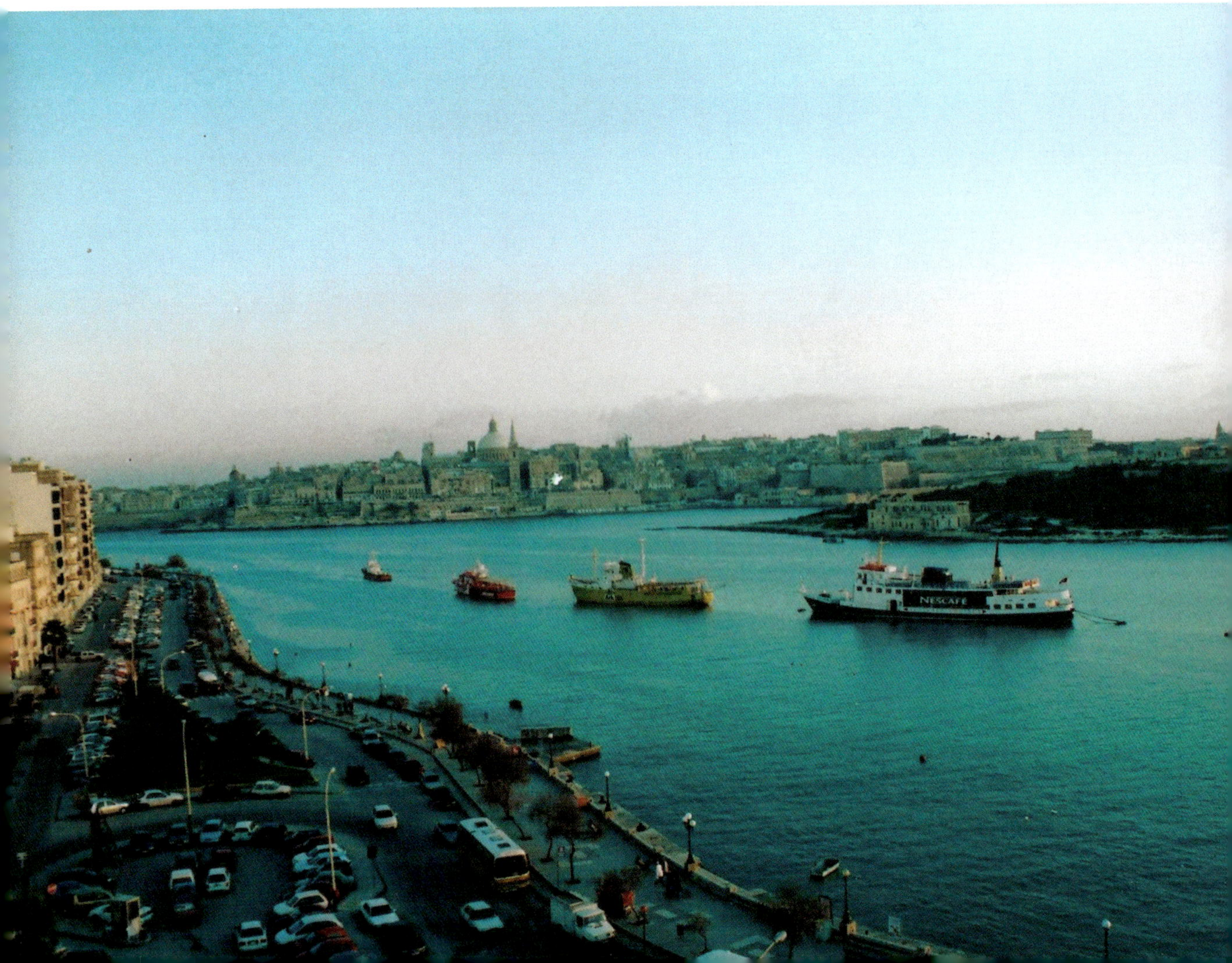
NESCAFÉ

Malta

My first trip to Malta was in the late eighties with my French girlfriend Roseline. We stayed in Sliema across the small inlet from Valletta and did daytrips from there by car. Malta has been ruled historically by the Greeks, the Romans, the Arabs, the French and the British, with influences from neighbouring Italy. It felt a little like all of these places on arrival. The capital, Valletta, is a beautiful small city of sandstone buildings; a joy to walk around. One of the highlights was a daytrip to Mdina, the old capital, the base of the Knights of St John in the 16th Century. The fine old stone buildings here in this silent old city were impressive. We visited some fishing ports and some ancient stones from 5,000BC settlements. The coast is all rock, so there were no real beach days. That trip was more a cultural holiday. My second time there was just after Malta joined the EU, becoming its smallest member state. I stayed with a work contact who'd bought a big apartment in Sliema looking over the harbour to Valletta. It was a weekend break for a bit of winter sun and some business lunches. Dinner at the Barracuda fish restaurant round in St Julian's Bay was memorable.

Would I go back? Yes, to do the Middle Sea yacht race around Sicily from there.

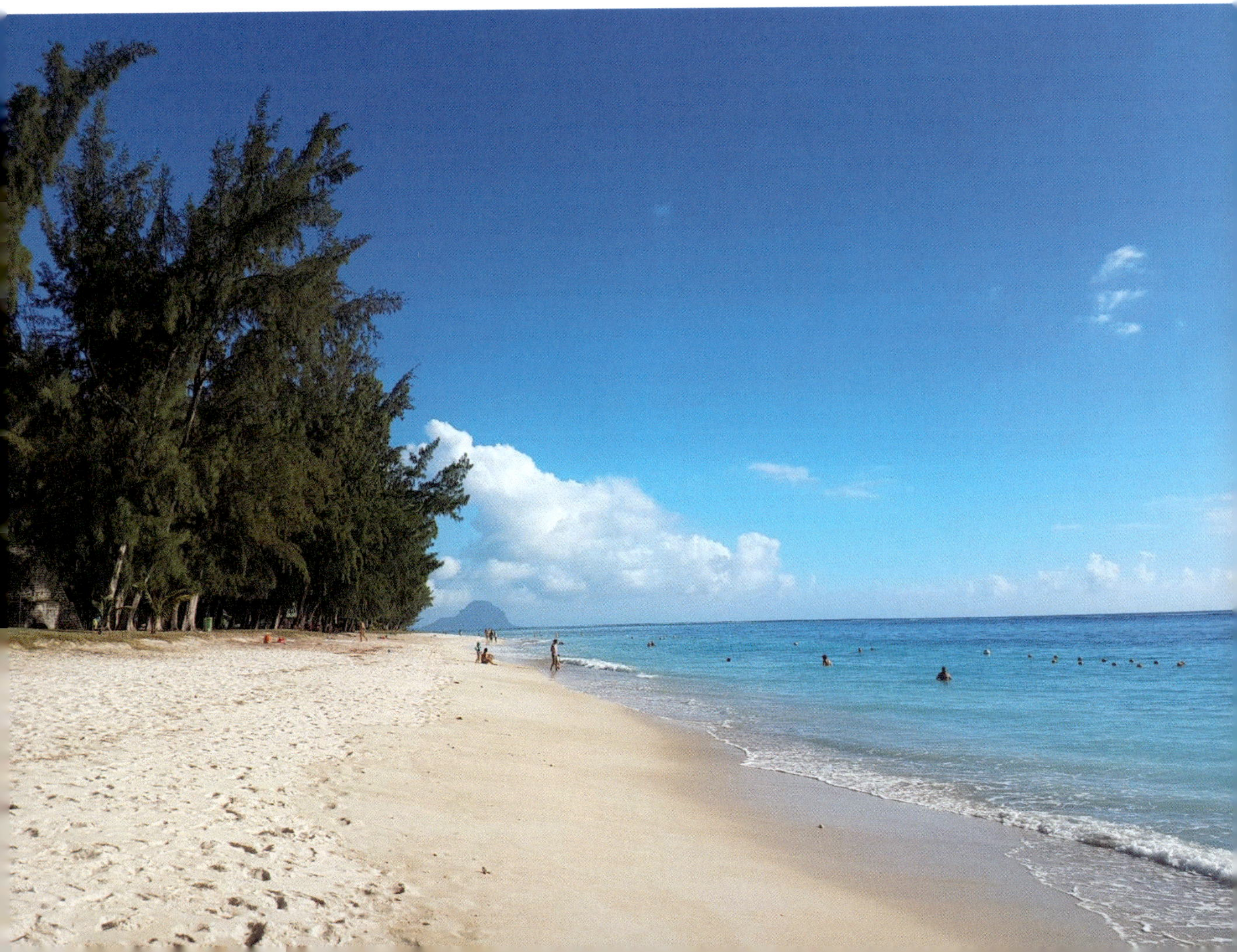

Mauritius

We were coming out of the depths of an English winter and I had some air miles burning a hole in my pocket, so I said to my good friend Helena, 'where shall we go?' It had to be somewhere warm and ideally a place I had not been. We settled on Mauritius and our mutual friend Jo, decided to join us. I was most curious to see the landscape. I had seen pictures of the island state and jungle covered mountains rising high out of the sea. Hels did the research on where to stay which turned out to be at three great spots on the island.

Our first place was called Chillpill Guest House, right on the waterfront, on the edge of a town near the airport called Mahebourg. This is the more weathered eastern side of the island. The sea is turquoise blue looking out to the reef and we mostly lazed about reading books in the sun. We went swimming in nearby Blue Bay and did a drive up the coast on one of the days. The forested mountains of rock and fields of sugar cane made for dramatic scenery. It was like something out of Jurassic Park. At night we would walk along the seafront to nearby fish restaurants and then enjoy drinks in the moonlight looking out to sea.

Next, we decamped to Black River on the west coast where we stayed in a great house with a roof terrace and a path down to a stunning white sandy beach. We swam here lots and being on the west coast it was great for sunsets. We walked up the beach each night to the boutique Bay Hotel for drinks and dinner: if I go back to Mauritius, I'll stay there. One of the days we hired paddle boards and paddled out to see dolphins. By the time we got to them we realised we were miles out to sea and had a long paddle into the wind back to the beach.

The last place we stayed was Grand Baie, a lagoon full of boats at anchor on the north end of the island. There were some good beaches here as well and we hired a Hobie Cat and went out for a sail.

Would I go back? Yes, especially to get to Reunion for a helicopter ride through the mountains.

Mexico

Mexico was the last country left in Central America for me to visit. For most people, it would be their first. My friends Johnny and Sarah were going with their daughters, my goddaughters Poppy and Flo, for a couple of weeks over Christmas. So I gate-crashed. They flew into Cancun from Spain. I hopped over the Gulf of Mexico from Houston to meet them on this north east corner of the Yucatan Peninsula. Our destination was Tulum, further down the coast. Sarah had organised a couple of different locations for us to stay at. The first place was Zamas at Tulum Beach which was a wonderful spot and right opposite a great Mexican restaurant. They had a sign saying, 'Best fish tacos in the world.' A bold claim, but they are the best I've had anywhere. The food was, in fact, amazing everywhere we went and might just be the best I've had anywhere in my travels. We ate in that first hotel quite a bit too and would sit watching the pelicans constantly diving for fish. Tulum has a great feel to it with boutique hotels and simple guest houses all along the coast. We hired bikes and rode everywhere.

A few miles up the beach are the ancient ruins of a large Mayan city. It's hard to think of anywhere else with such a significant historic site on a pristine white sandy beach with turquoise sea. Iguanas crawling over the rocks make it extra special. The ancient square lighthouse, sitting high on the cliff, is truly impressive. It was built to guide ships through a gap in the reef by lining up the windows on the back with those on the front. We went snorkelling the next day and swam with turtles. It was great to see how the ancient lighthouse worked from the sea.

We moved further down the beach to another great guest house where our rooms were on the sand. The door mat to your room was a dish of water to wash the sand off your feet. The food was good here too and the bar next door served amazing fresh ceviche, Chilean raw fish in lime juice. We would take early morning walks for miles up the beach passing the remnants of all night new moon parties along the way.

We needed to go into Tulum main town every few days to get money from the bank.

There weren't many cash machines. While you waited in the queue for the bank teller, there were lots of posters with pictures from CCTV images of hold ups. Underneath each mean-looking guy with a gun in his hand were the words 'Do you know this man?' I looked around at everyone in the bank to confirm I didn't recognise any of them. The other reason to go into the main town was the fantastic Burrito Bar. Their burritos were the best ever.

This part of Yucatan is home to a vast network of interlinked underwater caves called cenotes and you can swim in them. Some are big holes in the ground, others are completely underground. It was a very different experience from swimming in the sea.

A trip to Yucatan would be incomplete without seeing Chichén Itzá. It features in lists of wonders of the world, depending on which list you look at. It is famed for its distinctive pyramid. As ruins go, this ancient Mayan city is better than most. The big court area, where they played a game akin to Quidditch in Harry Potter, was very impressive. We went to the colonial city of Izamal, known as the Yellow

City, and saw the monastery. Not only is it yellow, it also boasts the second largest monastic court in the world after St Peters in Rome. You would not notice this fact if it wasn't for the sign. Izamal is a classic central American colonial town and it reminded me of Antigua in Guatemala. We stayed just outside the city of Valladolid, where we had another great meal in an old Spanish courtyard. On the way back to Tulum we stopped at the Mayan ruins at Coba, basically just piles of stones. But they were in the jungle and you could climb them and look out over the canopy. Not quite as impressive as Tikal in neighbouring Guatemala, but well worth seeing if you are closer to here than Tikal.

The last part of our trip was a couple of nights in a very swanky apartment in Playa del Carman before we parted ways and I headed back to Texas.

Would I go back? Yes. Happily, back to Tulum, Mexico City, Pacific coast, whale watching Baya Peninsula.

Monaco

My first visit to Monaco was in 1976 with my parents. There were no camping grounds or cheap guest houses, so we checked into the Holiday Inn. It was in an era before wheelie cases and my sister, aged ten, struggled with her case all the way through the crowded lobby to the front desk, where she dropped in on the marble floor and said loudly 'F**k this case is heavy!" She did not have to carry it from there.

Let's face it, Monaco is not a big country. Some would say it is just a principality. Either way, there is not a great deal to see once you have done the casino and looked out over the harbour. So, on my second visit in my twenties with Johnny, there was only one thing for it. That was to drive his Golf GTI around town as if we were doing the Monaco grand Prix. That done, we continued along the riviera towards Italy.

Would I go back? Yes, to the Grand Prix or into the Yacht Club after racing.

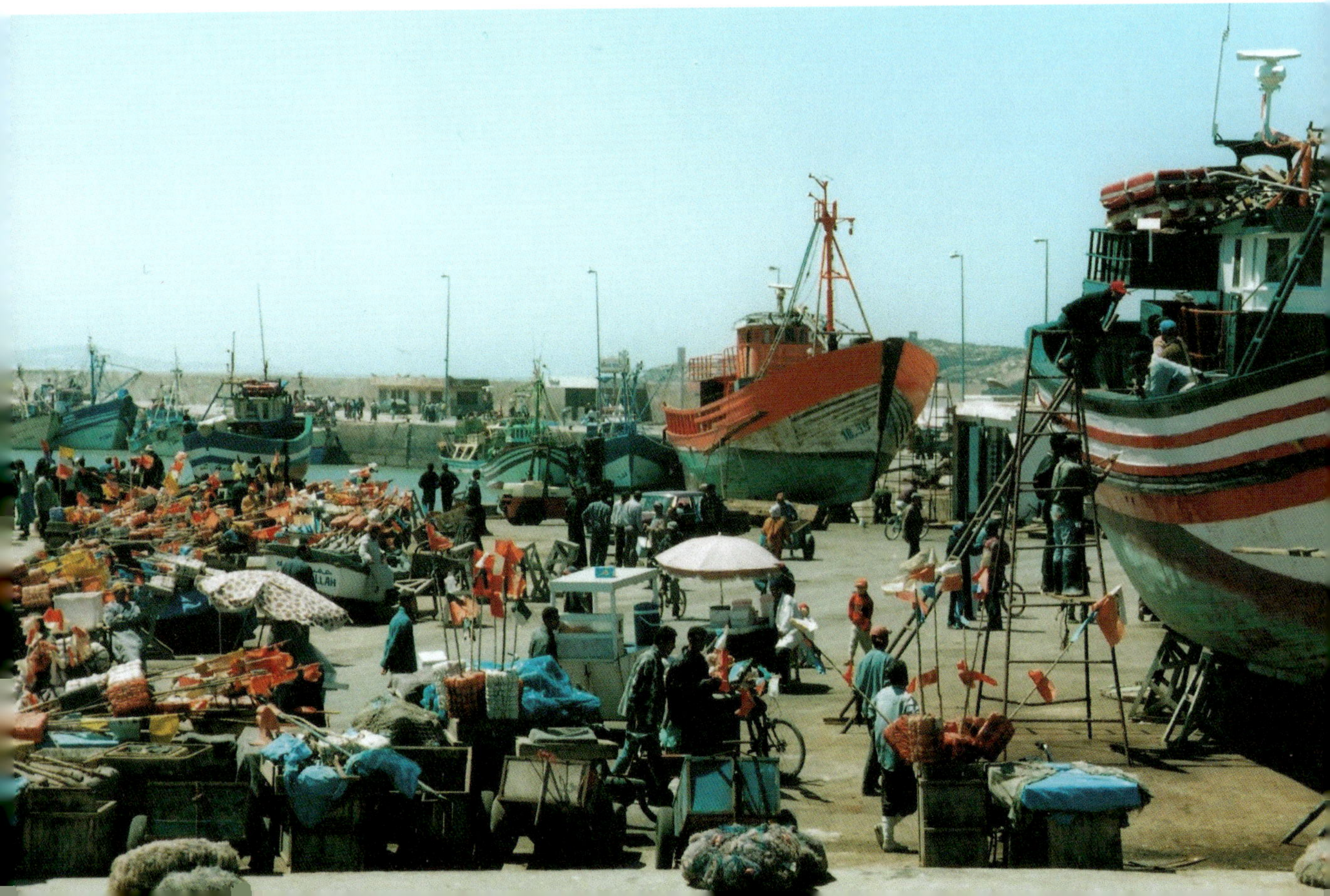

Morocco

I went to Morocco in the nineties with my girlfriend Katherine. We flew to Marrakech and stayed at the Ibis Hotel, which had a great garden and a pool and was just outside the city walls. On the first night we headed to the main Jemaa el-Fnaa square. At dusk it becomes one great big outdoor restaurant, with hundreds of food stalls cooking and serving food. We watched the evening unfold with ringside seats at a rooftop café on the edge of the square. The next day we hit the souk, or more accurately the souk hit us. I cannot remember ever being more hassled in my travels. Everyone wanted to take us to the best shop. The best stalls were those of people making an honest living selling local produce such as nuts and spices. I got so fed up with people offering me 'cheap carpets' that at one point I wheeled round on several people who had been relentlessly hassling me and said, 'where can I buy expensive carpets?' There was a moment's silence while they computed this and then a new bidding war ensued. We had to leave. Another day in the souk Katherine had her mind set on buying a handbag. After going round all the shops, she couldn't quite find what she wanted. Everyone was losing their patience and the one shop keeper who had seen us a few times said, 'come with me,' and took us through a labyrinth of alleyways to what was clearly the handbag factory. Thousands of bags. Everyone was lying down, and the foreman kicked them into action, and they started weaving and banging with hammers. There were no excuses now. Bag chosen. The weary shopkeeper got his sale.

For me, the highlight of Marrakech is the Majorelle Garden. The garden is a complete inspiration and is one of the top gardens in the world. Monty Don thinks so too. The buildings and garden walls are in cobalt blue, which really works in this setting. Pink bougainvillea against this blue provides such a contrast you never really see in a garden. So many parts of the garden are inspiring. A walk through the bamboo garden, with leaves on the ground forming a soft carpet, the sound of wind through the leaves, and the dappled light plays tricks with your senses. Next door to Yves Saint Laurent's classic Moroccan mud house which, with its tall palms, serves as a sympathetic backdrop to Majorelle.

Marrakech becomes a bit stifling after a few days, so we hired a small car with the aim of driving around the Atlas Mountains. We headed high up into the mountains first, where it was much cooler and lusher than the desert. Then our drive took us out towards the desert along the Draa River down the Draa Valley. The view is an explosion of palm trees growing all the way down the valley floor. A line of green across a vast brown landscape as far as the eye can see.

Our stop for the night was the world heritage site of Aït Benhaddou. This is where Omar Sharif first appears as a shimmer in the desert as he arrives on horseback in David Lean's classic film, 'Lawrence of Arabia'. It does have a unique film set quality and many films since have been shot here as a result, including Gladiator and Games of Thrones. I walked into the reception of the main hotel. which looks across to the mud village. They were full, but I was told they did have some Bedouin tents in the garden. They had the best view. I was thrilled, Katherine less so. In the morning we got up early and beat the tourists to walk around the ancient village made of mud. It was almost futuristic.

We hit the road and headed south towards the city of Ouarzazate getting closer to the edge of the Sahara Desert. The roads soon turned to gravel and then to sand. Our trusty little

Toyota Starlet soldiered on. Sometimes we would pull up in the middle of nowhere to survey what lay ahead and get out of the car to stretch our legs. Small children would emerge out of the hills, running down paths to see us. Seeing a car was a strange enough sight for them, let alone pale-faced tourists. They were weary but always had big smiles. We made it to Taroudant, a walled city on the southern edge of the atlas and stayed in a fabulous Riad. After a few days in the dry desert, it was an oasis with beautiful Islamic tiling, lush plants, and fountains.

The gem of this trip though, was Essaouira. This Portuguese fort city with walls butting right onto the rocks of the Atlantic Ocean was literally a breath of fresh air. It has been a favourite hangout for celebrities over the years, with Jim Hendrix being its most famous son. We stayed at a hotel in the battlement walls and spent a few days wandering round. The souk here is more authentic than in Marrakech, with better quality woodwork being made in workshops that are not hidden. I still have some great wooden chess boards and domino sets and when I open them up now, all these years later, the smell of the wood transports me straight back to those little factories.

At nightfall, the women would come out with their children to socialise in the square. It was a nice change to see in a male centric society. The fish was abundant in this ocean seaport. The fish market would set up on the front each morning. We went to a great fish restaurant called Chez Sam on the end of the harbour wall. The beach in Essaouira is a vast expanse of sand where the locals play football and the Berbers stand idly, looking like pixies in their coats. It has since become a kite-surfing mecca due to the strong winds that constantly barrel in from the ocean. We ate veg tagine a lot in Morocco, something that has never tasted quite right anywhere else since.

Would I go back? Yes, to see Tangier, Fes, Meknes and Casablanca.

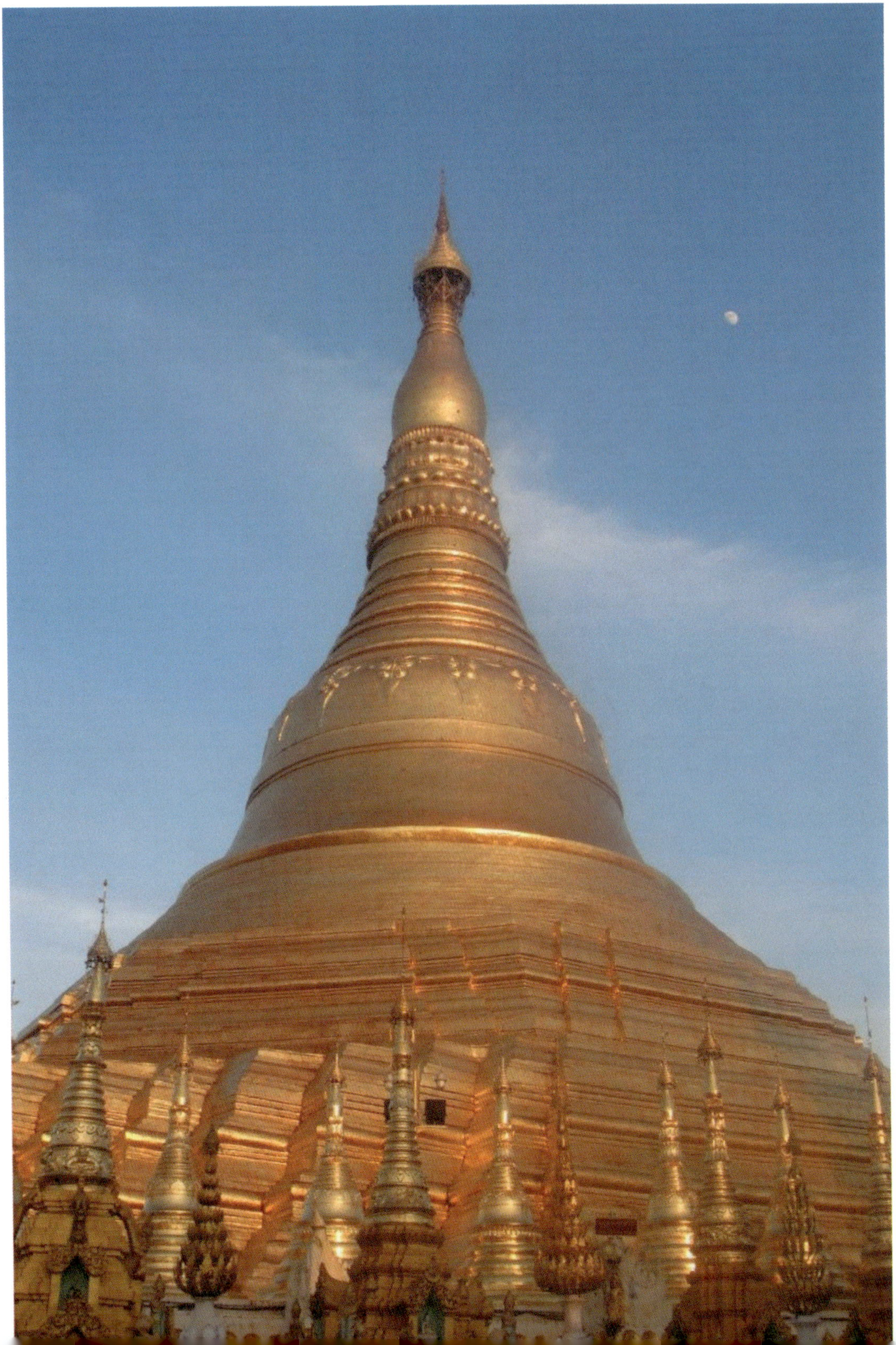

Myanmar

I had always wanted to go to Burma and the opportunity arose in 2013. My sister was going to be there on business and a few other friends were there too, so Miranda my girlfriend and I went. On the first night we stayed at the Inya lake Hotel, built in the 1950s by the Russians to demonstrate their technological prowess. On its completion, it was said to be the most modern hotel in Asia. There was a certain charm to staying in this hotel, with all its original detailing that had been left untouched. The parquet flooring throughout was stunning. From here, only a few years earlier an American tourist had swum across the lake to visit Aung San Suu Kyi, who was being held under house arrest.

The next day we flew up to Bagan, an amazing valley of 2,000 temples. We stayed in a fabulous boutique hotel with a great pool and hired bikes to go and see some of the temples. It was hard-going in the sand and when we saw electric bikes whizz by, we upgraded from the next day onwards. There are no mopeds or motorbikes in Burma. The regime banned them after a drive-by shooting. It is difficult to put Bagan into context without seeing it with your own eyes. Everywhere you look across the lush green landscape there are temples of all shapes and sizes as far as the eye can see. It was so hard to take it all in that we decided to organise a hot air balloon ride one morning through the valley. Unfortunately, the wind got up and it was cancelled.

The Irrawaddy River runs past Bagan and we walked down to the water's edge and found a fisherman who agreed to take us out in his boat. The food was great everywhere we went. All local produce of course. The Burmese salads were especially good. The people were friendly but there was an undercurrent of oppression. I remember a big army truck rolling into town one evening while we were sitting outside at restaurant having dinner. The atmosphere became tense all around and the silence lasted for a long time after the truck had gone. We headed to the airport, saw our flight handwritten up on the departures whiteboard, and flew to the capital, Yangon.

My sister was staying at the Chatrium Hotel and had arranged a room for us. Her boss had a permanent suite there and the staff all knew who Molly was. Soon they all knew who we were, and our service went up a gear. The hotel pool was amazing, with tall palm trees growing out of planter boxes in the pool. It was hard to get out of the water each morning. Yangon, Rangoon under the British, is a beautiful old colonial city that has been largely untouched. We walked around and went to the five star Stand Hotel for lunch. There was a quote framed from the 1911 'Handbook for Travellers in India, Burma and Ceylon', which declared The Strand to be, "the finest hostelry East of Suez". It was a very pleasant step back in time. That night we rounded up various friends who were in town and ended up with a table for twelve and quite a raucous night.

The star attraction in Yangon is the golden Shwedagon Pagoda, built 2,600 years ago. It is one of the most sacred Buddhist monuments in the world, said to hold the relics of four previous Buddhas. At nearly 400ft high, its golden glare dominates the Yangon skyline day and night. The main pagoda is estimated to be covered with up to sixty tons of gold and topped with 4,500 diamonds, the largest of which is 72 carats. Here, the poorest of people buy gold leaf to be offered at the temple. It was a surreal place to visit.

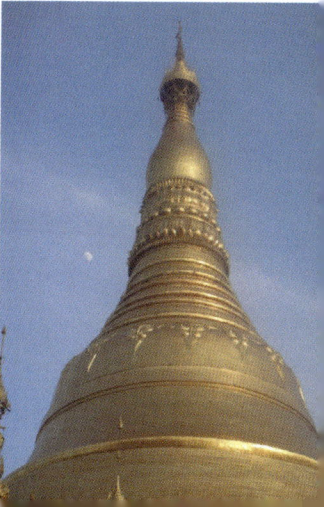

You needed cash to pay for most things, even in some of the big hotels. On our last lunch we pushed the boat out at the Kandawgyi Palace Hotel by the lake. I put my credit card on the table and was shocked to learn they did not take cards. We had to scrape together the cash we had on us and ended up paying in four currencies. The exchange rates vary depending on the size of the notes, $100 bills getting the most. You get around 20% less for $10 bills and all notes must be in crisp and new condition or they will be rejected. After all, if you are going to smuggle foreign money out of the country, you need to be able to pack it as tight as possible.

Would I go back? Probably, to see more of the country.

The morning after I wrote this chapter, I woke to the news of a new military coup in Burma. Aung San Suu Kyi was under house arrest and the country's future was again uncertain. Sad for the people and the country. I feel privileged to have been when I did.

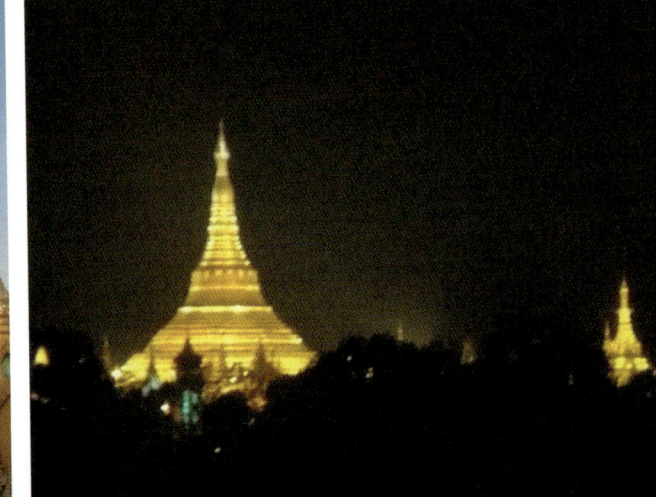

Netherlands

It is a little-known fact outside The Netherlands, that Holland makes up just two of the twelve provinces of this nation. North Holland is the province around Amsterdam and South Holland takes in The Hague and Rotterdam. I have been to the country many times and love it and the Dutch people. I visited fleetingly with my parents on our European trip in the seventies and my second trip, with the promise of interrailing to Scandinavia, was fleeting too. I was riding a bike down a shopping street and pulled out from behind a tram and had a head-on collision with another cyclist. The Dutch are the tallest people in the world and this guy was above their average. His forehead made contact with my cheek and I ended up in hospital. I went back to London for facial surgery in St Thomas's. Instead of seeing all the lovely Scandi people, I spent a week staring directly at Big Ben. The clock face was imprinted on my retina for longer and I avoided riding bikes in Amsterdam for a long time. I started going to NL a lot on business in the nineties, especially to the lovely town of Amersfoort. We often went as a team and would tack on a weekend in Amsterdam. We got to know it so well that when our Dutch business colleagues said, 'we'll show you Amsterdam', we'd say, 'we'll show you Amsterdam.'

Of course, there is much more to this beautiful city than smoking pot and seeing the Red-Light District which the liberal Dutch enjoy a stroll around after dinner. It is one of the best capital cities in Europe for walking. It is compact, bicycles massively outnumber cars, and the pretty network of canals add charm and open up the skyline. There are some great bars and restaurants and live music venues. Bourbon Street is a favourite, where people turn up from all over the world to jam ad lib. There's more of Vincent's pics than you will ever see in one place at the Van Gough Museum. And the exquisite almost photographic paintings of Dutch Masters in the Rijksmuseum are amazing. After dozens of trips here, I am always happy to go back. It is the perfect weekend city break.

I did a fabulous trip to The Netherlands one year with my parents. They were close to buying the Dutch barge, a Tjalk they had seen in France, so I suggested we go and see if there were any better ones in their homeland. Some of the best travelling you can do is when you have a project or a purpose as it takes you places you wouldn't go as a tourist. We drove all over the place, looking at the map for boatyards and marinas and banging on steel hulls to talk to people. We stayed in some lovely towns on the canals. We didn't find a better barge, but we learned quite a lot.

Groningen in the north of Holland is still a place I visit for work and it is a lovely train ride from Amsterdam across the flat countryside. To the west is Friesland, home of the Friesian cow. I remember one year when I was there, the farmers were protesting about something and made a statement by removing all the cows from the landscape for a day by hiding them inside. The dyke around the north coast is a great walk with the sea much higher on one side than the land on the other. A quarter of Holland is below sea level and another quarter is less than a metre above. You can see why the Dutch are big campaigners against global warming.

The south of Holland, near Maastricht, is great too with a surprisingly hilly landscape. Rotterdam, the largest port in the Europe, is a big modern city. A favourite place of mine is Middelburg in the south west region of Zeeland. I still go there occasionally on business and on the next occasion I will make more time for the beaches and sand dunes.

My last trip to Amsterdam was to board a 54ft yacht with friends for a passage to Copenhagen. We went up through the inner seas of Markermeer and Ijsselmeer with picture postcard scenes of old Dutch barques sailing. We emerged from the last loch and sailed through the Wadden Islands off the coast of Friesland along the northern coast. It turned into a wet and windy night in the North Sea but there is nothing like studying a chart at sea all night to get a handle on the shape of a coastline. It was a rough night but in this boat it was great.

Would I go back? Always.

Nicaragua

Nicaragua was the longest stop on my trip rattling through Central America with my pal Biggles. We were heading north from Panama City to San Salvador and this was the midpoint of our journey with Panama and Costa Rica behind us and Honduras and El Salvador ahead. We felt Nicaragua held the most promise. We flew into Managua from Costa Rica and headed straight for the classical Spanish city of Grenada, a great place on the edge of Lake Cocibolcha. This 100km-long body of water with an archipelago of islands in the middle was set to become an integral part of the Chinese-built and controlled Nicaraguan Canal project. The lake would be linked by canals to the Atlantic and the Pacific. At nearly four times the length of the Panama Canal it's an ambitious project which may never be completed. Sitting on the shores of the lake, you hope it won't be.

Granada is very Spanish and there are some good restaurants with lovely courtyard gardens. The paintings on the walls of buildings normally either told a biblical story or were advertisements. What do you do if you are next door to the shop that sells Coca-Cola? You paint your whole shop Pepsi! We went and climbed into the crater of a live volcano where you could barely breath for the fumes of sulphur.

After a couple of days in Granada, we went back to see the capital Managua. It was baking hot and lacked any real soul. The city was hit by a devastating earthquake in 1972 and large areas were never reconstructed. The civil war that raged through the sixties and seventies had also taken its toll. The Sandinistas took several years to overthrow the dictatorship with a violent campaign, only to have to fight a new war with the US-backed Contras. With the Russians then backing the Sandinistas, the Nicaraguan people became victims of a Cold War flash point. Monuments and paintings everywhere laid testament to what Northern Irelanders would call, 'the troubles'. The huge cathedral in Managua was at the epicentre of the earthquake damage and is still just an eerie shell. The place was deserted and being there that day, with seemingly no human life left, was like something post-apocalypse.

The next city, Leon, held much more promise. We stayed in a massive convent, converted to a hotel, and had a fun couple of nights out in lively bars. The symbolic murals in the streets of the struggles of war added to the atmosphere of this old colonial town. We could have stayed longer, but we were falling behind schedule and needed to hit the road with the pressure of flights at the end of our trip.

Would I go back? Was worth it, but probably not.

Norway

My first trip to Norway was around 30 years ago. I went by train via Denmark and Sweden, arriving in Oslo. It is a beautiful city at the head of Oslo fjord. Compared to London it was supremely expensive, with most things costing a few times more so I did not eat and drink like a king, but it's a fine place to walk around. It was nearly midsummer and pretty much light all night. You don't need to take a boat trip here because there are ferries going back and forth to the islands on the fjord.

The Norwegian people are probably the kindest I have met anywhere travelling. I remember asking the police sitting in car where I would find a bank with a cash machine. They said, 'jump in, we'll take you' and not only that, but they also drove me back to where I had first asked them. I love the sound of the language and how sometimes you can pick out similarities with English. I got a ferry over to the Vikingskipshuset to see the 9th century wooden Viking ships. I have been a couple of times since and I always marvel at how well they have survived.

I got a train to Bergen, home of Edvard Greig, on the coast. Norway is a great place to travel by train. Passing the fjords there were mirror images of the scenery in the water. Bergen has a seafaring atmosphere, and you feel you could be in a whaling community town on the north east coast of America. Somewhere like Nantucket. From here I headed north up the coast to Trondheim. There are over 1,000 fjords in Norway and many of them needed to be crossed by train to get to here.

The objective was to make it inside the Artic Circle, the land of the midnight sun, and that meant a train trip further north to Bodø. It never got dark. As a sailor, I wanted to go and see the strongest tidal current in the world at Salstraumen maelstroms. It was about 30km away. I walked out of town thinking I would hitch hike. There were no cars, but now that I was a few k's in, I was committed to keeping on walking. I finally heard a car coming, stuck my thumb out, and turned round to see it was a taxi. He stopped and I apologised for not meaning to hail him. I said I was hitchhiking and couldn't afford a taxi. He said he could see I was hitching and would happily give me a lift. He was going to Salstraumen anyway to pick up some tourists to bring back, so it was no skin off his nose. So, this taxi driver drove me 25km and insisted on taking no money. The fjord entrance in this place is a bit of a freak of nature and the tides can reach the colossal speed of 20 knots (40 kph), with big deep whirlpools 30ft wide forming on the surface. The sea here would swallow up most pleasure boats. The seabirds have a field day with confused fish whizzing round in circles. I watched in awe for about an hour and the same taxi driver had told his Scandinavian tourists that I might need a lift which I did and they insisted that I ride back to town with them.

I heard that people would be celebrating midsummer that night a few kilometres out of town, at a beauty spot looking over the sea towards the Lofoten Islands. So, early that evening, I started walking out of town. After about twenty minutes a blond Norwegian girl pulled up beside me in a bubble gum pink Triumph Herald convertible and said, 'Hey, do you want a lift?' I know, it sounds improbable. As we drove into the sunset, even I thought it was some kind of dream. But this really did happen. We got to the picnic spot and there were hundreds of people all set out on picnic blankets. Everyone was expecting to pull an all-nighter. I was the new guy from Australia joining their group. Not only were they all kind and generous, everyone was interesting and interested.

Shortly after midnight, the sun was low on the horizon and the light was turning golden for sunset. But instead of sinking below the horizon as it had done every day in my world forever before, it just stayed there. It just hung around. And then sunset turned to sunrise and it got lighter and lighter. I went back to my hotel for breakfast, taped my curtains to the windows and went to bed. Night time was the new day time. I would go out walking late at night. Or was it early in the morning? It all got very confusing. One night, or day, I walked past a nightclub. I said hi to the guy on the door and he beckoned me in. I said thanks but no thanks. I could see it was beyond my budget and so could he, but soon I was standing at the front desk being let in for free and given the normal free drink tokens for a couple of beers. They seemed to be pleased to have an Aussie in the house that night and the drinks kept coming. I looked out the big plate glass windows overlooking the harbour and a ship was coming in, in broad daylight. It was 2am. I have encountered a lot of the kindness of strangers in my travels, but never more than in Norway.

The train ran even further north to Narvik, from where there was a direct train all the way down through Sweden to Stockholm. I found my seat and in one of those great travel coincidences, the guy in the seat next to me was Canadian John whom I'd met and travelled with in China. We both just laughed.

I have been to Norway several times since and I still love it as much as that first trip. Work has taken me there for the most part, back to Oslo, Stavanger, Bergen and Tromso in the far north. I have got to know Oslo well, been to conferences, business cruises on the fjord, eaten amazing fish and reindeer in the restaurants there. I had a client in Tromso in the far north of Norway, deep inside the Artic circle. When we used to speak on the phone, he'd say, 'when are you coming to see us?' and my response was nearly always, 'when the sun comes up.' While the sun does not set here in the summer, it doesn't come up in the winter and when it does decide to show itself past mid winter, it is still a fleeting visit. But as we headed into summer one year I was running out of excuses, so I went. To put the scale of Norway's geography into context, it takes as long to fly to Tromso from Oslo as it does from London to Oslo. Tromso has been dubbed the 'Paris of the North' for centuries, maybe because early visitors were surprised there was any culture here at all. It is more a town than a city, but it's a fun place.

I have a theory that, the colder the water is, the tastier the seafood is. If there is a place to prove this theory, it's Tromso. Big chunks of meaty sweet-tasting fish, massive prawns, crab, lobster, langoustines, it's all here. I have only been in the summer, but I should go again in the winter for the amazing seafood…and the Northern Lights.

On a more recent trip to Oslo, I managed to leave my wallet back in London. Luckily one of my team was already there and had me covered. When the conductor came up to me on the airport express train, I stood up and opened my mouth to begin explaining, he stopped me, smiled, and said, 'Mr Linton, we've been expecting you.'

Would I go back? For sure, cross-country skiing, Lofoten Islands by Hurtigruten coastal steamer, see polar bears in Svalbard, more of the fjords, the Northern Lights.

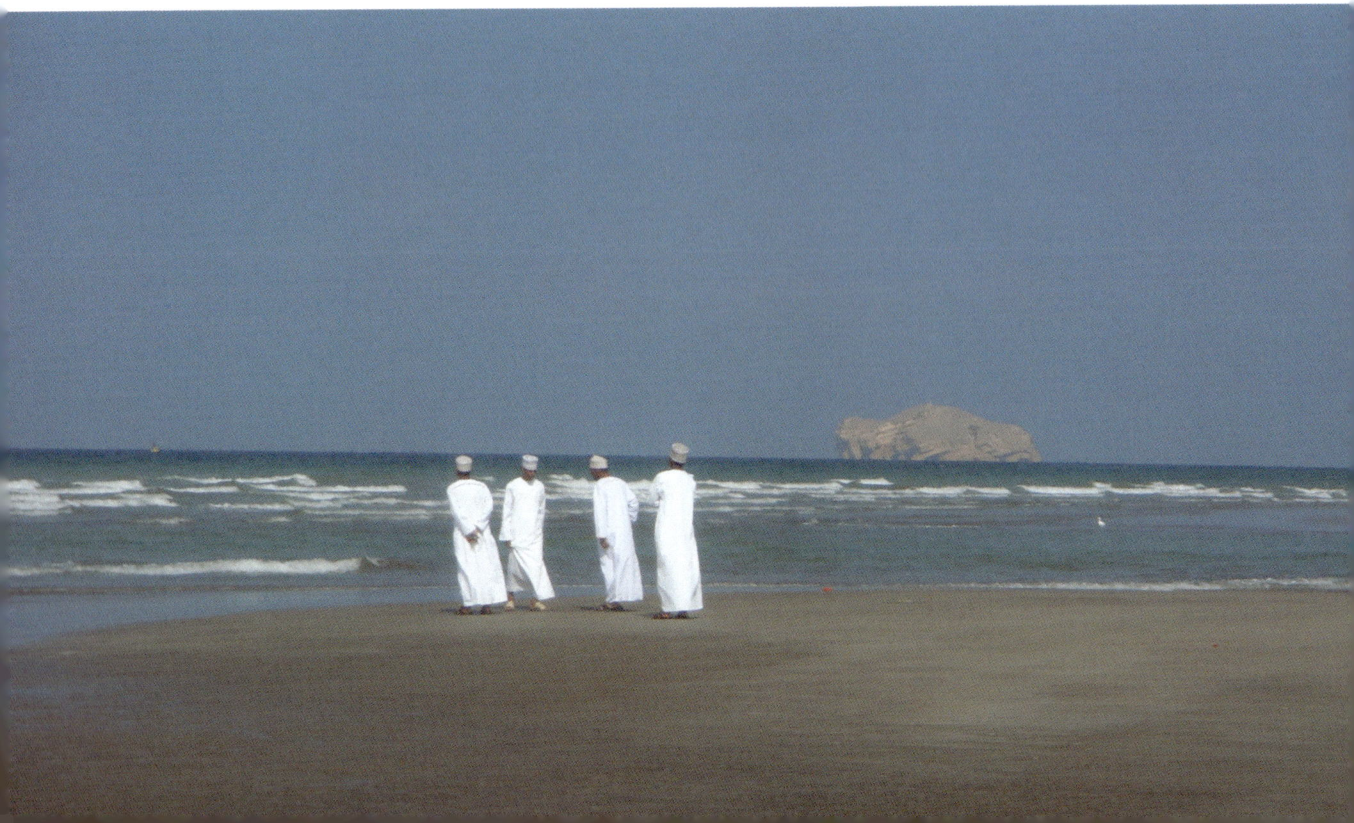

Oman

I went to Oman to write a book. A boring financial book, but I broke the back of the job there. I was already in UAE and wanted to see something more real than Dubai. It was for a few days over new year and the perfect place to walk and explore. I would enjoy the warm sun by day and hunker down over my keyboard at night. I flew into Muscat and stayed in an unexciting Ibis Hotel in the main part of town just along from the beach from the airport. The big hotel complexes are right on the beach here. Many tourists just fly in and laze in the winter sun by the pool in these compounds without seeing very much else. I did visit the Crown Plaza up on the cliff at the end of the beach one day for lunch and a snoop round suggested that guests mostly stayed put. I saw more tourists here than for the rest of my time in Muscat.

I found some cool local beach bars nearby where I would normally have delicious Fattoush salads for lunch. The large international embassy compounds were set along the beach here as well, their austere structures with CCTV everywhere creating a series of small prisons. The long sandy beach here was deserted, save the few groups of Omani men out walking. The water was warm to paddle in and I felt compelled to swim. After spending a while out in the deeper water, I waded back into the beach. A group of Omanis came up to me in their bright white robes and told me I should not swim here. Was I underdressed in just swimming trunks? No, the sea at that time was full of deadly sea snakes. They told me they are everywhere and then pointed to one lying dead washed up on the wet sand. That was my last swim in Oman.

I really liked Mutrah, the port with a sweeping Corniche around a small bay. It was a much more old-world Islamic setting with a fish market and an authentic souk set in a network of old alleyways off the main drag. There were no tourists shopping here and the silver was especially good. Beyond Mutrah is Old Muscat, dominated by the Sultan's Al Alam Palace. It is set on a small bay and a hill of rock in the perfect defensive position. There are mosques, museums, and ministries on the accessible side of this impenetrable palace. This part of Muscat is orderly and spotless.

Oman was a breath of fresh air after UAE. Dubai has a feeling of cheap labour shipped in to do all the menial work. The Omani people are the warmest and most relaxed I have encountered in the Middle East.

Would I go back? Yes, into the desert. To the enclave jutting into the Strait of Hormuz.

Panama

Panama was the start of my whistle-stop trip through Central America with my friend Biggles. We flew into Panama City from Houston. I was not expecting to see a skyline with more skyscrapers than America's fourth biggest city. I was also surprised to learn the official currency is US dollars. We flagged down a taxi and asked him to show us around town. We might easily have been at risk of been shown to the nearest girlie bar owned by his friend, but we took comfort from the fact that he had his young daughter doing her day at daddy's work. She sat in the front seat doing her schoolwork for a while but decided that acting as our tour guide would be more fun. We drove to the colonial old town and then walked around with our guide and her father. Some of the buildings had been restored and many were ripe for redevelopment. Our night out on the town after the taxi tour was large.

The next day we headed to the Pacific loch entrance at the Panama Canal. We were a bit hung over and it was proving challenging to take in all the facts and figures of the canal's construction at the visitors centre. We opted for a long lunch at the restaurant upstairs instead. We had a ringside table on the corner of the balcony where we watched all the Pacific-bound ships emerging out of the jungle and slowly into the lochs. All this fascinating activity happened right before us in between aperitifs, starters, wine, mains, more wine, puddings and coffee.

As much as another night in Panama City would have been welcome, we jumped on a night bus for the 600km journey to Bocas del Toro on the far north Caribbean coast. The bus journey to the 'mouths of the bull' was a bit too backpackerish for us. But with so little sleep in the last 48 hours, we managed to go into our respective comas. Boca was great. We arrived and had a big breakfast in a shack over the water on stilts. We flagged a guy down in a speed boat from our table and he motored over towards us and we asked him if he would take us out. Because of our tight schedule, we had dubbed this the 'throw money at it' trip. This was our first play. We didn't have time to go looking for tours and just grabbed the opportunity to go out on the water. Our need to keep moving would make us ever more resourceful on this trip. We offered a price, he gladly accepted. We paid the bill for breakfast, left the change, and jumped aboard his boat, which he reversed up to the restaurant. Half an hour later we were anchored off a tropical island and swimming off the fuzziness of a bad night's sleep. We went ashore and saw a sloth up in a tree, which was just as well as we had no plans for going sloth-watching over the border in Costa Rica. That night we boarded a plane and flew to the Costa Rican capital in firm agreement that there would be no more night bus trips.

Would I go back? Yes.

Poland

I went to a conference in Warsaw once and, while I was only there for a few days, I took as much time as I could to walk around early in the mornings and during some of the sessions for some fresh air. The most notable building is Poland's tallest, Joseph Stalin's Palace of Culture and Science. A group of us went out for dinner in the old town with its charming buildings. A business party was held on an island in the middle of the Vistula River: this turned out to be a bit of a washout, quite literally. There had been floods further upstream and they were working their way towards the capital so we were advised to leave while we could. For sure, the river level was much higher than when we arrived, so we spread out in a street of bars back in town. On my last day I went for a long early morning run around town. I often found it was a good way of seeing more of a place when time was short. I flew back to London seated next to William Haig, then UK foreign secretary.

Would I go back? Yes, and to see some countryside, maybe Gdansk.

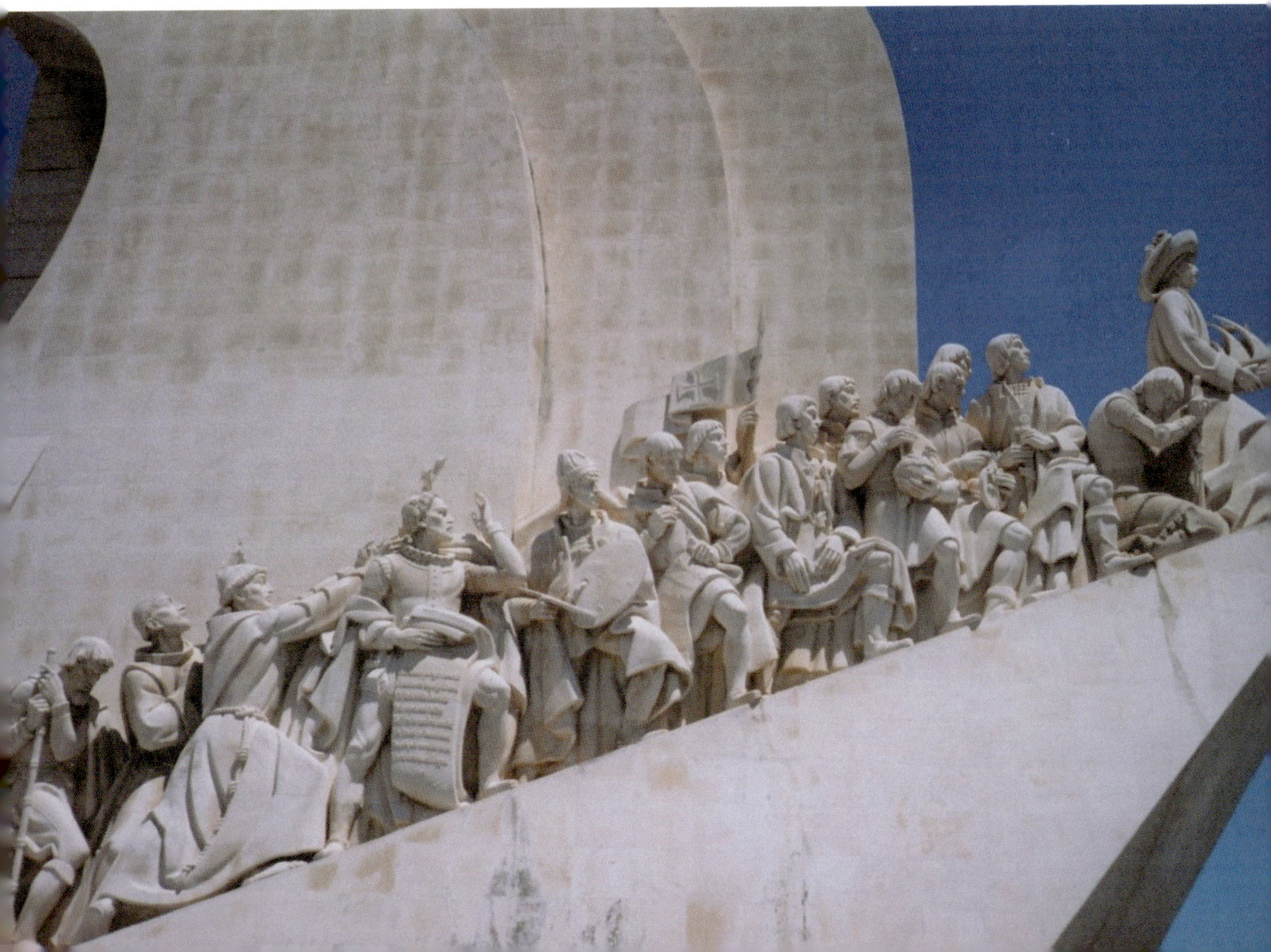

Portugal

My first time in Portugal was a trip to Lisbon with my girlfriend Katherine in the late nineties. It was Lisbon World Expo 98. The 17km-long Vasco da Gama Bridge over the River Tagus had just been completed and I was keen to see it. For its opening, 15,000 residents of Lisbon were seated at a table the length of the bridge, making it the world's longest dinner party. The new bridge was impressive, but the 25th Abril Bridge, built in the sixties and more central to the city, was more so. Iron red, it is still the longest suspension bridge in Europe. Only a few hundred metres shorter than the Golden Gate Bridge, it gives Lisbon a bit of a San Francisco feel. Add to that, the Santuário de Cristo Rei monument of Christ with his outstretched arms high above the riverbank opposite the city, and you've got a bit of Rio thrown in as well. But the similarities end there. Lisbon is a beautiful old city.

Built on a series of hills, the centre of Lisbon is a network of steep streets that will test even the fittest traveller. Our small hotel was on one of these hills and we would climb up into a lookout set in the roof and watch swifts circle round the surrounding red tiled roofs at great speed. You are compelled to climb up to the Castelo de S. Jorge to walk around the 11th Century terraces and look over Lisbon and the mighty Tagus River. Further along the river is Belém, with its medieval tower on the water's edge, the Henry the Navigator's monument, and Jerónimos Monastery. And all the while you are by the blue waters of the massive river which is now almost the sea. The trams are a fun aspect of Lisbon. You just jump on for the ride to see where they take you. Coming from Melbourne, also a city of trams, I felt very at home riding on these old rattlers again.

From Lisbon we caught a train to Sintra, a long-time royal sanctuary set in the cooler mountains 30km from the capital. The place is not what you would expect to see in Portugal. There are fairytale castles with classical gardens dotted over the lush surrounding hills. The gaudily Pena Palace is reminiscent of Neuschwanstein Castle in Bavaria. We continued on to the Atlantic coast and stayed for a couple of relaxing nights by the beach.

We went to the Algarve a few years later. From Faro we went to Sagres, famed for its beer, and to the rugged cliffs of Cape St Vicente, mainland Europe's most south-westerly point. The highlight of this trip was the drive to Tavira, an old Portuguese town towards the Spanish border, stopping at some old costal forts on the coast on the way. The big surprise is how green this hot weathered landscape is. There were carpets of wildflowers that you might expect to see in the Alps in spring.

Recently, we had my dad's 80th birthday in Lisbon. It was my parents' first time there and we had a great weekend walking round. Johnny rode his motorbike from the Costa Blanca in Spain to join us. We had some amazing meals, and the Portuguese wines were really good. The highlight was Ramiro's Fish Restaurant, which might just be the best seafood restaurant I have eaten in. The food just kept coming. We had the goose barnacles, and it is tradition to have the small salty 'house' steak sandwich at the end of the meal. I was sceptical, but it worked.

Would I go back? Yes, back to Tavira, Oporto and to see a bit of the interior and vineyards.

Qatar

Qatar was the third country in my Middle Eastern book-writing trip. After Oman and UAE, I flew into Doha and checked into a hotel with views over the great bay. The Doha Cornice wraps around this bay for a few miles. Qatar is a small peninsula 100km long that juts out into the Persian Gulf. It is one of the richest countries in the world, due to the fact that it just happens to sit on the largest liquid natural gas deposit on the planet. One in five of the pots you heat on your gas cooker in the UK will have been heated on Qatari gas. Doha is modern skyscrapers at one end of the bay and the new Museum of Islamic Art by the old town at the other. I spent a few days here, walking around and catching the odd traditional boat across the bay. The souk was good, but a little touristy. I preferred my time in Qatar over Dubai.

Would I go back? Probably not.

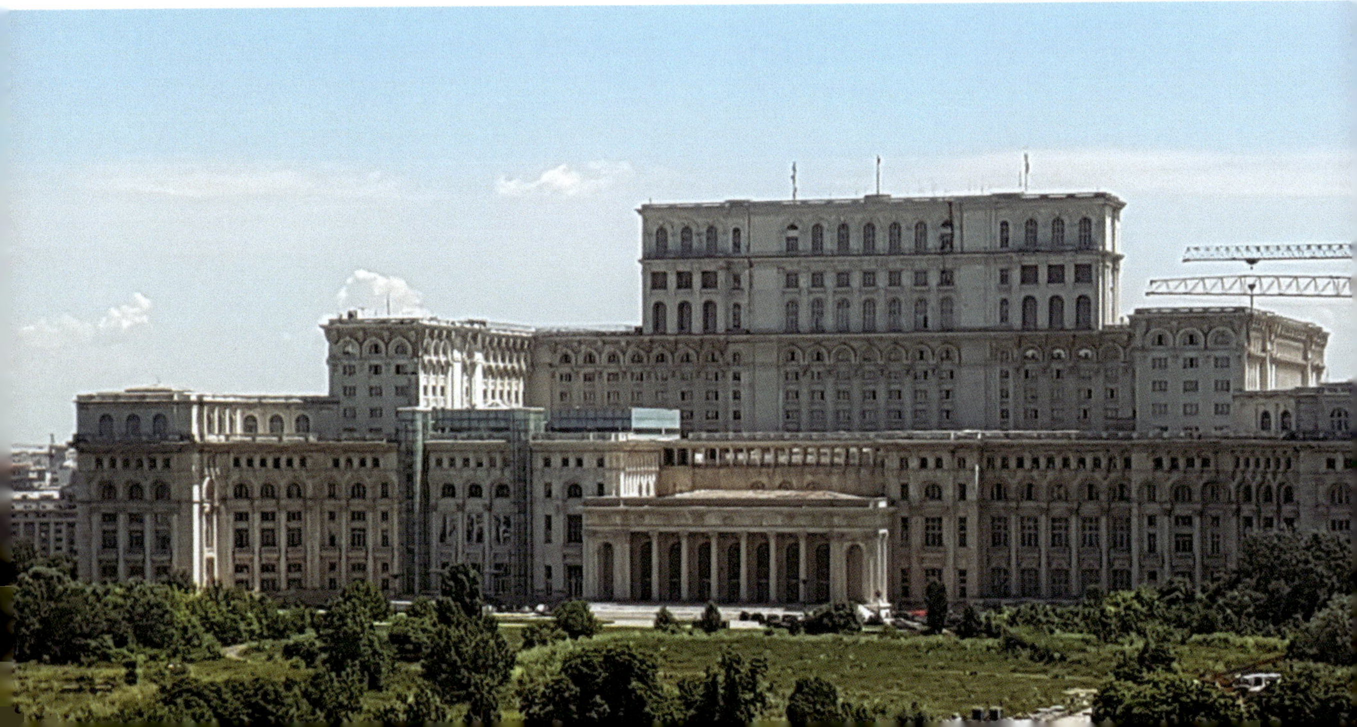

Romania

I was invited to speak at a conference in Bucharest and jumped at the opportunity to visit somewhere new. It was held at the Marriot, one of the most opulent hotels I have ever stayed in. As you walk in you are confronted with the grandest sweeping staircase you will have ever seen in your life, made of solid white marble. This luxury hotel masks the sinister fact that it was built by Nicolae Ceausescu as an administrative spill-over to the Palace of the Parliament for his VIP guests. At twelve stories and 3,000 rooms, that is a lot of people in your pocket.

My room on one of the higher floors looked straight at Ceausescu's Palace; the Parliament building ironically called the 'Palace of the People.' More like, 'the palace for one.' The scale of this building takes ages to comprehend. It is massive. I struggled to get used to seeing the sheer size of it from my hotel room while I was there. It's the biggest building in the world that isn't an aircraft hangar. And the heaviest building in the world; so much so, that satellite images indicate it is sinking under its own weight. I went for a walk around its perimeter one evening and it took over an hour. I was tempted to go on a tour but it all just felt too chilling. There were heavily gated vehicle entrances that lead into it underground, and you could look right into them, imagining the harrowing things that would have occurred here during the regime's darkest days.

Each night I walked into the old part of the city on the other side of the eerie monolith for dinner, shunning the over-the-top bars in the hotel. The food was hearty – well it was basic meat and potatoes – and the wine was earthy. It was a million miles from my hotel, but I liked the contrast.

Would I go back? Yes, to explore the countryside.

San Marino

I was staying with some friends who had bought a house in the hills in the region of Abruzzo and one of the days I went for a drive. I didn't really have a plan when I set out but when I stopped and looked at the map, I saw San Marino shaded indicating its differing status. I remembered as a child having San Marino stamps and as I drove in the direction of this dot on the map, I became more curious to see it. I didn't know that much about the status of the place until I read about it when I got there.

It turns out that San Marino is a micro-state and one of the world's oldest republics. The steep winding road takes you up to the medieval walled old town, with 11th century citadels, perched improbably on a mountain of rock. This country is basically a castle on the peak of a mountain with spectacular 360-degree views of the Italian countryside. I parked the car for a couple of hours, wandered around, had a light lunch and left thinking I had visited the smallest country in the world. As it happens, there are three that are smaller, two of which are in this book.

Would I go again? No.

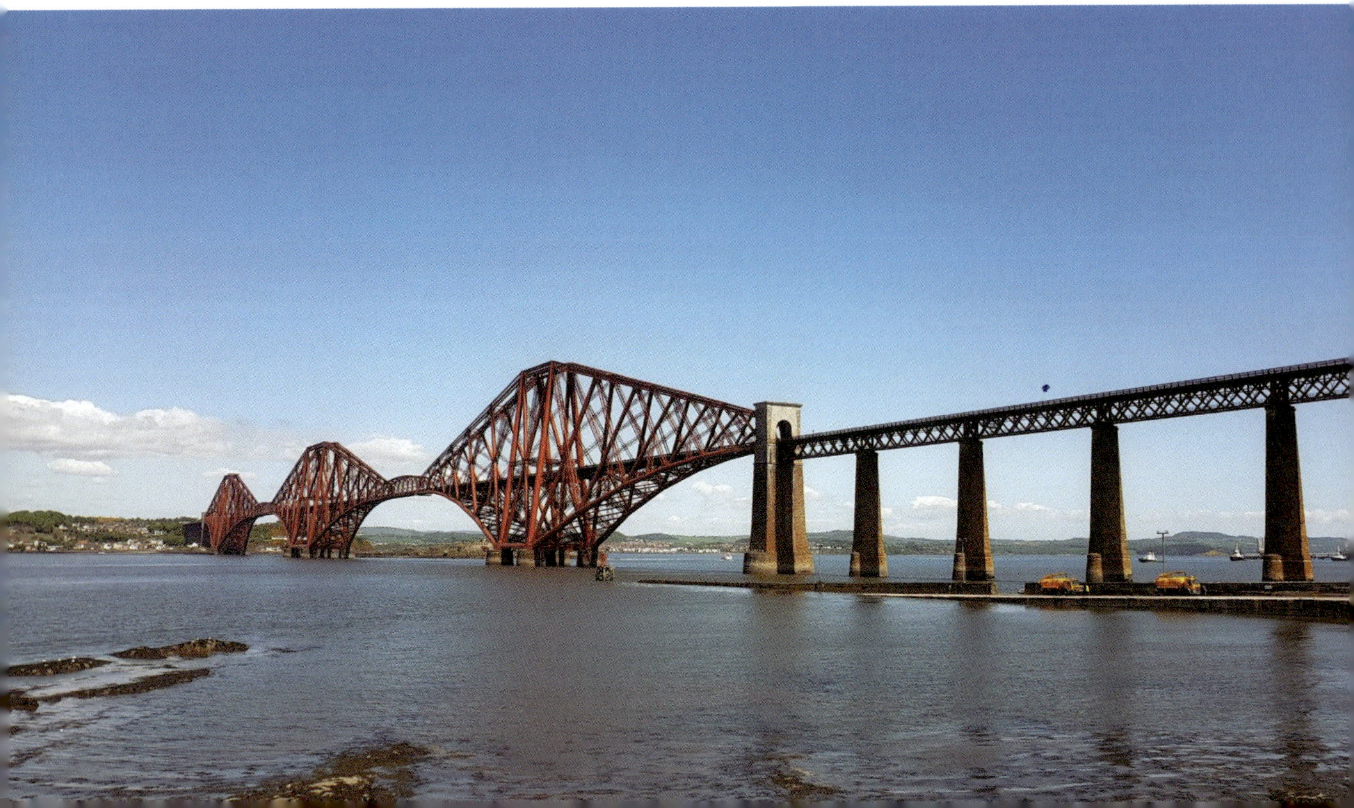

Scotland

Look up most lists of countries and Scotland is counted as part of the United Kingdom. But ask any Scot if Scotland is the same country, or nation, as England and you will get a very clear answer. And for most outsiders, it is even more confusing. Great Britain is England, Scotland, and Wales. The United Kingdom includes Northern Ireland. And the British Isles adds the Republic of Ireland, though Ireland is definitely not British. The Six Nations Rugby tournament each year adds France and Italy, confirming that Scotland and Wales are separate nations. Scotland fields a national football team in the Football World Cup, but is part of Team GBR at the Olympics. Most of all, how can San Marino be a country and Scotland not be? So, in my book, Scotland is a country.

My first visit was in the seventies with my parents on our trip from Oz. We arrived in Edinburgh where, according to my childlike diary, we were kept up by bagpipes. I have thought, ever since then, that they sound the most romantic from afar. We did the inevitable touristy things, 'we went to the castle and saw the jails and everything'. We all had a look through one of those telescopes you put a penny in. I remember mum looking through it and saying she could see there was a sale on in one of the shops in Princes Street. We left and picnicked by the Forth of Firth bridges. We needed a new car radiator in Perth and the went on to Pitlochry for the night and saw the castle the next day. It was the most beautiful place we saw on that trip to Scotland.

We went to Loch Ness in search of the monster and then on a wild goose chase to a place called Achnasheen, almost on the west coast. A 'real card' of a barman who'd served my parents in a London pub had apparently got a job in a pub here and they thought it would be fun to surprise him. The surprise was that the pub had shut down. We went back to Inverness, home to the finest spoken English language, so mum kept telling us in the car.

I lived in England for many years before going back to Scotland. While all my trips were on business, they were always great fun. I went to Edinburgh a few times to see clients and really love the place. It is such a beautiful city, especially with the long twilight nights in the summer. I had some fun times in Glasgow too. I wrote a column in the Mail on Sunday for a short time and one of Britain's high street banks, launching a new product, flew a group of journalists up to stay in a castle for a couple of days. There was shooting clays followed by some fine dinners. I really cannot remember what the new product was, but it was great fun.

My favourite trips were to see a client in Arbroath on the east coast. It is the home of the Arbroath smokie, a wood-smoked haddock produced in a small smokehouse with a creamy texture that does taste smoky. I would drive up from Edinburgh and often stop in Dundee on the way back. I would normally stay in St Andrews where there were lots of accommodation options. On my last trip, there was an American Fathers and Sons Golf tournament on and everywhere was booked out. As a last resort, I walked into the big Scores Hotel right on the edge of the 18th green. The lobby was full of Americans milling round and chatting loudly in their caps and plus fours. I told the woman at reception that I couldn't find anywhere to stay. Inevitably they were booked out. Then she said wait a minute, I have a single room right up in the roof and the booking just cancelled. I asked how much, and she wrote down the price with the words 'please keep it quiet' beside it. Clearly my transatlantic comrades were on a different tariff. The next morning, I got up early and walked the course and the sandy beach beside it. Back at the hotel, I had a fine breakfast of kippers and poached eggs looking over the 18th hole. I have never really been into golf, but it took on a certain charm that morning.

Would I go back? Yes, I must! To sail the Western Isles, hiking in the highlands, to land on the beach at Barra.

Serbia

My criteria for having visited a country is to have set foot in it and at least got a feel of the place, however short my visit. Being in transit in an airport does not count. Staying in the airport hotel, which I have done quite a bit, doesn't count either. Crossing it by train is questionable. And what if the country you visited didn't exist as a nation when you visited it? Serbia is all of this for me.

I was interrailing in my twenties and needed to get from Athens to Vienna and the train route took me through what was then Tito's Yugoslavia. It was a massive country encompassing the nations we now know as Slovenia, Croatia, Bosnia and Herzegovina, Montenegro, Macedonia and Serbia. Yugoslavia was around 1,000km long with four languages and two alphabets. The first train left Thessaloniki in northern Greece and took several hours, heading north through the countryside to arrive in Belgrade. From the train you could see that the people were poor and there was little on offer on the train or in any of the station stops. I remember an abundance of red peppers. The landscape turned from villages of minarets in the south to churches further north.

I had to change trains in Belgrade, then the capital of Yugoslavia and now that of Serbia. I had a few hours to kill but unfortunately it was the middle of the night. Train stations tend to attract a rough element much the world over. There were uniformed men walking around with Alsatian dogs on heavy clinking chains demanding papers from anyone who made them suspicious. I began to feel I could easily be in the wrong place at the wrong time so I ventured out into the dark street in front of the station and the interest I had to explore the city dissipated. It was my first real experience of Eastern Europe, at a time when it was austere and unknown. I was happy to board my train. I shared a cabin for six with a German couple heading home. The seats opposite each other slide down to make a bed and I fell asleep in this safe cocoon that transported me through the night to Austria.

Would I go back? Definitely to neighbouring Montenegro, Macedonia and Slovenia

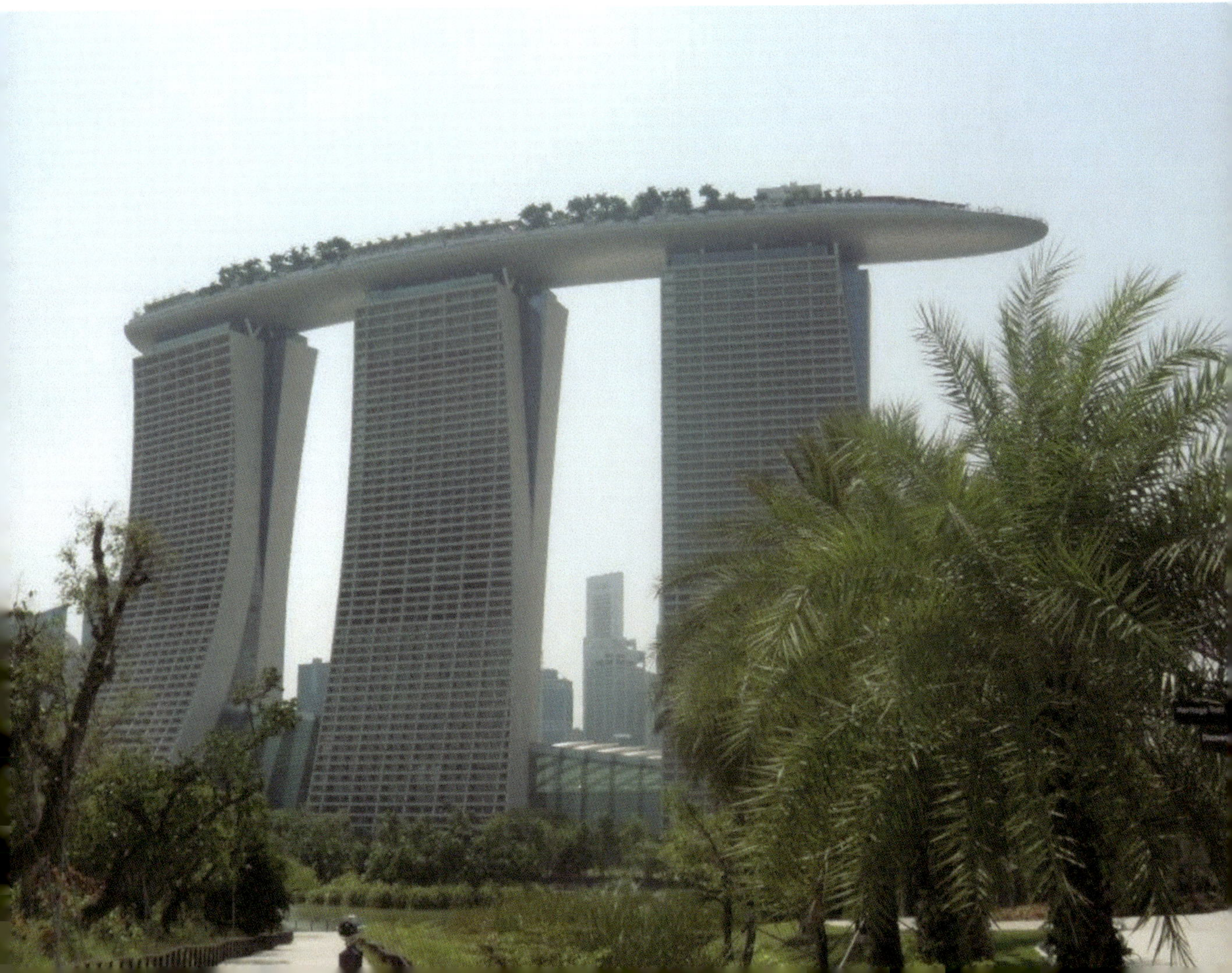

Singapore

The first foreign country I visited from Australia was Singapore. We were on our way to Europe for our long family trip in the seventies and Singapore was our stop-over. This island state has changed a lot since. On that first trip we stayed in the five-star Shangri-La hotel at the top of Orchard Road. My parents felt that our first time in Asia deserved a bit of luxury. Apart from eating out at night at some street markets, my main memory of that first visit was the hotel. The pool was amazing, and our room was on a higher floor than anything I had experienced before. Recently, I had a business meeting near the Shangri-La and I paid a visit to see how it matched my childhood memory. It has barely changed. It feels a little dated now, but it is still a beautiful hotel in a jungle-like setting.

I have been back to Singapore many times since and stayed for a few weeks at a time for some of those trips. For the ex-pat lifestyle, Singapore is as good as it gets. I have had so much fun there it is hard to know where to start. The main island lies one degree north of the equator and in recent decades has grown by a quarter through reclamation. This is emphasised by the fact that the Fort Canning Lighthouse is now 2km from the sea. If it was still operational, it would be obscured to most ships by skyscrapers and a blaze of lights. Singapore is a very modern city but some beautifully maintained colonial buildings and Chinese shophouses remain. Going to Raffles Hotel for a Singapore Sling is kind of compulsory.

The city feels like a high-rise metropolis sprouting out of the jungle. When it rains here, it is nearly always torrential. The street gutters, a few feet deep, give you a clue. It really is true that it can be raining on one side of the street and sunny on the other. The city is spotlessly clean due to the punitive fines for littering and there has been a big civic effort to plant trees. One of my favourite spots, where I spent many mornings, is the Botanic Gardens up in Tanglin. Even with the general greenness of the city, the 183 acres of grounds, just a short walk from the centre, still feels like an escape. There are some spectacular big old trees that would now not be found in the neighbouring jungles of Malaysia and Indonesia. Once you get to know Singapore, there are some great walks with a wildland feel to them. There are loads of hikes you can do in big nature reserves a few miles drive from town. There are even otters in the river in the centre of the city. I literally ran into one on the steps to the river towpath once. The city is a less oppressive than most other major cities and a great place to live.

Being on the equator, Singapore is never cold. Most places have a big pool. I bumped into a friend from London in Starbucks on one visit who insisted I come and stay. The pool in his complex was 50m-long; an Olympic pool, right in the centre of some of the most expensive real estate in the world. I also spent a lot of time in more recent years staying with my then-girlfriend Miranda, in a lovely garden flat in Spring Grove. The complex was the old colonial American Embassy situated between the Tanglin and Orchard districts. We sat out in our jungle garden most nights having barbecues and drinking wine. In the mornings we would blow away the cobwebs playing tennis. One weekend we went out on a friend's motor launch to a nearby island and had lunch on board. While we were having lunch, two Laser Picos on the roof were rigged and launched, a windward mark was laid, and we spent the afternoon dinghy racing. We headed home weaving through all the ships at anchor at sunset. A magical day.

I have stayed in several of the hotels around Marina Bay, the gateway to the city, most notably the Marina Bay Sands. The hotel comprises three 55-storey towers with a 1,000ft long boat-like sky park on top, housing the world's scariest infinity pool looking down over Singapore. The casino in the basement takes more money than the whole of Las Vegas strip. It did feel a bit like staying in a tourist attraction and there are some much nicer, more exclusive hotels in Singapore.

The Fullerton Hotel, the massive Old Post Office and Raffles have a much nicer feel. There were some great parties in old world venues like the Singapore Cricket Club. The annual White Party over by Gardens on the Bay was also fun.

There are so many food choices in Singapore that it was easy to go out for dinner every night. My favourite speciality was black pepper crab. Just before you get to Changi airport, there's a strip of restaurants on the beach looking over the tankers anchored out to sea. This would often be my last stop for dinner for black pepper crab before my night flight back to London. It beats the airport lounge hands down.

Would I go back? Always.

Slovakia

While I was in Budapest, I was near enough to Slovakia to visit a client based in the city of Nitra. I had been to the Czech part of what was previously Czechoslovakia but not the Slovakia bit. I was happy for an excuse to visit. It was ninety-minute train ride to Nové Zámky inside Slovakia and my client was waiting for me in a big black BMW to drive me the 20km to Nitra at speed. Not only was he driving very fast, he kept chatting and looking over my way instead of the road. He might have been able to drive this journey with his eyes closed but I got a taxi back to the train all the same.

So, most of my time in Nitra was spent in an office. But with the freedom of being able to get a taxi back, I aimed for a later train and went for a walk around the town. It was a nice break after a long meeting. Nitra is nestled in a valley on the edge of some heavily treed hills. The focal point is the medieval castle on a smaller hill in the town. I walked to this through the old town with its smart baroque buildings. I felt as if I could have been in a town in Hungary or the Czech Republic which is not that surprising, given it is almost exactly halfway between the two. Having got a feel for the place, it was time to jump in a taxi to get back to my train back to Budapest. That was my day trip to Slovakia.

Would I go back? Probably not.

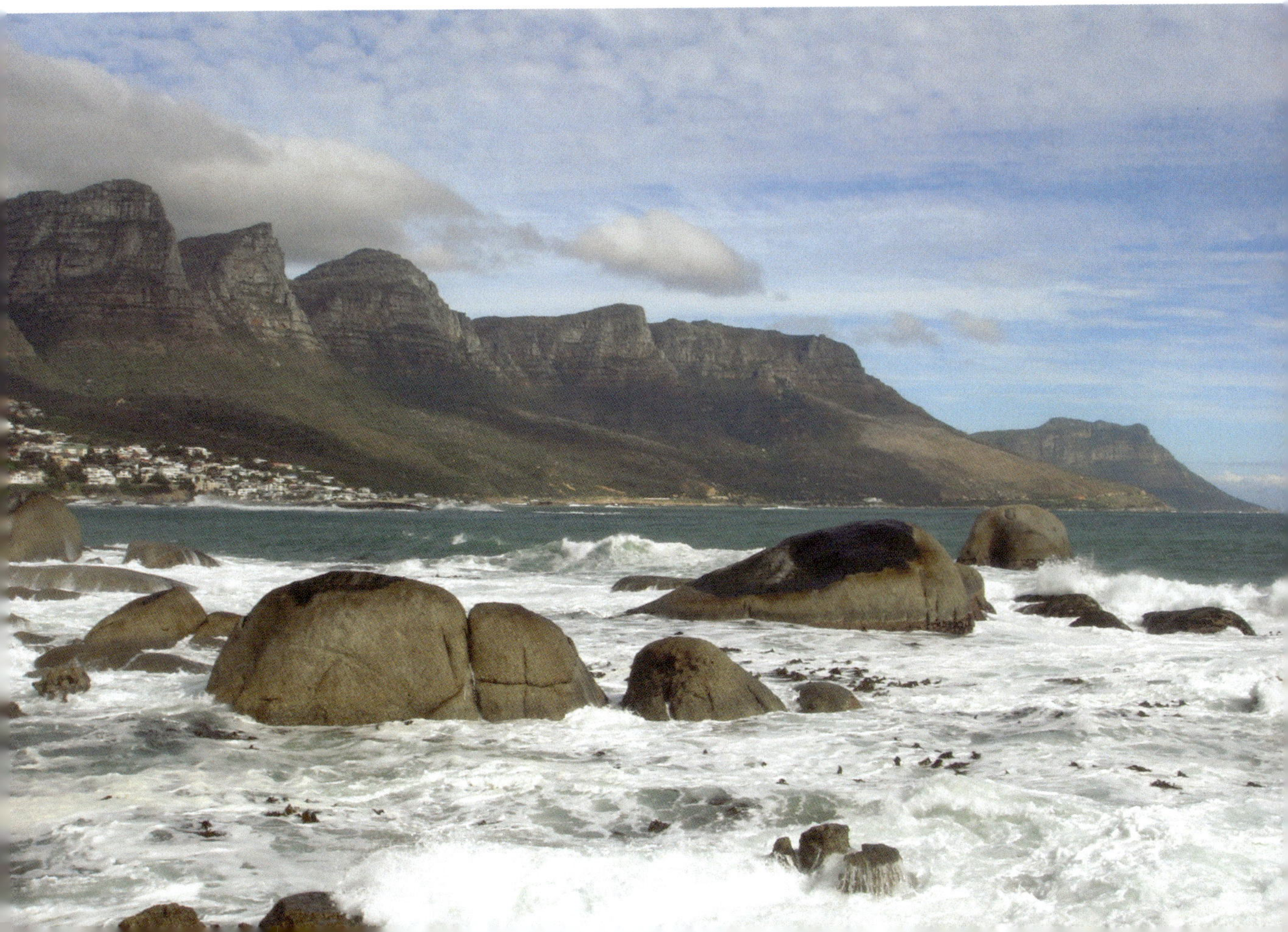

South Africa

My company bought a business with a lot of clients in South Africa and an opportunity came up to sponsor a conference there, so I went. I flew into Johannesburg and stayed in the Stanton business district in the very ritzy Sandton Sun hotel. It was attached to a shopping mall and there was a larger-than-life-size statue of Nelson Mandela in a square out the front. I felt a bit couped up there and wanted to go for a long walk, but was told it wasn't safe.

We held our own training event for clients in a small hotel in one of the neighbouring districts. We were twenty minutes into the day and there was a power cut. The whole area went down. The venue staff shrugged their shoulders and the delegates understood, but without a working projector we were running out of things to talk about. One of our clients had offered to drive to his house and get a portable generator and as the morning went by this was looking like the best option. We were up and running an hour or so later and gave presentations in the dark for the rest of the day.

The next night, after the conference we sponsored had ended, we went out on the town. We started at a restaurant called Carnivore in Muldersdrift, on the outskirts of Joburg. The menu was straight from the wild plains of Africa with ostrich, springbok, crocodile and a load of other animals. I felt relatively unadventurous choosing the springbok, but it was very good. We then hit the bars in Soweto with some people in our group who had local knowledge. I remember quite a few long taxi rides that night. Joburg, the city of gold, is hot and sprawling.

I hadn't come all the way to SA not to see Cape Town, so I took the two-hour flight there. I checked into the Radisson at Green Point, which had the most amazing terrace where the big surf waves of the Southern Ocean broke right before you. Sitting there you frequently felt as if you were about to be engulfed by the sea. I did get refreshed occasionally by a fine saltwater spray. After hot dry Joburg, this place was a breath of fresh air. I holed up in the hotel for several days and loved staying there. You could sit up at the bar and eat the most amazing food and drink local wines from the bottom of the list all night, and still not believe how cheap your bill was. With an increasingly favourable exchange rate, South Africa is cheap cheap for Europeans. I walked into town to the Victoria & Albert Waterfront Dock and wandered around the city centre. One day I walked the other way around the shore through Clifton to Camps Bay for a swim in the icy sea followed by lunch at the Bay Hotel. I was shocked, walking around Clifton seeing all the exclusive homes with spectacular sea views. It was disconcerting seeing razor wire and signs indicating armed guard protection. I am not sure I could ever feel relaxed living amongst the extremes of wealth and poverty and the high rates of serious crimes. I never felt entirely safe walking around places in SA.

For me, the best part of my trip here was to see the Cape. It took a couple of hours to drive down to the final point of the Cape of Good Hope. The high road skirting the mountains is a trip along some of the most dramatic scenery that I have seen in the world. I was surprised to learn that it is not the southernmost point of the African continent. But, as you look out to sea, it's clear that the Cape is the meeting point of the Atlantic and Indian oceans. These two great oceans of dramatically different temperatures collide here to produce one of the greatest concentrations of sea life on the planet. I drove to Simon's Town on the Indian Ocean side. It is lovely small harbour lined with waterfront restaurants, but the main draw here is the thousands of jackass penguins at the Boulders Beach Colony. You walk down to the beach on raised walkways and watch these human-like creatures waddling from place to place in their tuxedos. The seafood restaurant lunch was good, but I would probably have been just as happy sitting there with a sandwich watching these guys. Driving back to Cape Town there were great views looking over the silvery water of False Bay. The road winds through beautiful scenery at Fish Hoek and Nord Hoek, and then Table Mountain guides you back into Cape town. On my last night, I sat outside on the hotel terrace with the roar of the surf breaking and the stars brighter than ever. It was winter in Europe. I sipped my big glass of wine and thought, I could get used to this every winter. Sadly I haven't been back....yet.

Would I go back? Definitely, vineyards Stellenbosch, Garden Route. Durban, a route into Namibia.

South Korea

I was already in Asia for Christmas and there was a business opportunity in Seoul, so I made a detour. It was bitterly cold, and the city was grey and drab. I only ventured out for business meetings, or to check out some nearby electronics malls, or to meet up for dinner with a friend living there. I passed on anything touristy. It didn't seem to hold much interest and it was just too cold. The technology did interest me. At the time over 80% of Korea's GDP was produced by just four companies, Samsung, Lucky Goldstar, Hyundai, and Daewoo, known collectively as the Chaebol. And it was clear that Seoul was a testbed for these four aggressively competing companies. Electronics was so heavily embedded here, from phones to robots, heating controls to the toilet in my hotel room, which had about a dozen settings including heating, flushing and drying. It was another world.

The Korean BBQ restaurants were fun, though they did smell like you were actually sitting in a BBQ. You cooked your own meat at your table and a flue hanging down above you took most of the smoke away. We went out in Itaewon, which was lively thanks to the presence of American GIs stationed nearby. I was there for New Year's Eve and we went to a big party at the Hyatt Hotel. It was quite fun, but hungover the next day I was ready to leave. My seat on the old 747 plane flying out was 1B, a big armchair in the front row on the lower deck. In the nose of the plane, in front of that, was just a wardrobe. I opened the doors and looked to my fellow Korean business passenger and said 'Huh, no pilot.' It didn't really break the ice, so I read a book all the way to Tokyo before boarding my BA cocoon back to London.

Would I go again? No.

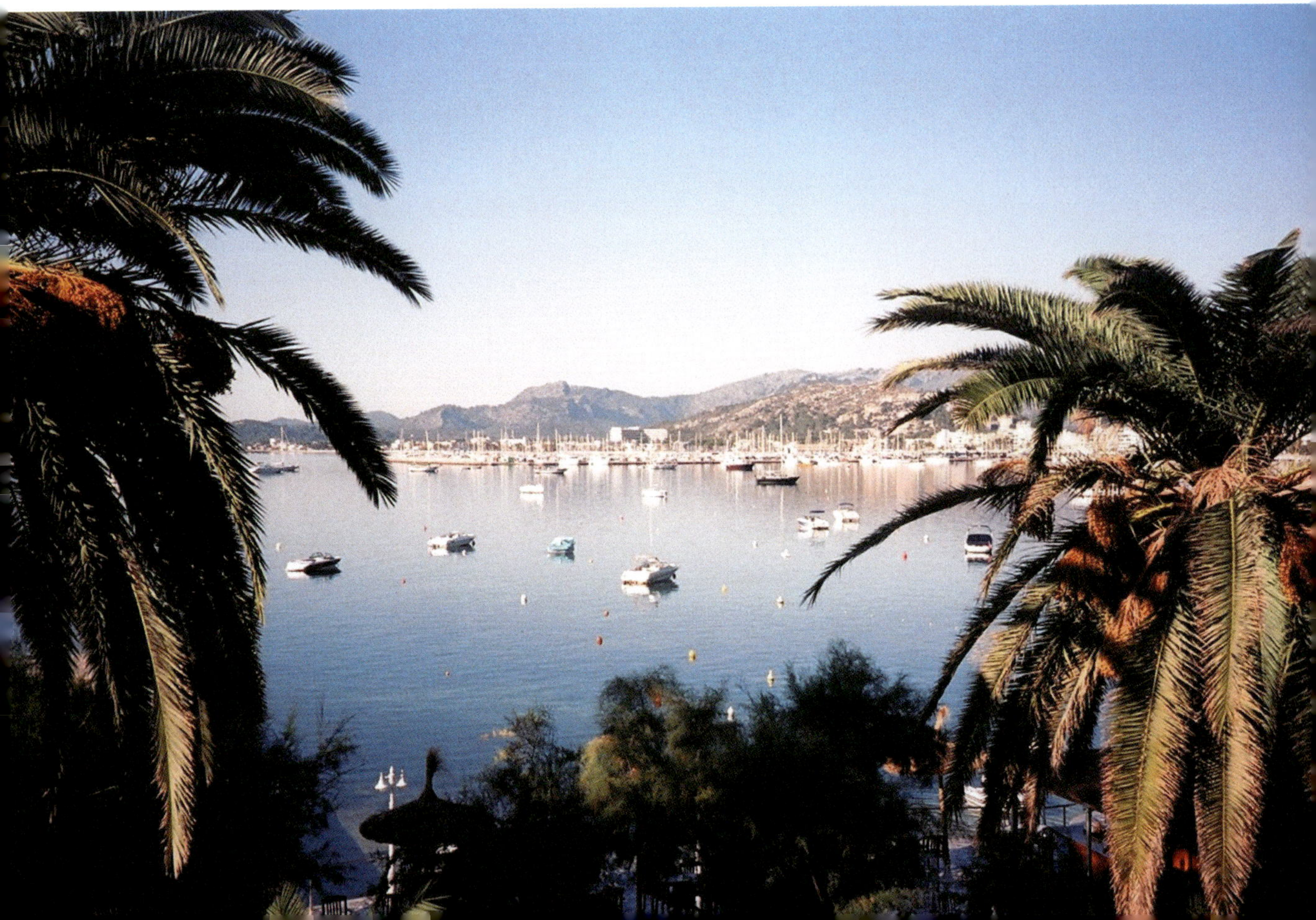

Spain

Spain is the country I would happily live in. I have been so many times that it is difficult to know where to start. My first trip was with my parents in the seventies. We drove to Barcelona, Madrid and San Sebastian. After that, my many trips are probably best described geographically rather than chronologically. Virtually dead centre of the country is the capital Madrid and I have been several times, mostly on business. I normally stay in a great family-run hotel in Sol, a district that is full of bars and tapas restaurants. The Spanish eat late and getting a restaurant booking before 10pm can be a challenge. In fact, Madrid is the only place where I have experienced traffic jams at 5am, with everyone heading home from the closing nightclubs. It is a great city to walk around day and night. My favourite cultural thing there is the house, now museum, of the 19th century Spanish painter Sorolla. His paintings, especially the beach scenes, are very atmospheric. One year on a conference here we had dinner in the Opera House with opera singers serenading us. The Americans, typically early eaters, really struggled with the late dinner schedule. We also went to the ancient city of Segovia, famed for the Roman aqueduct which has remained in good condition. Here we ate the regional specialty of roasted whole suckling pig, so tender that it is cut up at your table with plates instead of knives.

So, starting in the north of Spain and working clockwise... I did a trip one year with Katherine from Bilbao to Santiago de Compostela, driving along the north Atlantic coast. The first thing to see was the new Guggenheim museum in Bilbao, designed by Frank Gehry. It's amazing. As you look down the streets you get glimpses of its bright silver reflective shapes like pieces of armour. Jeff Koons's Puppy, a West Highland terrier with flowers growing all over it, was a stunning example of street art. We had lunch down one of the side streets at a fantastic tapas bar, where helmets of the construction workers, with their names painted on, lined the top of the walls all the way round the ceiling.

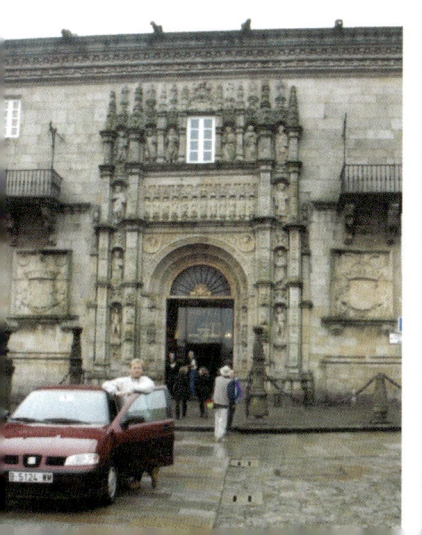

We had Spanish friends from the coastal city of Gijón, the largest in Asturias, so went to visit them. This is cider country and in the bars they hold the bottle high in one hand and the glass low in the other, and pour, to aerate it. There are several hundred bars in town and our friend Julio would choose a place based on the amount of crab shells on the floor at the bar. A pile of shells indicated that the crab was abundant and good. Not many shells, not so good. It seemed the whole of town was out for the evening.

Next, we headed to Santiago de Compostela with its ornate cathedral at the end of the famous Camino pilgrim route. We pulled up in front of the Hostal dos Reis Católicos Parador to the side of the cathedral. Luckily, they had a room. It has been taking in pilgrims for over 500 years, making it one of the oldest hotels in the world. There are lovely courtyards and colonnades in the Parador and just walking the corridors to your room is like walking round a museum full of oil paintings and antique furniture. The stone wall between out room and our bathroom must have been five feet thick. Galicia is the north west corner of the Iberian Peninsula, pushing out into the Atlantic as a finger like its relatives, Brittany, Cornwall, and the west coasts of Ireland and Scotland. Its climate is similarly wet and sea mist frequently rolls in, as it did when we were there. The landscape is not what you expect in Spain, the sea mist making it the same emerald green as its foreign cousins. We headed back east to the lovely beach at Llanes and then on to San Sebastian for our last night, where we stayed up by the lighthouse. It was raining and watching the bright beams of light reflecting millions of silvery drops as they swept the night sky was magical.

I came back to this part of Spain for a debauched few days for my friend Johnny's stag weekend. We had a big night out in Bilbao, ran the bulls in Pamplona and caused havoc in San Sebastian. We visited a vineyard, where on the tour one of the guys stripped off and wrapped himself in the shrink wrapper. The stag 'lost' his shorts in the middle of an outdoor public swimming pool. He then had the pool all to himself which the Spanish thought was even funnier than we did. We were running late for the airport and only just made it. When we dropped the keys off at the car rental desk for our two people carriers, we said 'Ahh… two things. First, we need to run for our flight…second, we crashed the cars into each other…. Sorry.' Most of the guys worked in insurance and said when we were hiring that the extra insurance was a rip off. We all had to put more in the kitty back in the UK for the excess.

One year Johnny and I went skiing at Baqueira-Beret, the highest resort in the Pyrenees. It costs a fraction of the skiing in the Alps, the skiing is almost as good and the food and wine is better. Aragonese is the language; a sort of cross between French and Spanish. The problem was knowing which words of which language to use and when to use them. You had to guess.

Barcelona is the biggest city on the Mediterranean and one of my favourite cities in the world. The combination of Spanish culture, amazing food and a vast seafront makes the place a winner. 'Barna' is the home to Gaudi, his most famous work being the iconic La Sagrada Familia cathedral. As construction projects go, this one is huge. It was under construction during my first visit over forty years ago and is still being worked on today: in fact building has been underway for a hundred years or more. When Gaudi was questioned on the slipping time frame before his death in the 1920s, he's said to have replied, 'My client is not in a hurry.' Sure, the Spanish Civil War didn't help progress, but the scale and ambition of the project is so astounding, it wouldn't even get started if it was proposed now. The building is really a series of artworks and irregular shapes and the intricacy of the design is mindboggling. The best part is a tour of the project, taking you right through the areas of fabrication in progress. It is great to feel part of a working project. It wills you to revisit La Sagrada on every trip to the city. The proposed completion date is 2026 to mark the 100th anniversary of Gaudi's death, so a visit every year is now starting to be rewarding. I can't wait to walk freely around the finished building. There's more Gaudi to see in the city. Park Guell is super impressive and the façade of the Casa Battlo building is unmistakably his work.

Apart from eating and drinking, some other favourites are Mercardo de la Boqueria, the main market off La Rambla, and down to the port and for a walk around La Barceloneta, wedged between the port and the beach. I also had a great day with my goddaughter Poppy, who now lives in Barna. We saw the gardens at Park del Laberint d'Horta. As the name implies, there is a great maze to get lost in there.

Leaving the Costa Brava and heading south you come to the Costa Blanca and the wonderful city of Valencia, Spain's third city. There is a little less buzz than its older sister in the north, but it's a beautiful place to walk around, and maybe a little more safely. Apart from some beautiful old buildings, Valencia is interesting for its City of Arts and Sciences built on the old riverbed and completed just after the millennium. It is futuristic, but it sits well with the city. The food in Valencia is more rustic and less about tapas. It is the spiritual home of paella. I spent a lovely weekend here in a beautiful boutique hotel: it's a great city break from the UK in spring or autumn.

Further south, about halfway to Alicante you come to a bump in the coastline jutting out into sea and pointing towards Ibiza. This is Javea, and inland is the town of Jalon. My friends Johnny and Sarah left the UK to set up an amazing retreat up in the mountains here and as godfather to their daughters, I have been to Caserio del Mirador many times. It is a beautiful part of Spain with olive, almond and citrus groves all around. It's a great place for hiking and climbing and you are only 20 minutes' drive to the beach. Climbing to the top of the Penon rock right by the sea at Calpe is breathtaking, both for the exertion and for the rewarding view. This was the Northern Rock to the Ancient Greeks, the southern one being Gibraltar, one of the Pillars of Hercules. In Greek Mythology, Hercules pushed the rocks apart, dividing Africa from Europe and joining the Mediterranean to the Atlantic.

About 100km out to sea lies the island of Ibiza, less cultural and more party central. Though away from all the raving, it's a stunningly beautiful place. A few of us met up in Ibiza for a weekend and chartered a speedboat. We had a ball. We headed straight to the island of Formentera, anchored up and went for a great lunch at Beso Beach restaurant. It's like fine dining, with tables on the sand all laid up among the trees. We headed off to some secluded bays, swam off lunch, had more drinks and then on to the beach clubs Blue Marlin and Mirage. We baulked at the 500-euro cover charge for a table and left. At the end of our Rockstar day, we settled for dinner at the restaurant opposite where our boat was moored in the port.

On the day we were leaving we went to the Jockey Club restaurant right on the beach by the airport. I had the most amazing tuna salad, and the drinks were flowing. We checked our flights and there were massive delays. The French air traffic controllers had called yet another strike. At least this one was at the end of the holiday not just before it. It was time for dinner, and I just reordered exactly what I'd had for lunch. It was just as good the second time round. We went to check-in for our flights. My friends flying Sleezyjet were given a bench in the airport for the night. Luckily, I was in the BA cocoon and was taxied to a five-star hotel with a terrace right on the beach. I had a leisurely breakfast in the sun and worked from there for the day before flying out. Probably the only time I have been grateful to the French Air Traffic Controllers for striking.

Beyond Ibiza lies the largest of the Balearic Islands, and for me the jewel of the Mediterranean, Mallorca. Of all the places I have been in the world, this would be the one I would choose to live in. It has everything. The capital city of Palma is beautiful, with its cathedral looking over bright blue sea. There are hundreds of great bars and restaurants. Bar Abaco is a good over-the-top experience. There are, maybe, a hundred shoe shops. I have certainly waited outside a lot of them. The Zara in Palma has big steps at the front full of men sitting looking at their phones. Apparently, the shopping is good there. Palma is great by night, and dining at the restaurants along the front of the port looking at the cathedral all lit up is special.

Mallorca has so much variety. The package tourism is confined to two main areas. From the airport, the Germans go left, and the Brits go right. A night of clubbing in Shagaloof is still an experience. Leaving Palma and heading clockwise round the island, your first good stop is Illetas. My then-girlfriend Jane and I went a couple of times to her parents' place there. I have also stayed in the old Illetas Hotel here. One night we watched a band playing from our balcony. They had Earth, Wind and Fire tracks down to a tee, because it was Earth Wind and Fire! A fan had flown them in for their birthday party. The swimming is lovely from here and I would swim out to the islets off the shore.

Next is the upmarket marina at Portal Nous. Good for restaurants and people-watching. Lunch at the beach bar at Cala del Mago, the other side of Magaluf, is always fun. Port Andratx is on the western end of the island and is therefore great for sunsets. St Elm further round is a lovely beach spot. And then you are onto the north coast where mountains plunge into the deep blue sea. The village of Deià up in these mountains was put on the map by the English writer Robert Graves and has been a mecca for the rich and famous ever since. After that is Valldemossa, followed by Port Soller. With its trams and plane trees, surrounded by mountains, it always feels a bit autumnal. The large monastery at Lluc is a tranquil spot before you drive down a long straight road into the beautiful town of Pollenca. Port Pollenca is another favourite spot and I have stayed at the Hotel Illa d'Or a few times. The paseo into town each night on the paths by the beach in front of old Spanish villas is obligatory. From here, the coast all the way back to Palma is flatter, wilder, more agricultural, and without tourists. I love it. The interior of the island is also great, and I have climbed a few of the peaks while hiking here. For me, Mallorca beats the Riviera hands down.

Further south along the Spanish mainland coast is the Andalucía region, famous for flamenco. Among my favourites here is the coastal town of Nerja. There's great hiking and some rewarding climbs here. The main peak looking over Nerja took me three attempts on different visits to climb. Malaga is another lovely Spanish coastal city, though I have normally only been passing through en route to business conferences in Marbella. Inland is the Andalusian capital, Seville. And what a place it is. I have only been a couple of times but sitting on the rooftops of beautiful old hotels looking out over this historic Spanish city is captivating. The alleyways below are full of bars and restaurants. My friend Biggles had his 50th birthday weekend at an amazing beach restaurant at Conil on the Atlantic south coast. This party weekend also took in Jerez and Cadiz, two more great places.

Spain does not end here. The Canary Islands lie over a thousand miles south, off the coast of Africa, and are the perfect place for winter sun. My first trip was to Tenerife. We attempted to climb El Teide Volcano but the altitude and the heat made it a challenge. The landscape is like something from Mars. The film epic, One Million Years BC, was shot here. Think Raquel Welsh standing amongst the volcanic rocks in a fur bikini. It is the highest point in Spain at over 12,000ft, and would be over 24,000ft if you measured it from the sea floor. The deep water attracts pilot whales, and we went on a great trip to see them. They were so curious that they would swim up to the boat. Another year we did a staff trip to Lanzarote, staying in Puerto del Carmen. We went climbing mountains in the moonscape here, for team building. A couple of us went for a swim off the shore and drifted a long way out to sea. With the currents, it was challenging to get back to the beach.

My last trip abroad was to the Island of Fuerteventura between lockdowns in November 2020 with my friend Hels. We stayed in the lovely town of Corralejo which has great plazas with live music, lots of bars and restaurants. The beaches and swimming are the best I have experienced in Europe. I am going back next winter!

Would I go back? Over and over and over. Must see the Alhambra in Granada, Vigo and surrounds in North West.

Sri Lanka

I was having breakfast in Penang in Malaysia when I made the snap decision to go to Sri Lanka for a few days on my way back to the UK. I had a five-hour layover in Bangkok between flights, so I went into the city for lunch before flying to Colombo. I met some Aussies in a curry house there and they said, 'we are heading down the coast tonight to go surfing, come with us.' After breakfast in Malaysia, lunch in Thailand and dinner in Sri Lanka, I thought, why not?

We found a driver with a small minibus and paid him to drive us to Hikkaduwa, about 100km south of the capital. In those days, Sri Lanka was in the midst of a bloody conflict with the Tamil Tigers and I had been warned at the airport of all the 'no go' areas, largely in the north of the country. We were completely in the safe zone and after a long day's travelling, I fell asleep, lying lounging on a bench seat for two behind the driver opposite the sliding door. The van stopped and I stirred in the sudden silence and the sound of distant voices getting louder. Slowly the door was being opened an inch or two with the barrel of a gun. It was pointing right at me. At first, I didn't know what it was and as the door opened further, there was a man with a machine gun pointed to the floor of the van but in my direction. Still half asleep, the situation suddenly hit me, and I sat bolt upright. I jumped aback against the wall of the van, which caused him to jump aback with his gun now pointed right at me. This was that moment that people talk about where you see your life flash right in front of you. And it's true. I was just waiting for him to pull the trigger. I had no time to question it. He was standing there in khakis, showing the whites of his eyes. He was young and seemed as fearful as I was. The whole thing probably only lasted a few seconds, but even now the recollection is one of slow motion over minutes. Slowly he lowered his gun. My heart was still pounding, and I was gasping for breath. Another soldier flashed a torch around inside the van. It became clear this was a military roadblock and a group of Aussie surfies wasn't what they were looking for. I was now wide awake and relieved to get out of that van at Hikkaduwa. Even now, the seat opposite the door is not the seat I go for in a minibus.

That night we checked into a guest house by the beach. We ran down the sand and jumped in the surf in the bright light of a full moon reflecting on the waves. I remember getting out and lying on the beach, staring up in the stars with the waves crashing on the shore. It was one of the most amazing days in my life with meals in three countries, but most of all the feeling that I had dodged a bullet. I felt more alive than ever.

The next day I had breakfast by the beach with all the cows wandering round the fishing boats, and then went further down the coast to the 16th century Portuguese city of Galle. The fort was meant to be the big attraction here, but I wanted to see the cricket ground. Galle had resurfaced as a childhood memory of Australia playing Sri Lanka here. It was a bit of a dustbowl then, just like a country ground in Oz. It is hard to think of a more picturesque setting for a professional sports field anywhere in the world. The ground occupies the beginning of the neck of land that leads to the fort, so that you have sea at both ends. On one side of the cricket ground is the old city leading down to the fort. Galle, for me, had an almost Caribbean feel which I loved. I walked round the bay along the beach to another neck of land and had a long slow drink at the beautiful Closenburg Hotel. This was originally an official residence of the P&O Steamship Company, highlighted by some of the insignia and motifs still in evidence. As I had been in the Eastern and Oriental Hotel in Penang only a couple of days earlier, I felt like I was tracing some historic British colonial route. This place had a classical old world unassuming feel about it. I would stay here if I went back.

I decided to get a train back up to Columbo instead of a minibus and really enjoyed rattling through all the villages along the coast. I went back to the curry house for lunch and spent a couple of days wandering around the city. Some of the residential districts reminded me of Hampstead in London, with its similar road signs to NW3. There were quite a few Morris Minors driving around as well. Walking along the seafront here at night I would stop and chat to families. Sri Lanka is not a place you'd imagine being held up at gunpoint, but overall the people I met were incredibly friendly and welcoming.

Would I go back? Yes. To stay in the Closenburg, to visit Kandy and Anuradhapura.

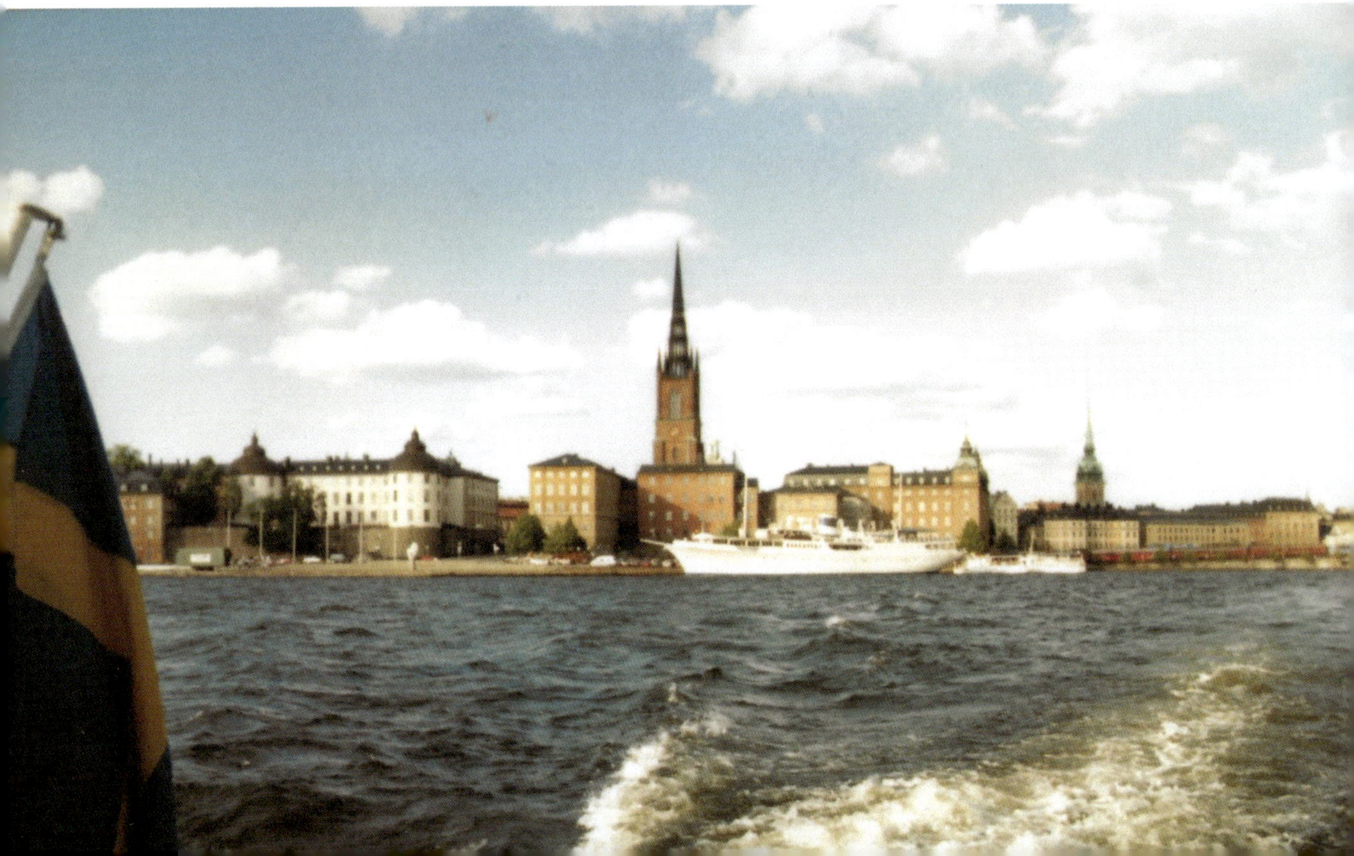

Sweden

My first trip to Sweden was inter-railing. Leaving Helsingor in Denmark, the boat train did the 3km sea crossing to Helsingborg in Sweden. I headed up the west coast to Sweden's second city, Gothenburg, a city I have been back to several times since. A business contact took me sailing around the archipelago in his yacht. The rocks in the sea here are smooth grey boulders and you wedge a steel peg in a crack to tie your bow line to. That day, he packed a picnic lunch and we walked to the highest point on a small grassy island. We sat down to lunch on rocks around a big rock. It was the perfect natural table and chairs. He said 'I know the Vikings sat at this table to eat a long time ago, just like we are doing now.' As busines lunches go, this was a pretty good one. Gothenburg is a lovely city, with canals, covered markets, and great restaurants and bars. At the top of town, a powerful statue of Poseidon stands in a fountain looking down the main boulevard. It was not far to Oslo, my next stop.

Having run into my Canadian friend John by coincidence, the train trip from the north of Norway to Stockholm was a great catch up. We ended up staying on a square rigger sailing ship, the 'af Chapman.' It is a youth hostel moored off the Island of Skeppsholmen. Stockholm is built on fourteen islands and the archipelago around the capital has 30,000 islands. I remember walking home one evening and a guy was standing fishing off a bridge in the middle of the city. I asked what he was fishing for. He said, 'wild salmon', very matter of fact. The old town on the island of Gamla Stan is full of beautiful buildings and great fun on a Wednesday night; what the Swedes call 'Little Saturday'. It's like a mini weekend in the middle of the week.

The best thing to see in Stockholm is the Vasa ship. This 17th century mighty wooden warship was raised from the seabed in its near original state in the 1960s. It is the world's best preserved sailing ship of that era, with intricate wooden carving. Walkways have been built around, over, and through the ship to give you a true appreciation of it. It is so awesome that it is worth a trip to Stockholm just to see it. Malmo and Lund in the far south of Sweden close to Copenhagen are also beautiful cities where I spent some time. There are 96,000 lakes in Sweden and some lovely islands. I spent a few days in Kalmar one summer, staying with a friend who grew up on the neighbouring island of Orland. She complained that it was a pain that they had to use the bridge to the island in summer. In the winter they just drive across the sea!

Would I go back? Yes, to marvel at the Vasa ship again, sail around the Stockholm archipelago, go to the Ice Hotel.

Switzerland

Switzerland is largely about skiing for me, though I have done several trips there that were not. We camped with my parents in the seventies on the slopes of the Jungfrau near Grindelwald. I am sure it was a two-man tent. I went to my cousin's wedding on the shores of Lac Neuchatel and I stayed with Biggles when he lived in Zug. He had to leave for making too much noise, including complaints for flushing his toilet in the night. (A common rule in Switzerland.) What if you have a gastro infection or need to have a chat to God on the great white telephone? That trip we went to Lucerne. A man had crashed his speedboat into the covered wooden bridge and set it alight a few years earlier. He had become a national pariah and got a hefty jail sentence. As I walked over a bridge in Lucerne, I found a 12ft marijuana plant tied to the railings, as you do. There are some lovely small cities in Switzerland, including Basel, Fribourg, and the capital, Berne. My favourite is Lugano in the Italian speaking part of the country. I have some clients here and am always happy to visit. This small city on the shores of Lac Lugano is like a clean and ordered Italian town. It is very stylish. The food and wine are twice the price of course, but this Swiss region, Ticino, is the only place in the world to produce white merlot and it's stunning. You never tire of looking down the lake that narrows to a point in the distance between the mountains. At an international conference here one year I swam from the hotel out to a buoy and back on the first morning. I kept swimming into fish. By the end of the conference, we had a morning swimming group going.

When smoking was banned in public venues in Italy, the Italians came to Lugano to party. It took another five years for Swiss law to catch up. This is the country where women only got the vote in 1971. In 2009 the Swiss voted in a referendum to ban the building of minarets. Speeding fines are levied based on your salary. One Swedish hedge fund manager was up for a one million dollar speeding fine. He was doing 290 km/hr. Fine over the border in Germany, but not in CH.

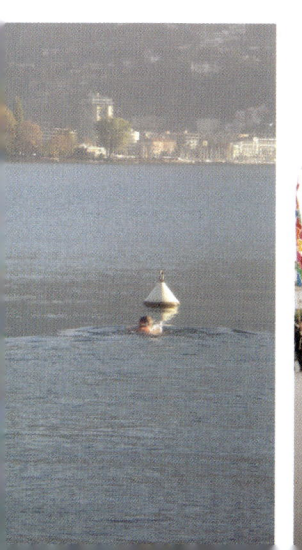

There have been quite a few business trips to Zurich and many more to Geneva where several of my friends live. I have had some fun times there. But Geneva has mostly been a stepping-stone to the ski slopes. I have friends in the swish ski resort of Villars and have skied in St Moritz, which has a shopping street of fashion emporiums to rival those of Milan. Maybe this is in case you forgot to buy clothes before leaving Milano. But my favourite place in the Alps is Verbier, and I have been lots. It is an easy train journey along the lake, past the chateau on the water's edge at Vevey, then a change to the alpine train which winds up the valley. It is always exciting to arrive here. I am lucky to have several friends with chalets in Verbier. Mostly I stay with my Irish friend Ann. Her place, Chalet Dunmore, at the end of town is fabulous. The skiing in the Four Vallées area is amazing, especially off-piste and being high up, it's snow sure. One year I had my birthday in the local pub there. Word got out and we ended up booking the whole place for thirty people. I can't wait to go back.

Would I go back? Yes! To ski and see friends.

Tanzania

My flight from Nairobi to Tanzania flew past Kilimanjaro with its unmistakable snow-capped flat-topped peak rising above the clouds. This majestic mountain, nearly 20,000 ft tall with a diameter of over 30 miles at the base, rises gradually out of the hot plains of east Africa. It is an amazing sight. The plane stopped in Zanzibar, but I didn't get off. This was my eventual destination in the country, but I wanted to see the port of Dar es Salaam first. I also wanted to arrive at Zanzibar's historic capital Stone Town by boat.

Dar es Salaam has become quite a modern city for the most part and I saw no tourists there. I walked along the coast to the fish market which sits on the beach off Barack Obama Drive. I could smell it before I could see it. It was interesting to see the fish being landed and watch the intense bartering going on. I was the only tourist there and with my blonde hair and pale skin I attracted some attention. As I walked around the market, I noticed I was being followed so I walked over to the nearby bus station and aimed for the gap between two parked buses. My tail took the next gap between the buses. I did an about turn and walked a convoluted route back along the coast. It may never have come to anything, but I was happy not to find out. It was hot and I wanted some peace and calm, so I had lunch in a lovely tranquil garden at the Hyatt Hotel.

The next day, I got the boat to Zanzibar. Leaving Dar es Salaam, the sea was like glass and the clouds reflected bright white in the water. It was like an oil painting. As we approached Stone Town, I was pleased I had followed my instinct to arrive by boat. It grew bigger as we got closer. The sea was a beautiful blue green. There was immigration on arrival to the 'Peoples Republic of Zanzibar', despite the island being part of Tanzania. I found a room in a guesthouse and set myself up for several days there. Stone Town is a lovely place by day and by night. It still has the feel of an old trading port. There was a makeshift boatyard on the beach close to where I was staying, where they would chop logs of wood by hand into planks for boat repairs. I could check in on the slow progress of a repair each time I walked past. The beach was lovely here with the fishing boats laying at anchor. The main park on the waterfront was a great municipal spot. In the afternoon, stalls would set up selling local arts and crafts and then in the evening it was the turn of all the food stalls. Stone Town's most famous son is Queen's Freddie Mercury, and his childhood home in the main street of town has become a bit of a mecca.

After a few days of sitting still, I hired a moped and headed out of town with the aim of seeing as much of the island as I could. I crossed the island and about 5km from the eastern coast my bike started behaving like a kangaroo and I ran out of fuel. It turned out the fuel gage didn't work, and the moped had been supplied to me virtually empty. It was baking hot and I was in the middle of nowhere. I started pushing the moped on the hot tarmac road. It was not like pushing a bicycle. I finally made it towards the small town of Paje on the coast and to my relief there was a petrol station. Problem was, they were out of fuel, a common occurrence in Zanzibar. There were stations to the north and to the south on the coast, but the problem was no one knew which one had fuel. I locked the bike up, bought a large bottle of water to drink and to hold the fuel that I hoped to find. I plumped for north, started walking, and stuck my thumb out. A local stopped and drove me to the next town where there was a queue of cars waiting for fuel, the drivers hoping it would last for their turn. It was a reminder that this beautiful island in turquoise seas was still in the third world. The mopeds seemed to be allowed to jump the queue, so I downed the rest of my water, shook my bottle empty to dry it, and walked up offering it for filling. With the lid on this dirty pinkish mix, I managed to get a lift back to where my empty moped was parked. The fuel truck was now there filling up the station, with an even longer queue waiting.

I was happy to be back on the road, but I was now hot and starving hungry. There was a cool beach shack and kite surfing centre down on the sandy beach, so I went there for a welcome local tuna salad. Before and after lunch I swam in the emerald green water. It was most welcome. I hit the road again and filled up with more fuel at the same station I had been to with the water bottle. It was probably more fuel than I needed, but I wasn't taking any more chances. It was great to be back on the open road riding all the way up the east coast looking out to sea. The next land due east from here is Java, Indonesia. I stopped at some of the amazing deserted white sandy beaches. The beach at Pongwe had goats running round in the seaweed and I looked across to the exclusive Pongwe Island lodge, nestled on a rocky outcrop sitting in the sea. I loved riding along the empty roads through miles of countryside. At times it reminded me of Asia or the Caribbean and I rode on for 50 Ks, letting the view wash over me.

I rode into one town and there was a group of girls at a bus stop. I asked them for directions, and one asked me if I could give her a lift to one of the resorts where she worked. The bus was late, and so was she. She jumped on the back and we chatted for the few kilometres to the resort gates where she got off. I was determined to get to Nungwi at the northern tip of the island and pressed on. I stopped and admired the view. The sun was getting low and I thought I had better get back to Stone Town by nightfall. On my way out of town I got waved down by a young policeman who smelt blood. He didn't like my paperwork and said my licence wasn't valid in Zanzibar and held me there. He threatened to lock me up for the night and said there would be a court hearing tomorrow. It was all getting very boring, so I sat and read my book, which I am not sure was the right move. A local go-between told me how much it would cost to fix the situation. I was happy with the concept of a bribe, but not the amount. After a fairly long negotiation with standoffs in between we agreed a number and I left, heading back to town while cursing riding on the potholed road in the dark as well as having being robbed of my dinner money. The next day, I left Zanzibar and flew to Mombasa.

Would I go back? To Tanzania yes, to see the Serengeti and to climb Kilimanjaro.

Thailand

Thailand is the only country in Asia that was never colonised. I have been many times due to my sister, Molly, having lived there for several years. My first trip was after my travels around China in the late eighties. Arriving in Bangkok after a few months of relative restriction was welcome. I headed to the backpacker street, Kho San, found a guest house and spent some time chatting to other travellers. A local Thai woman approached a group of us and offered to be our guide and show us round the Royal Palace. We thought 'why not?' and agreed a price. Walking round the grounds of the palace I got chatting to her telling her I had been travelling around China. She mentioned she had shown a Swiss girl round the palace a few weeks ago. On the off chance, I asked 'She wasn't called Florence?' She laughed and said yes and then opened her handbag and pulled out an envelope. It was like some magic trick. This was an envelope addressed to Florence, which our guide had kept for the Chinese stamps. It was my handwriting and my name on the back. I had sent Florence a postcard in an envelope from China.

A big city was not what I needed. I wanted a relaxing time on a tropical island. The money was getting tight at the end of this trip and the cheapest option was Ko Semet. I found a hut right on the beach to spend a week winding down. I ran into a great group of travellers, mostly relaxing after long trips as well. Two English girls I had already met a few months earlier in Queensland and Hong Kong. One was a hairdresser working her way round the world. She had cut my hair in Queensland and I saw her sitting on the beach when I arrived. I walked up and asked, 'Any chance of a haircut?' We laughed. There were two Swedish journalists I kept running into in China. One had a small typewriter. I fixed it in China and again here. There was a London cabbie who had us in hysterics with his stories. We were a real gang and barely moved from our village of huts that week. The sea was so warm it was like swimming in soup. At night we would sit around drinking beers, chatting and laughing for hours under the stars with sound waves breaking in the background.

My next trip to South East Asia was on my way back to London from Oz. This time I went south from Bangkok to the island of Koh Samui in the Gulf of Thailand. I opted for a beach hut again and hired a moped for the week. It was great. I then went to Phuket on the Andaman Sea side of Thailand and toured around some of the islands here including the infamous 'James Bond Island' in the bay of Phang Nga. This is the spot where Roger More lands his seaplane and parks it on the beach. He meets The Man with the Golden Gun, who welcomes 007 by zapping his plane into flames with his gun from the top of the rock.

I went back many times when my sister lived in Bangkok. She had some great pads with cool swimming pools. My favourite was the one that had an old 25m tiled pool in the garden. It was a joy to swim in every morning. We got to know the city well of course, and would go out at night to some great bars including those looking over the river and sky bars. Restaurants were mostly street food, Soi 38 Street off Sukhumvit was a favourite. Molly had a great house built down in Hua Hin, a couple of hours south of Bangkok, and we had some fun family Christmases there as well. She insisted on light green tiles in the pool against my recommendation of dark blue. She's scared of deep water and sharks.

One year I joined Johnny, Sarah and my goddaughters for a trip to Koh Lanta. I made a new friend Ali on the boat trip to the island and she has been a sailing and skiing buddy ever since. Koh Lanta was dreamy, and we did some great trips out to some of the islands. The cast geography here has left a series of small mountains rising out of the sea. The most memorable of these was Emerald Cave. You arrive at this island of rock hundreds of feet high and swim into a cave which emerges onto a beach in the middle of the island surrounded by high rock walls. It's amazing.

Would I go back? Maybe, but I have been a lot now. Perhaps to do the King's Cup sailing regatta.

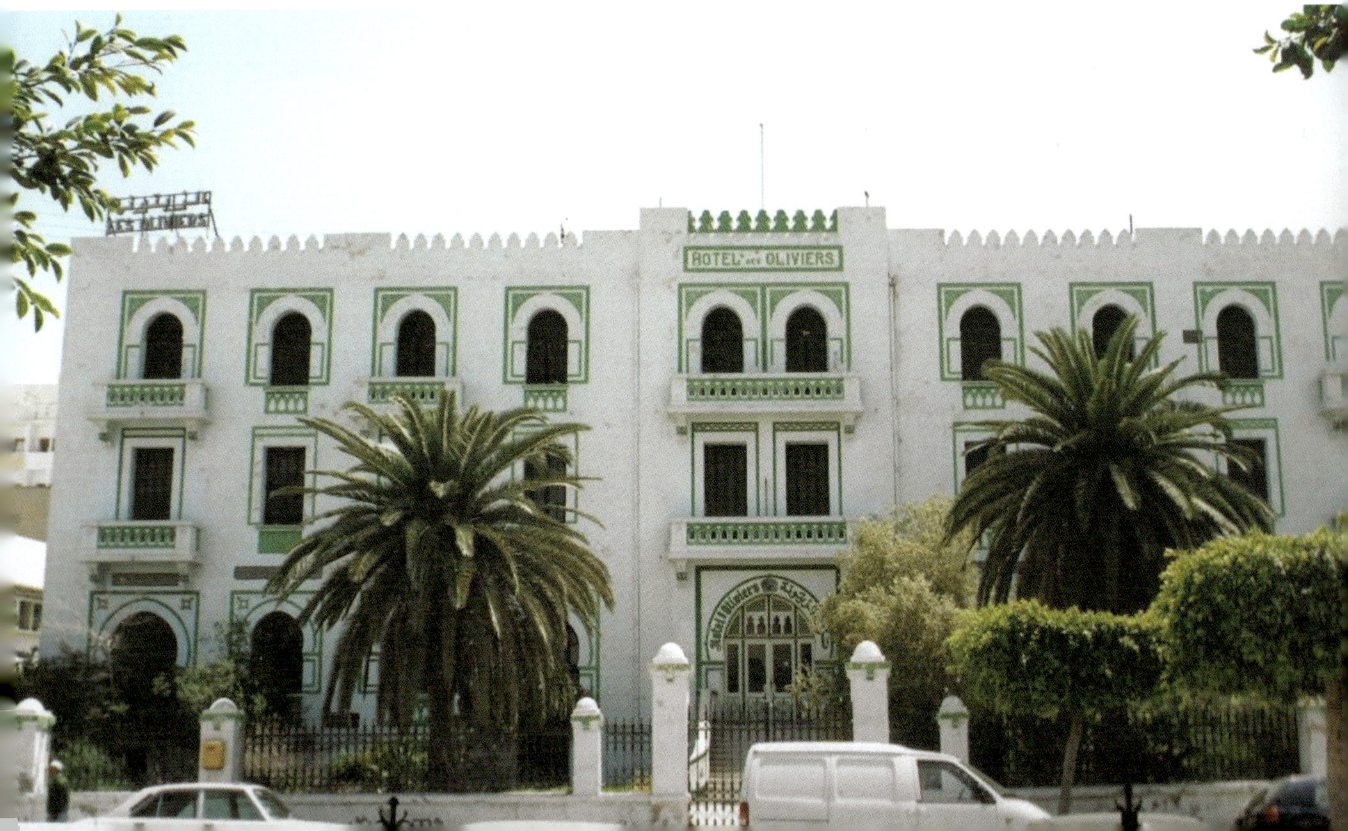
HOTEL des OLIVIERS

Tunisia

I went to Tunisia in late 2000 with Katherine. We wanted a week away somewhere a little more interesting than the usual Mediterranean haunts. This was my first taste of North Africa. It was a package holiday to Monastir where we stayed in the Alassio resort near the Mediterranean port city of Sousse. Our plan was to venture out to see sights each day. The first day we walked for several miles along the beach to Monistir. It was a lovely small city set on a small peninsula with the well-preserved Ribat Fort. We walked around the backstreets and soaked up the atmosphere of this calm place. Sousse was our other spot for escaping from the resort and we ventured into the city a few times for lunch, markets and the occasional dinner. The quality of the produce in the food markets was better than in the resort so we would often make our own salads for picnics. Freshly squeezed strawberry juice in Sousse was my go-to. The olive oil is the best I have ever had. If you ever see olive oil from Tunisia, buy it!

We did two longer day trips. We took the train from Sousse to the port city of Sfax which also had some amazing buildings and bustling markets. The train passed through El Jem, which has the most complete Roman amphitheatre in Africa. Our other trip was inland to the ancient desert city of Kairouan. We went to the taxi station in Sousse and got a louage, a shared taxi, which was an old Peugeot estate with three rows of seats. It was a long straight road inland to the desert. On one stretch we could see an ambulance with its flashing light on ahead of us. We gradually caught up and overtook. In a low voice I said, 'if we are in a road accident, maybe get a taxi rather than wait for medical help.' The 50km trip inland was well worth it. The Uqba Mosque at Kairouan is special as seven visits to this place in your lifetime is worth one trip to Mecca. Quite convenient if you live nearby. The building and marble floors are largely in their original state and the Aghlabid water reservoirs looked as if they had just been built. They are considered one of the biggest feats of hydraulic engineering of the Middle Ages.

Ten years after this visit, the political situation erupted in Tunisia. Deeper into the interior of the country a young street vendor selling his crops had become so exasperated from being fined and moved on by the authorities that he set himself alight. His death sparked an outpouring of grief and civil unrest leading to the Jasmine Revolution and the ousting of the regime. This in turn sparked the Arab spring across the Middle East. Five years after that came the tragic terrorist attack just up the beach from where we stayed, killing 36 people, mostly holidaymakers lying on sun loungers on the beach. Inevitably, the tourist industry has collapsed. It's a great shame because Tunisia is well worth seeing.

Would I go back? Maybe as a route into Libya. I would quite like to see Tunis too.

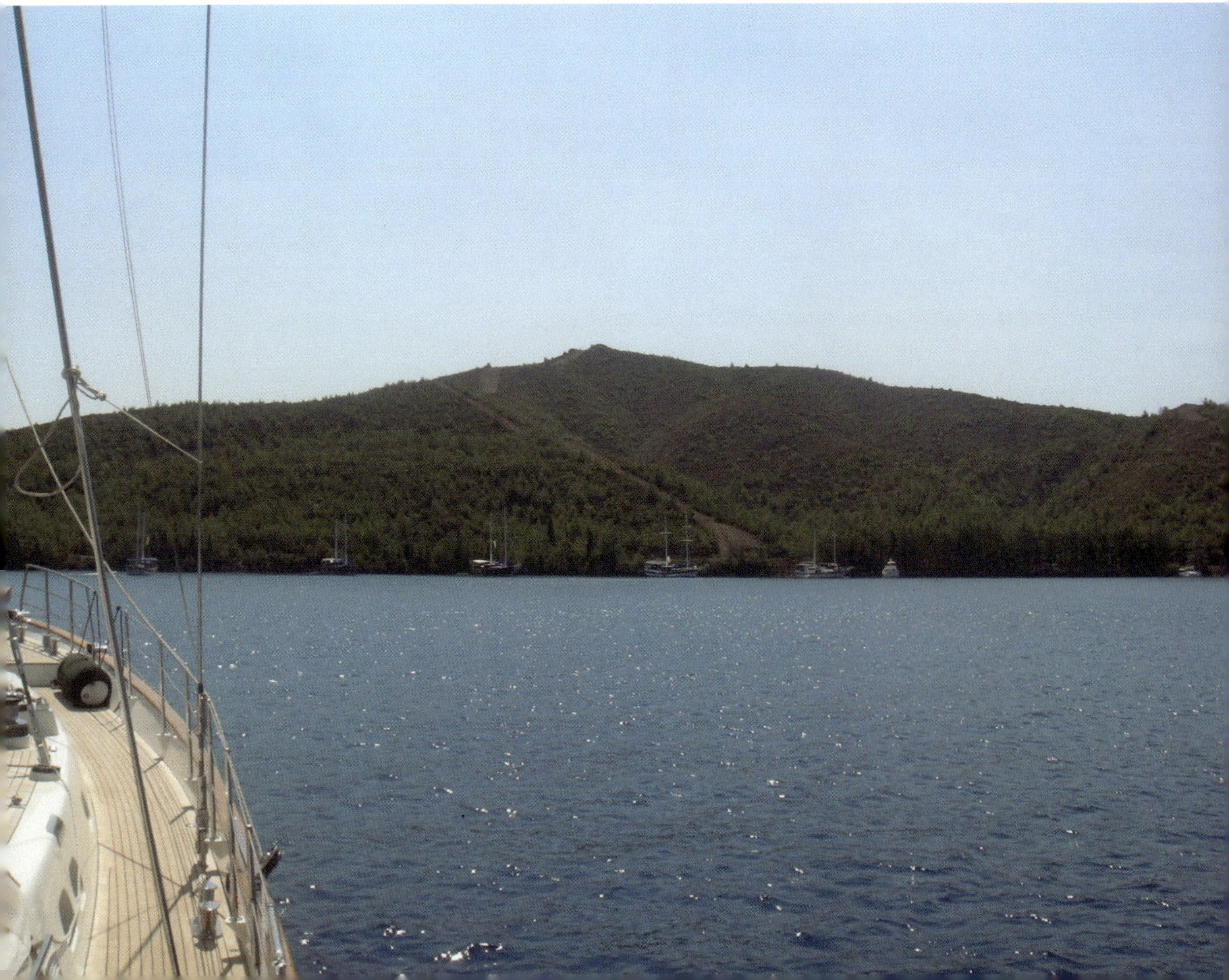

Turkey

I went to Istanbul with my girlfriend Ann Louise in the early nineties for a long weekend break. We stayed in the atmospheric district of Sultanahmet just by the Blue Mosque. This mosque is big and the Hagia Sophia Mosque at the other end of Sultanahmet Park is even bigger. We went inside both, but the sheer scale of the 6th century Hagia Sophia Mosque was breathtaking. Built as the Cathedral of Constantinople, the largest church of the Byzantine Empire, it was converted to a mosque when the city fell to the Ottoman Empire. With so many worshippers and tourists, finding your shoes when you come out is a challenge.

Continuing up the hill in a line from the mosques you come to the opulent Topkapi Palace, home to the sultans for four hundred years. There are commanding views over the Bosporus from here. Facing the other way, you look through the minarets growing out of the mosques. Topkapi is full of treasures, but the thing that has stayed with me are the cabinets housing emeralds, each the size of a fist. The harem complex is the most ornate interior imaginable. We caught a ferry across the Bosporus, from Europe to Asia Minor, to Uskadar. And it did feel like arriving in a different continent.

A highlight of Istanbul is the Grand Bazaar, one of the largest souks in the world, covering over sixty streets with thousands of shops. We went back round it each day we were there. The spice market with bright coloured mounds of brown, orange, gold, and yellow at the front of the stalls was fascinating. There was row after row of vendors selling fruit, nuts, sweets, and, of course, Turkish Delight. The practical sections of the souk were also interesting. Different areas selling things like glass light shades, metalwork and pottery. In the woodwork area, one section of several workshops sold long wafer-thin wooden baker's paddles for retrieving bread from ovens. I had the idea of getting one of these remodelled into a Pizza paddle for my friend Biggles. He liked making pizza in his Aga oven back in London. I chose one of the workshops and picked out a paddle like I was selecting a surfboard. With a pencil, I drew the lines I wanted cut with the bandsaw to make a smaller paddle with a longer handle. All the other shopkeepers came and watched. Tourists did not normally buy bread-making paddles. I didn't haggle for the paddle and paid the price it would have been before it was reduced in size. Armed with latest 'must have' kitchen utensil we left the souk for the day. I imagined returning the next day to see the hundreds of long bread paddles transformed, the local market sacrificed for a new moneyed tourist market.

We had good food in Istanbul, especially fish in the restaurants in the Kumkapi district. One last treat was a day at the Turkish baths. Relaxing it was not. After lying on a marble slab and being rubbed up and down vigorously by a Turkish wrestler for a few hours I left feeling dazed, like I had done ten rounds with Mike Tyson.

My second trip to Turkey was to go sailing with Miranda. We flew into Bodrum and spent a couple of days staying in the lovely fishing village of Gumusluk. The sea lapped right up to the steps of our villa. This was a great spot for water front restaurants and beach bars, with lots of yachts anchored in the bay. One of the days we climbed up the rocks at the entrance to the bay where a huge Turkish flag furled and unfurled in the hot breeze.

After a few days we went to meet friends to join the boat for a week. It belonged to Miranda's friend's father. He normally chartered the yacht out for a small fortune but had kindly put her at our disposal for the week. We left the dock in the tender and as we approached our home for the next week, I was beginning to feel as if I had died and gone to heaven. Kestrel is a 106ft Turkish Gulet, built in 2004 and designed by the famous boat designer Ron Holland. We were six, but there was room for twenty-six, and there was a crew of four. The bowsprit was so high out of the water that it was almost too scary to dive off. Our skipper was happy to let me helm the boat and I was more than happy to do so. She was a challenge to manoeuvre in confined spaces in windy conditions and we had to pass up on some of the smaller popular bays. Our crew were great fun. The power of Kestral under sail was immense and it is still one of the best sailing experiences I have had.

Would I go back? Yes. Back to Istanbul, more sailing, to see the rock towers at Cappadocia.

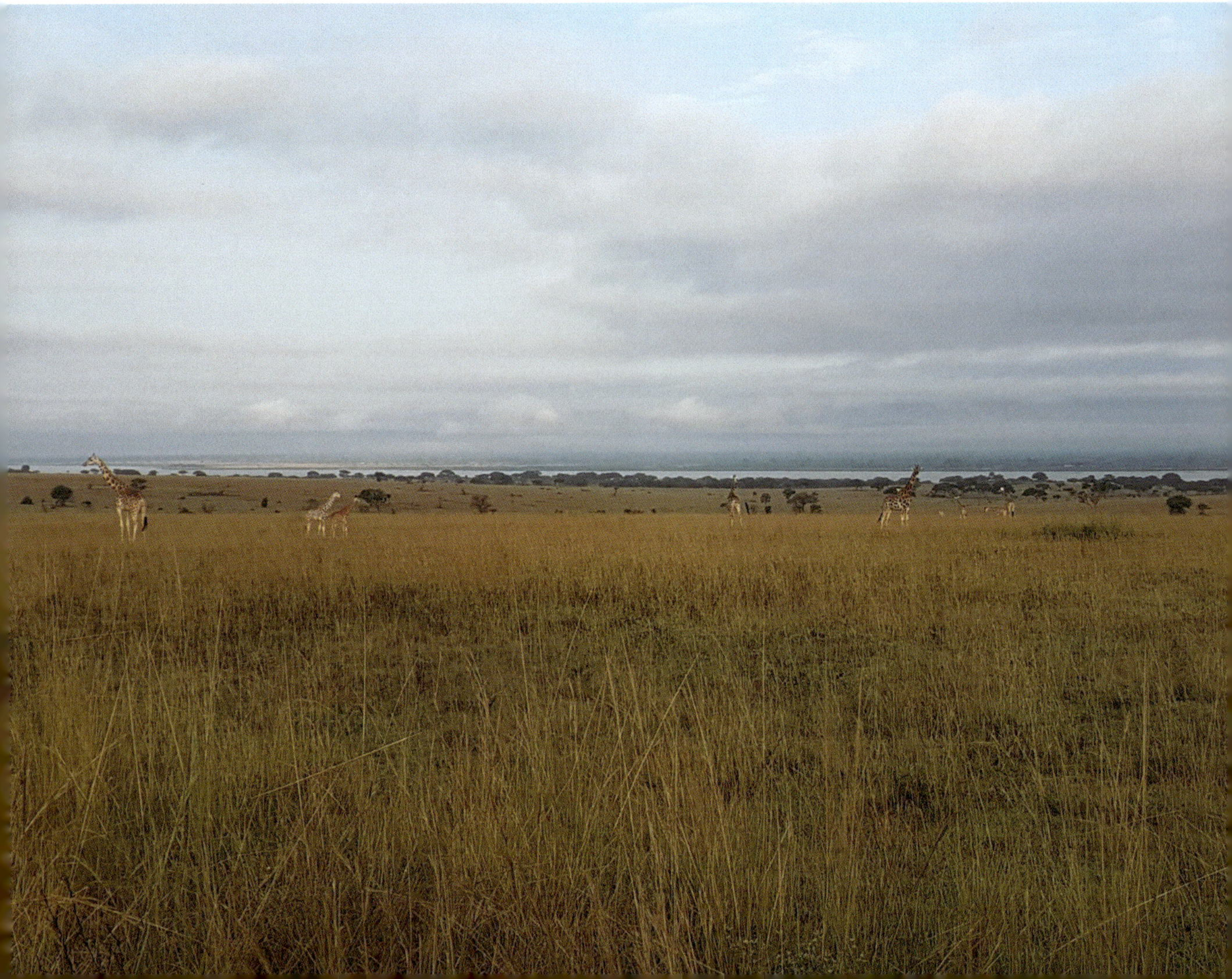

Uganda

A friend of mine, Lucy, set up a charity in Uganda rescuing abandoned babies and placing them in families. There are over 50,000 children languishing in orphanages in Uganda. On the face of it, these orphanages, largely supported by the church, look like charities but they are mostly scams. Lucy saw the injustice of the system while she was working in Uganda. She quit her job and set up her charity, Child's I Foundation. She was passionate about placing unwanted children within loving families and changing the system in Uganda. CIF had already saved hundreds of babies found abandoned, often in bins or rubbish piles, and placed them into families. After years of struggle, Lucy was winning. Her charity was growing, I was helping her raise money and she needed help growing her team and managing people. My friend Linzi had spent years in senior human resources roles in global companies and she agreed to help. So we went to Uganda to learn more about the work of CIF on the ground.

We flew into Entebbe on the edge of Lake Victoria and drove into Kampala. There is something about Africa that makes you feel alive from the moment you drive out of the airport. I wound the window down and looked out at the children playing everywhere along the road. The thing that struck me immediately was the stark contrast of the deep red earth and tropical green vegetation. We stayed at the Makindye Country Club which would have been quite something back in its heyday. I liked the feeling of its former glory. It was a bit run down but anything more luxurious would have been inappropriate with our work there. We had an old pool and tennis courts, and lovely grounds which were great for impromptu meetings with the charity staff. The charity had a baby centre nearby, where abandoned babies were looked after while families were found for them. The Ugandan men and women who work here are amazing people. They all had big smiles, constantly laughing amongst themselves, but were mostly quite shy. These people were on Lucy's mission and were passionate about their work and the best practices from UK social care that they were learning. Hearing their humble life stories, their calm demeanour, and optimism for the future was heart-warming. We had taken out big cases of toys from friends in the UK whose children had outgrown them. It was almost overwhelming to present them to the centre and watch the children interact with them. There were banana trees in the garden with big bunches growing on them.

The baby centre was high security. There was a growing trade in the smuggling of babies. High profile westerners, such as Madonna, had adopted in Africa. Seemingly good intentions were having unintended consequences. A child could change hands for thousands of dollars or more, with a number of people profiting in the chain along the way so the compound needed to be secure. Another risk was that the charity, and Lucy, were becoming a target with many of the orphanages claiming their business models were being undermined. As part of our leaning about the bigger problem in Uganda, Linzi and I went to an orphanage undercover, posing as tourists wanting to give. The place we saw was mostly funded by the church. The scenes of abandonment are a bit too harrowing to recount, and looking back now it is heart breaking to relive the memory of that day. But it was necessary for us to see what we were up against. We also made some visits to the homes where we had placed children to meet them and their foster carers or adoptive parents. It was always humbling how readily people would invite you into their homes where they had so few comforts. I was helping Lucy to attract high net worth donors and seeing everything first-hand really helped me in presenting our cause to them.

We mostly stayed in the country club at night, talking over everything we were learning and we met some interesting characters there too. We did make it into Kampala one night though and went to this fabulous outdoor restaurant. They had a brass band of about a dozen locals accompanied by vocals, bongos and percussion instruments playing Afro beats. The overall sound was brilliant, and the energy of people dancing was mesmerising.

Lucy had been pushing herself to the limit with the charity and all the pressures of keeping everything going. Linzi and I were starting to feel our own brains exploding with the intensity of it all too, so we decided some rest and recreation was needed. This was also a good time for us to sit down with Lucy and understand the future of this great thing she had created, which was now becoming bigger than her.

We hired a driver and his van with a lifting roof for a safari, heading several hours north to Murchison Falls National Park. Driving out of Kampala, we were pulled over by the police. A driver with tourists on board was likely to be earning good money. It was easy to forget at times that the people of Uganda were ravaged by Idi Amin in the seventies. While these times are long gone and Uganda now has a bright future, there are still undercurrents of fear when the law is involved. These men in uniform needed to find a problem with our vehicle and they soon homed in on a bald tyre. The resulting negotiations were conducted away from us, but to be fair the tyre was bald. At the next town we stopped at a garage – well, by a pile of old tyres and some tools laying on the ground. We swapped our bald tyre for a less bald one. While this repair was underway, I chatted to an old man drying his coffee beans out on a blanket to dry them in the sun.

For the last couple of hours of our journey after Masindi, the roads had turned into rivers in places with the rains and we were up to our axels in mud a lot of the time. We finally made it to the Nile River Lodge and our rooms were like tree huts with balconies on stilts right at the edge of the Victoria Nile. We had the place all to ourselves, it was magical. No phone, no internet, and very little electricity. I would lie in bed at night and hear the hippopotamuses grunting in the river below.

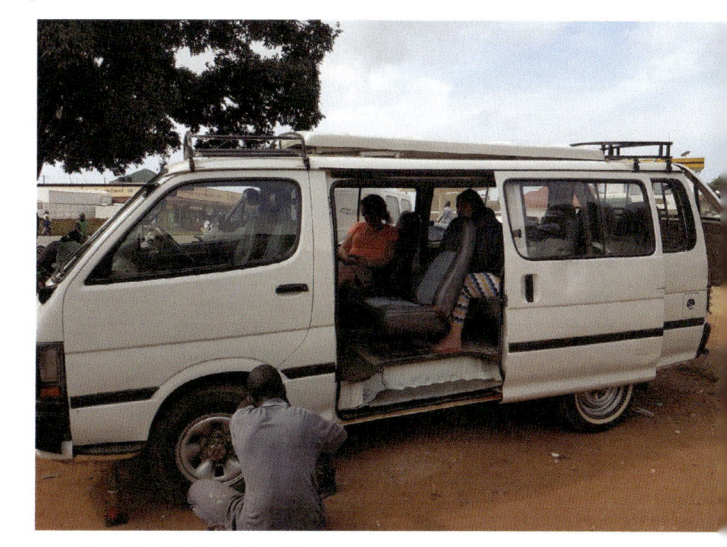

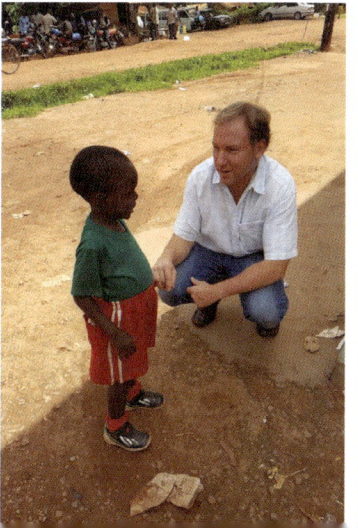

At around 4am, the morning would come alive with a cacophony of birds and monkeys. There would be a knock on the door soon after and a soft voice would say 'your shower is ready'. The water had been heated over a fire and tipped into a bucket in the outdoor shower. There was a tap with a rose under the bucket and I made the most of a few minutes of warmth. The water smelt of charcoal as it ran over me. I had to compete with monkeys trying to steal the soap; well for that matter anything.

At breakfast Linzi told the hotel guys that there was a bright green snake in her shower when she walked in. Ah they said 'a mamba, it's dangerous but it doesn't bite.' I looked it up in my guidebook: 'The venom is the fastest-acting snake venom, meaning bite victims have little chance of survival.' I decided not to recount that to the girls and talked about the day ahead instead. I kept having visions of us driving through thick mud for a few hours to Masindi trying to keep Linzi alive in the van. The vision kept re-occurring for some weeks.

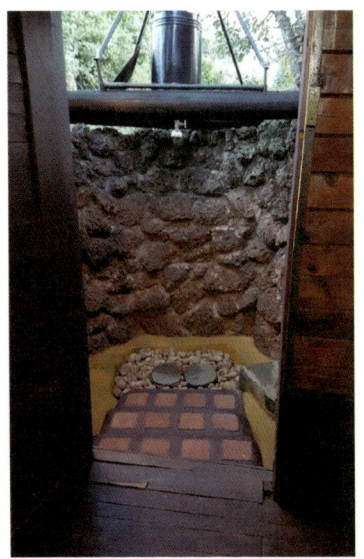

We crossed the Victoria Nile on a motorised platform to a peninsula of land bounded by the White Nile on the other side. Both rivers run into Albert Lake and are so crocodile-infested that you can actually see them in the water or very well camouflaged on the riverbanks. This was my first safari experience and I was excited. We also had a park guide who was super nice. He had a big smile and a rifle slung over his shoulder at all times. We saw so many wild animals as we drove around standing up in the van, lots of giraffes, water buffalo, antelope, and more hippopotamuses than you can imagine.

On the other side of the lake is the Democratic Republic of Congo. Our guide told us that poachers would come across the water to take baby hippos for food. You have to be seriously hungry to want to wrestle a baby hippo from its mother. The best moment of the day was reserved for our encounter with a bull elephant. We stopped on the road, sensing something in the trees, and suddenly there he was. He had a spot behind his eye that was weeping down his cheek. He was in musth, a time of a large rise in reproductive hormones which can lead to highly aggressive behaviour. We froze in the hope that not moving might calm him. He was huge. He could have tipped our van over without any effort. The rifle would be useless if he decided to charge us. He started stamping and throwing dirt on his head and then wheeling round to face us. He was not happy with us there and we were beginning to agree with him. I was dreading the van not starting, but luckily it did and we were off. It was an amazing experience.

The next day we went up the Victoria Nile in a small boat to the falls. On the way we saw hippos fighting, their splashes like a series of mines going off in the water. They would lock their big molar teeth, seemingly fighting to the death. We hoped our captain knew what he was doing because our boat wouldn't stand a chance against these beasts. Our captain's desire to get us as close under the falls as possible was our next part of the assault course. These are not your usual 'pour off the top' kind of falls. This vast river is forced through a 20ft gap in the rocks, creating some serious rapids at the bottom. Just to the side of the rapids, our eager captain landed us ashore to take us on a short walk into the bush to show us where Ernest Hemingway had famously crashed his plane. Being a bit of a fan of Ernest, I was happy to stand on the crash site and it seemed safer than the falls and the hippos. The black and white colobus monkeys here were fascinating and the bright green and red birds living in holes in the cliffs were too. The whole place was a treasure trove of wildlife.

There was a thunderstorm in the middle of the night on our last night at Nile River Lodge. It was so loud I thought my tree hut room might roll into the river. I imagined swimming with the hippos and crocodiles. The lightning was so bright the room was filled with fluorescent white bright flashes for hours. And then came the rain. The storm was biblical. It was so loud on the roof that, if I'd screamed at the top of my voice, no one would have heard me. I wondered how the girls were faring. And I also wondered where green mamba snakes went when it rained this hard… I tucked my sheets tightly round me, just in case warm dry beds were their refuge of choice.

At breakfast we wondered if the roads would be drivable. As it happened, the deep mud was mostly washed away in the night. On the road back to Kampala there was an overturned truck which no one seemed to think much of. In the rain we followed a logging truck with a group of guys hanging on at the back by the skin of their fingers. I loved my time in Uganda. It is among the poorest countries I have been to, but it is also one where the people seemed happiest. It has a great future.

Would I go back? Definitely, for all those smiling faces, the charity, to see gorillas.

United Arab Emirates

I was writing a text book related to my work over the Christmas break in 2009 and I figured the Middle East would be a good place to do it. It would be warm by day to go for walks and relatively quiet in the evenings to type away at my computer. Dubai was my entry point. I had been through the airport several times in transit but had never stopped over, with the prospect of getting Asia or Oz, or back to London always winning out. I did not know what to expect but I somehow felt that Dubai wouldn't be my kind of place. There was a plethora of hotels and I logged on each day and just took the best deal going. I stayed in the world's tallest hotel on the hundred and something floor, at a couple of places down by the beach at Jameriah, and up at Media City, near the famous palm.

The new parts of Dubai were still under construction, meaning walking from place to place was difficult. The city is not really designed for pedestrians so I found myself gravitating to the beach which I could walk along. So, this is where I did my long walks each day. I had fancied getting out sailing on a traditional wooden dhow and saw lots of them parked up on the beach, but none going out. The old part of the city, where you could catch boats along the river, was my favourite. The Gold Souk was a more authentic old world Middle Eastern experience. On Christmas day I went skiing in the snow dome. It seemed like the most ridiculous thing to do, so I figured why not? Inevitably the skiing was very limited, but there was a chalet bar half-way down the slope where it was quite fun to pull in and have a drink. I turned up in shorts and a t-shirt and hired all the kit you would wear skiing. After the novelty had worn off, I walked to the beach and had lunch. I went to the Palm Jumeirah on the monorail and saw the aquarium. Seeing a whale shark in a tank there was a bit upsetting.

The highlight of Dubai was the Burj Khalifa, the world's tallest building, which was just opening.

It was to be called the Burj Dubai, but the city was close to going bust in the global financial crisis and needed bailing out by its much wealthier neighbouring emirate, Abu Dhabi. The oil wealth is concentrated there, not Dubai. So Burj Khalifa was a nod to Khalifa bin Zayed Al Nayan, the emir of Abu Dhabi and president of UAE. I went up it the day it opened to the public, catching the lift up to the observation level on the 148th floor. The total height is a whopping 2,720ft tall. You really do feel like you are in an aircraft. Watching the Dubai Fountain display on the ground below was surreal. It was so high up that you could barely make out cars on the road below.

I caught a bus to Abu Dhabi and checked into the Radisson, which has its own private beach. I had a couple of meetings with clients at the Abu Dhabi Investment Authority, one of the biggest sovereign wealth funds in the world. Their building may not be the tallest in the city, but it is the prettiest and my meetings were on the top floor. I liked Abu Dhabi much more than its brash neighbour, Dubai. It was a nice city to walk round. You could actually walk around without being cut off by new multi-lane highways through the city. And it still has an Arabic heart and soul.

Would I go back? Probably not.

United States of America

My first trip to America was to New York in the late eighties. I ended up living in the Big Apple for a year a couple of decades later. I have been to more than half the fifty states in the many trips I have done to and around the US over the years. It is difficult to know where to start, so I will work my way down the east coast, then the west coast and then the middle states.

I had just finished university in London and heard about a gig whereby you could fly to New York and back as a courier. Not that exciting, until I learnt that the return leg could be on Concorde. This was in the days where documents had to be signed physically and the quickest way to get them across the Atlantic was as accompanied baggage. I brought back twelve mail sacks, which I never saw. So, I flew to NY with just hand luggage wearing as many warm clothes as possible. It was winter and it was its brutal self on the US east coast. I remember flying down the eastern seaboard of North America for the first time. Looking out the window it was white all the way and the sea was frozen for most of it.

I think you never forget your first trip to a place and that trip to New York was special. Your first time in New York is like being in a movie. So many 20th century icons leap out at you. In the late eighties it was not that safe a place. I got off the bus at 42nd Street Station and guys in hoodies were already after my bag and my pockets. I walked to the YMCA on the East Side by the United Nations building. There were several locks on the inside of the door of my room. Gun crime was high, and mugging was rife. I met up with Johnny, who was doing a course there for his first job. We did all the touristy things, like up the Empire State building, the World Trade centre, the Metropolitan Museum of Art, Central Park, and the Staten Island Ferry. Money was tight in those days, so we spent our nights in cheap dive bars, delis, hamburger joints or pizza parlours. Half of it was to escape the freezing temperatures outside. A Danish girl I met in the Met was staying with her American cousins and they invited me for dinner in a lovely apartment on the upper West Side.

Her uncle was just like Woody Allen. He and his wife took great pleasure in simultaneously explaining the cataloguing of their vast wall of books. "These are the ones I've read, and she has to read. Those are the ones I've read, and he has to read. These are the ones I love, and she does not…." and so on for a good twenty minutes. Their son was a journalist on the New York Times, and he had to go back to work and asked if we would like to come and see the paper. We got a tour round and I got to press the button to start the print of the next edition run. There were guys everywhere bundling and stacking up papers and loading them into trucks. It was a frantic atmosphere. The security guard showing us out of the complex found out I was an Aussie and then kept asking me about Crocodile Dundee. I had a friend up in Boston, so I flew up to stay with him and his college mates in a beautiful old house. We went up to Salem, the home of witchcraft, on the Massachusetts coast. There was what they call a snowmaker over Boston on my last night and we woke up to deep snow. I needed to get to the airport for my flight back to JFK. The airline kept cancelling flights and I was worried I would be stuck overnight and miss my Concorde flight out to London. The crew wanted to get home too and the last flight out of Boston was so empty that I sat in the front seat chatting to the airhostesses for the entire flight. I arrived super early for my flight the next day and waited in the Concorde room looking out of the glass windows viewing the supersonic beauty. There was an array of food and drink on offer and as I was loading a plate up, the pilot came and introduced himself to me. He welcomed me to flying Concorde. Out of over forty passengers I was the only fist timer. I had become a bit of a Concorde bore in the run up to this trip, having read all the books and learned all the facts about this amazing plane. When I went up to cockpit, I literally knew what most of the dials were. I am sure the flight deck all agreed 'what a weirdo' when I went back to my seat. Still, I was happier than ever. The flight took 3hrs 15mins back to London. I got the tube back into London and met some friends in the pub.

I have been back to Boston a few times. I did a road trip one year, taking in the states of Connecticut and Rhode Island. Newport R.I. is a kind of a rite of passage for anyone who sails. I had a great weekend one time in Provincetown, a lively old seaside resort, on Cape Cod. The whale watching out on the boats here is easily the best I have done. We were constantly surrounded by humpback whales feeding right next to us. It was amazing. Another weekend I went to the island of Nantucket. Fortuitously, it was the weekend of the Nantucket Wine Fair. I still have the etched tasting glasses. The European wine stalls were all the rage with the visitors and the American ones were empty. This coincided perfectly with the love affair I was having with American reds at the time. I visited Greenwich and Stamford in Connecticut a few times and made some good friends there as well.

Long Island also holds some fond memories. Walking the beaches at the Hamptons and seeing the amazing holiday homes. On a recent trip to New York, I went and stayed with a friend at Shelter Island right at the top of Long Island opposite Sag Harbour. Her father was an architect and the home they had built there was great fun. I loved my time on Shelter.

When I asked my mother at the turn of the millennium what was the one thing she wanted to do in her life, she responded 'Fly on Concorde and see the Taj Mahal.' The next day I booked tickets to New York, flying back on Concorde. Dad had been to NY in the early sixties on his way back from Europe to Australia. Mum had never been and had no real desire to go to America. I felt it was time for her to see New York. We stayed on the Upper West Side and did the usual touristy things, including going to the top of the World Trade Centre. We had a meal at Windows on the World on the 107th floor and stood out on the observation deck for ages at sunset. We watched the planes flying past and helicopters flying below us. Who would have believed that a year later these two amazing buildings would be razed to the ground in the September 11 terrorist attacks? I remember watching on TV in horror as waiters waved the red and white checked tablecloths from the windows of that restaurant. New York has never been quite the same since.

Another thing that would never be the same was visiting cockpits in airplanes, something I asked to do a lot. On the way back from that trip with the three of us on Concorde, the year before 9/11, I managed to do 'a landing.' I joined the flight deck as we entered the Bristol Channel at Mach 2.03, 2,200 km/h. I was seated behind the captain in the jump seat with a headset listening in on all the radio comms. Air Traffic control came on, 'BA1, we have switched to south runway for you.' Concorde's higher landing speed meant she needed an empty flight path ahead of her and the terminal was on that side of Heathrow. Four Olympus fighter jet engines made taxiing a bit more of a challenge. Air Traffic Control transmitted 'BA1, please come down onto your flight path' and then again, a few minutes later. The first officer turned to me and told me not to worry. They always got told they were too high. As a delta winged aircraft, being too low and putting on a bit of extra thrust was not really an option. We had to glide in like a bird. They had given up explaining this to the control tower. We banked over London, aiming for the bright line of lights in the distance. The nose went down, so we could see the runway and we came in quickly to touch down and reverse thrust to bring us to a halt. The kinetic energy formula dictates that the square of the speed is a bigger factor in stopping a plane than its mass is. To this day, landing in that cockpit on my second Concorde flight is one of my greatest experiences. For years beforehand in London, I could hear her and would say Concorde's coming and a couple of minutes later she would be over us. On her last day in service, I went to a good spot in Richmond to watch the four of them land one after another for one last time.

I made many trips back to New York before I lived there. There were trips out to New Jersey, Pennsylvania, Delaware, and Baltimore in Maryland. I used to stay in West 44th street by the New York Yacht Club. I even stayed in it once. When I moved to New York, I took an apartment a few blocks from Columbus Circle, 40 floors up with expansive views over the Hudson River and all the way down 8th Avenue to lower Manhattan. I actually had a view of one of the decommissioned Concordes on the Intrepid Aircraft Carrier Museum in the distance. Of course, you really get to know a place when you live there and there are too many great restaurants and bars to mention. At weekends I would rollerblade round Central Park, ride my bike out to places like Coney Island or visit museums. There was never a shortage of things to do and I was always flying off somewhere.

A few years after living in New York, I did a great road trip from Savanah, Georgia up to NYC. In Savanah, I sat on Forest Gump's bench where, 'life was like a box of chocolates.' We visited some of the great plantation homes around Savanah. I had done other trips to Atlanta, Augusta and Athens, a university city known for its music scene. The B52s and R.E.M. were born out of there. The countryside is beautiful too. Charleston in South Carolina was another lovely seaside city, very upmarket, with beautiful weatherboard homes. I had read that a young Ted Turner used to drive from Atlanta to the yacht club here, towing his trailer sailor yacht behind his Ferrari. What a guy. Driving up through North Carolina, Virginia and West Virginia brought us to Washington DC. With all my trips to America, I had left it so long to go to the US capital that I was excited to see it. It was freezing cold. The Potomac River was frozen solid. Given that New York is further south than Rome and here is further south still, it always amazes me how cold the North American continent can get. Washington has a very European feel to it and there were some fun nights out in cool bars and great restaurants. The trip to New York from here was driving through freezing rain. When I dropped off the hire car, it was covered in inches-thick ice.

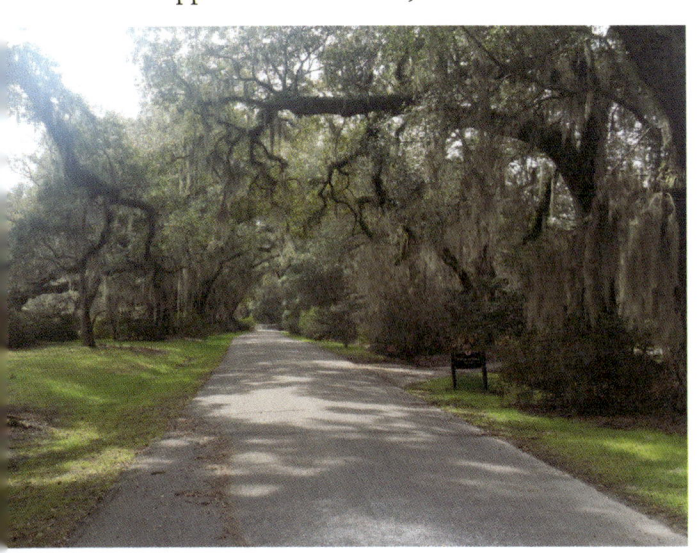

The final state on the east coast is Florida. I have spent quite a lot of time in Miami Airport, the main flight hub for the Caribbean. My first time in the city was meeting up with Biggles after I was freezing to death in Chicago. We hired a Ford Mustang convertible and went to a giant record store to buy CDs for road trips. When we came out of the shop the car was gone. I thought, 'Great we have this brand-new Mustang and in under an hour it gets stolen.' We went back into the shop to ask if they could call the police and they told us the car had been taken to a pound. Apparently, they read our licence plate out, which of course we didn't recognise, over the PA system in store while we were spending a small fortune with them. They gave us the address of the car pound and we got a taxi to this God forsaken place. This was at a time in Miami where a wrong turn off the freeway could take you into a dangerous neighbourhood. Tourists got shot. The car pound was in one of those kinds of neighbourhoods. They told us we had to pay cash. We said we didn't have any and they pointed to an ATM in the wire fence. Car back, roof down, sunglasses on, we got out of there and headed down to the Florida Keys with the CDs, which had turned out not to be not such a bargain, playing loud enough to put it all behind us. I drove down to Key West one day and went to Ernest Hemmingway's house. I drove back through the Everglades on a starry night with the roof down and The Cure playing full blast. We stayed in South Beach in Miami's art deco district. It was a fun time.

My mother was adopted at birth and only a few years ago discovered she had a sister and a brother, Joe, living in California and a sister in Salt Lake City, Utah. Mum and dad were staying with me in New York and then went on to Utah. I was speaking at a conference in Seattle the following week, so I flew to Salt Lake City to see everyone. My mother's new-found brother-in-law was very big into guns. He insisted on showing us all his weapons. It was pretty scary. We drove up into the mountains and mum, Joe and I went on these parallel zip wires about a mile down into the valley below. I went on to Seattle, home to Boeing, Microsoft, and Starbucks. I went out to the Microsoft campus in Redmond and did the history of Microsoft tour in Building No 92. I arranged a meeting in the Starbucks by the Nordstrom store and after sitting there for thirty minutes realised there was a

Starbucks on three streets surrounding that block. We were in different Starbucks. Seattle is a beautiful city, surrounded by the water, inlets, and the islands of Puget Sound. I have never seen so many conifers. Lunch at the Public Market right on the waterfront was a treat. I would like to see more of Washington state and Oregon state below it.

From the south of Oregon, running all the way to Mexico, is magical California. If this state were a country on its own, it would be the fifth biggest economy in the world. I have been to San Francisco quite a few times and have done some great trips from there. Down to the Big Sur, Carmel, Monterey and Santa Cruz to the south and the wonderful vineyards of Napa and Sonoma north of the city. Probably the best trip was with my parents to see the redwoods up the northern Californian coast. We walked down to one glade in the Redwood State Park near Orick where a group of trees were all over 350ft tall. The diameter of each tree was over 20ft at the base and they would take a minute to walk around. They were so tall that looking up you could not make out where the tree ended. Driving through the forests was amazing. A couple of trees in parks had been tunnelled so you could drive through their trunks. San Fran is great city with all its hills and the bay. The Golden Gate Bridge frames it all. Riding round on the cable cars was great fun and the Cable Car Museum, the working engine room for all the moving cables, is fascinating. Fisherman's Wharf is always a fun place to eat out at night.

I had not been to Los Angeles before I moved to New York to live. I was at a conference in Marina del Rey by Venice Beach for a few days and was really beginning to wonder if I had chosen the right location in New York. I have been to LA a few times since and I like it even more than San Francisco. The beaches are amazing, and you can see why LA's brightneess attracted Hollywood movie makers decades ago. I would roller blade on long paths along the beach from Venice to Santa Monica, and on one day I hired a bike that was like a cross trainer. You can easily spend days just driving around the streets of residential districts like Belair looking at the amazing homes. I stayed at some great hotels and had some fun nights out with friends in West Hollywood. Sure, it is a very material place, especially when you walk down a street like Rodeo Drive in Beverley Hills, but there is no denying the star quality of LA. A trip up the coast to Malibu and a walk along the beach looking at the beach homes of the rich and famous is also a bit of an experience.

Further down the coast is wonderful San Diego. This is Top Gun territory and with jets flying in over the beach you can be forgiven for hearing the movie soundtrack playing over and over in your head. The Gaslamp Quarter is a fun night and lunch at the Hotel del Coronado on the beach was also good. The trip back up to LA took in a stay at the lovely La Jolla and Laguna beach, where I saw some clients.

From LA we did a road trip along Route 66 into Arizona and on to the Grand Canyon. Nothing prepares you for your first sight of the Grand Canyon. It's vast, strangely silent with the wind in the trees, and it wills you to want to climb down into it. Unfortunately, we didn't have time. From there it was a drive back to Las Vegas in Nevada, stopping to see the Hoover Dam, the largest concrete structure built in its day. I had been to Vegas before, but I always wanted to drive across the desert and see the bright lights in the distance on approach. It's a crazy place, but it is unique, and I was happy to see it again. I also went skiing in Vale and Breckenridge in neighbouring Colorado one year.

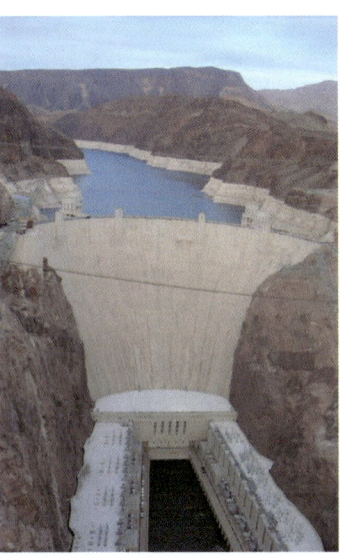

Chicago is one of my favourite cities. It is hard to think of a city anywhere in the world that has more street art than here. Anish Kapoor's stainless steel 'Bean' is my favourite. The windy city can be brutally cold in the winter, but on the edge of the lake in the summer it is a great spot. My first trip here was in the days of futures trading on exchange floors the size of aircraft carriers. The open outcry in the trading pits was mayhem and we were given a special tour through them. I was too scared to scratch my nose for fear of buying a ton of pork belly futures. On my last trip I walked out onto the glass bottom floors extending out of the Willis Tower, and looked down 108 floors to the ground below. It felt so unnatural to take the tentative steps out over a glass floor with nothing below you. The sound of the wind and the glass box cracking added to the adrenalin. With wobbly legs it was easier to crawl than it was to stand. But this was nothing. That night, the tightrope walker Nik Wallenda, walked across a wire between two buildings 500ft up without a safety net. Crowds of us watched from the streets below in disbelief as he took seven minutes to do it. Chicago is the 'windy city' and he faced 25 mile an hour winds that cold night. To top this of he did another leg between two buildings bind folded. Only in America.

Drinks in the bar at night at the top of the John Hancock Centre, where the brightly lit grid of roads extend to the horizon like fairy lights is also a sight to see. Dinner at Gibson's Steak House is a favourite and there are some great rhythm and blues bars around town too.

Drawing a line down the approximate middle of the US takes you from Chicago to Houston. And I did this as a road trip one year, taking a few days with some business meetings along the way. I drove out of Illinois and headed to Indianapolis for lunch. I stopped by the speedway circuit, famous for the Indy 500-mile race. Leaving Indiana and crossing over the mighty Ohio River I arrived in Louisville, Kentucky, home of the Kentucky Derby. I met up with some business colleagues for meetings and friends for dinner. Next was the drive to Nashville, Tennessee, home of bluegrass music, and then on to the spiritual home of the 'King', Memphis. I stayed in the Peabody Hotel which has a fountain and pond in the lobby with resident ducks swimming around. There is a bit of a ritual where at 11am each morning the ducks come down in the lift and waddle through the hotel to the pond. At the end of the day, the clock strikes 6pm and they all leave the pond, waddle through the hotel back to the lift and up to their home on the roof. Everything in this hotel, and I mean everything, has a duck motif on it. Memphis is enormously fun at night. The Rendezvous restaurant next to the Peabody serves their renown smoked ribs and the main music drag of Beale Street is full of bars with live bands and many an Elvis lookalike.

I hit the road the next day, driving along the mighty Mississippi River into the state of Mississippi. The cotton farms interested me, and I wandered out into a field to pick some. The balls of wool are really just like the cotton wool you would buy. I crossed the Mississippi River into Arkansas and drove to Little Rock, where I had lunch and wandered round the Clinton Presidential Library. I had a meeting set with Walmart, the supermarket giant, at their head office in Bentonville. I stayed round the corner from the very first "Walton's" store, still in its original state, in neighbouring Rogers.

The next morning, I drove north, where the countryside became very scenic into the state of Missouri and then into a prairie-like landscape across into Kansas. It was great to get into what felt like the heart of the Midwest, stopping off at the odd deserted hick town along the way. Think rusty sign squeaking while blowing in the wind. It really is like that. I drove into the state of Oklahoma, had a meeting in Tulsa, and aimed for Dallas. I stayed a couple of nights here and had dinner with clients each night. I have been fleetingly a few times, but it was good to get to know Dallas a bit better. I stayed in Turtle Creek where there are some great parks and the Katy Trail.

Houston is a city I have spent a lot of time in. It is America's fourth biggest city and will likely overtake Chicago for the number three spot soon. Six of the twenty most populous cities in America are in the state of Texas. I didn't like Houston that much when I first visited. It is a great sprawling city with freeways up to ten lanes wide each way. Getting around without a car is impossible. But after many years of spending lots of time in Houston and now knowing it well enough to drive around pretty much all over without a map, the city has grown on me. The food is top quality and prices are reasonable and I now have a long list of favourite haunts. It is a great place to go on business. I have come to like the brashness of the place. The map of the world in the bar at the Hilton Hotel Downtown has the American continents smack bang in the middle, rather than Europe. Everything is bigger, the cars, the trucks, the steaks, the hats. I would go shooting at the gun club where you take you own steaks to BBQ afterwards. Each guy's steak is bigger than the next guy's. On weekends it was good to get out to the bay beaches down to Galveston. And I have done weekend trips to San Antonio, Austin, a very happening city, and New Orleans in neighbouring Louisiana. One of the best things to do in Houston is to visit NASA. It took many visits to Houston before I decided to go. One recent trip from London to Houston with my girlfriend Amanda, we spent a great day at the Space Centre visiting Mission Control and seeing the massive Saturn V rocket. I would happily go back to NASA now with every visit to Houston.

Would I go back? Yes. Want to see Oregon, Montana, Wyoming, Maine, Yellowstone.

Uruguay

I went to Uruguay for new year. Some newfound friends in Argentina had a holiday home in Punta del Este, and they invited me to join. Punta was a place I had heard about, being one of the stopping points in previous Whitbread Round the World yacht races. It had looked great in the race coverage, so I was keen to see it.

I left Buenos Aires, crossing the Rio de La Plata to the historic city Colonia. The river at this point is over ten miles wide and at the so-called mouth is over 20 miles wide. It is not the Atlantic Ocean for sure, but it is a bit too wide to call a river too. If the water was not the brownish colour that is, you would say it was the sea. Colonia del Sacramento is a Portuguese settlement and it still has a real colonial charm with its cobbled streets and old buildings. I spent a few hours wandering around and had lunch before heading off to Montevideo.

The capital was better than I imagined. The city is centred around the Plaza Independencia, with the main streets meeting here. The variation of architecture is the real surprise, with a mix of classical colonial, French renaissance, and art deco. It is a lovely city to walk around. The Mercardo del Puerto is more a of a meat market than a fish market and the 'parrillada' grills serve up a meat platter beyond the wildest imaginings of even the most dedicated carnivore. I was staying by the Mercado Mundo, and went for dinner in the food hall. In the evenings it turns into dance central with people of all ages getting up from their tables. It was great fun.

The holiday home in Punta del Este reminded me of some of my childhood holidays. The pool had a huge cycas revoluta palm growing as a centrepiece beside it. There was an outdoor kitchen. We never ate inside. And we had our own parrilladas BBQ for cooking.

It had a wind-up handle for raising and lowering the grill. Genius! Punta is a neck of land, jutting out into the Atlantic, about a couple of kilometres long and only a few hundred metres wide. We had beaches either side of us. We would go for drinks at seaside bars where the speciality was white sangria. A jug of white wine and fruit. I was sceptical at first, but I grew to like this whole new idea of a fruity white. It seemed right for the place. We went for some lovely long beach walks further up the coast, but had the most fun eating and drinking in the sanctuary of the holiday home. It was a great place to spend new year and I was lucky to be part of it. All the neighbours came, and my Spanish was seriously tested. I got the bus back to Montevideo and spent another night there before heading back to Buenos Aires.

Would I go back? Probably yes.

Vatican City

If you have visited St Peter's in Rome, you may not have realised that once you walk into the main piazza bounded by the colonnades that extend from the cathedral-like outstretched arms, then you have entered another country. If you are inside the cathedral or Michelangelo's magnificent Sistine Chapel you are also inside the country of the Vatican City. I have done these things a few times and I might have ignored the Vatican City as one of my countries but for the fact that I have been deeper inside the city's walls.

If you are a lapsed Catholic or not deeply religious, one of the best things about a visit to St Peters is going up to walk around on the roof. The obvious thing to do when you get up there is to go to the front of the cathedral and look between the backs of the thirteen colossal statues that sit atop the main façade. Christ plus twelve apostles? No, for some reason St Peter is replaced by St John the Baptist. I guess Peter got the cathedral. Anyway, the view over the piazza, the colonnades, down the street to Castel Sant'Angelo and the River Tiber, to the skyline of Rome beyond is quite something. But, even as a child on my first visit in the seventies, the view that held my interest most is the one from the back of the cathedral down into the private garden, with its perfectly clipped swirly patterned hedges. What goes on there? I often wondered.

So, it was fortuitous that I should be invited to a wedding in a chapel inside il Vaticano. Suited and booted, invitation and passport in hand as our means of entry past the Swiss Guards in their stripy uniforms, our names are on the list. We can get in. The small chapel filled up with lots of Italian relatives and us, a small group from London. It was stiffing hot inside and through the service most of us were on the verge of fainting. The Pope had been invited but he wrote to say he was sorry he couldn't attend as he would be doing a tour of his native South America. Television in the recent days had confirmed he really couldn't make it. You sensed he might have shown up otherwise. And of course, all the Italians thought he was there in spirit. Once out, the wedding party and guests spent ages saying hello to each other, which afforded me the opportunity to partially explore the gardens without raising too much suspicion from the guards. It felt special essentially having the grounds to myself. An immaculate old Mercedes 190SL convertible pulled up to drive the bride and groom leisurely through the streets of Rome to the reception at the Villa Miani. We followed in taxis to join them and survey the Vatican City from this stunning location.

Would I go back? Suspect it might have been a once-in-a-lifetime experience.

Vietnam

As I was already nearby and leaving Phnom Penh, I flew to Ho Chi Minh City in Vietnam for a few days of exploration. This city, formerly Saigon, held a bit of a fascination for me and I wanted to get a taste of Vietnam for a future visit, with a bit of the time I had. The first thing that strikes you about this place is that it is a city of mopeds. Some are their very own fashion statement, from chavvy Burberry-checked seats to bright painted colours. There are even dedicated moped river ferries. Wait for the traffic lights to turn red at a crossroads and within seconds hundreds of them have backed up, raring to go when the lights change to green. You come to learn, after ages of waiting for a clear path that never comes, that the only way to cross a road is to go for it. You step out into a sea of oncoming mopeds and walk your line with a strong conviction and determination and that sea of mopeds will part for you as if you were Moses and had done it yourself. Half will go in front of you and half will go behind you. It is almost poetry in motion. I didn't see any accidents in the days I was there and statistically you would expect to see many. I was surprised to find so many lovely old French colonial buildings like the Notre Dame cathedral, City Hall and the Main Post Office, which was beautiful inside.

I felt compelled to visit the War Remnants Museum and see a sample of the US military hardware that the Viet Cong had captured during the Vietnam War. Located right by the big plain Independence Building, with the large remnants proudly on display around the grounds, it serves as a reminder that, here, communism has prevailed. Almost opposite is a large Vietnamese restaurant, but the real food was to be found in the street markets. I have never seen so many frogs on the barbie. Seemingly too many for the idea of eating these four-legged creatures to have been solely inherited from the French.

Would I go back? Yes, to Hanoi and Halong Bay.

Wales

So, the last country in my list of 80 is Wales. Like Scotland I have given it its own status as a country. If you are Welsh or follow rugby, Wales is a country regardless of the fact it is lumped into Great Britain in most world countries lists. I am ashamed to say, given all my travels, Wales has largely been neglected by me, something I intend to rectify with some road trips there very soon.

In our university days, Johnny's stepfather had a cottage in a village called Meifod in mid-Wales and we went there to escape civilisation a few times. When ordering beers in pubs we would say 'We are not from London', which was partly true. The atmospheric Lake Vyrnwy, the water supply of Liverpool, was nearby. It was dammed in Victorian times, so all the construction is more historical than your run-of-the-mill modern reservoir. The gothic revival straining tower with its green copper roof adds to the magic of the place. On one of my trips with some friends we went tandem cycling around the lake. We also climbed Snowden and had a great day's white water rafting through the rapids on the raging River Dee emptying into the lake, Lyn Tegid, at Bala. I have been to Cardiff a couple of times for conferences. The Italian restaurants in the city centre were memorable. And there was Fishguard, en route to Ireland, but I confess Wales needs and deserves more of my time. I will make it up to you Wales. I promise!

Would I go back? Yes! Millennium Stadium for rugby, Brecon Beacons, Pembrokeshire, coast all the way up to Anglesey.

Where Next?

Well you have probably guessed by now....anywhere new!

There is a long list of new places that I want to go to and quite a few I have been to that I cannot wait to revisit.

Who will I go with? Anyone who will join me and of course there will always be some great people along the way. Just think of all the amazing kindred spirits around the world we will never get to meet. It is true the world is becoming a smaller place. It is easier to travel than it was when I first started. But this makes it harder to find magic undiscovered places. And we will have to start looking beyond the top destinations. But they are there, we just have to find them.

So, as we emerge from a year of lockdown for travellers, it is time to get planning. I know where my next place is. Do you?

Here's to the next 80 countries and thank you for reading my book.

This book is for me, but it is for you too.

Safe Travels!

D

Acknowledgements

It is hard to know where to start in thanking people, there have been so many along the way in my travels. My parents were instrumental of course and taking Molly and me traveling for six months around Europe when we were children stood us in great stead. Mum and dad had experienced the kindness of strangers in their travels and have themselves been great givers to travellers ever since. It is the unwritten rule of travellers 'give to people travelling where you can, and it will come back to you from somewhere, somehow, someday.' In recent years, I have met some amazing young people out seeing the world on a tight budget and been more than happy to buy them a drink or a meal to help their money stretch further. It's a privilege to help and it is a payback for all the kindness I have been shown myself along the way. So, to my parents who instilled this spirit in me, I am eternally grateful. And they have been great fun to travel with over many years too.

Molly, my sister, living in Oz and Asia for several years really enabled me to explore that amazing part of the world. There have been many friends I have travelled with, the most significant ones I have mentioned, and their enthusiasm and humour has made these travel adventures much more enjoyable. Thank you. And to anyone I have missed out, I apologise and thank you too.

In terms of putting this journal together I would like to thank my dear friend Chris Bird, a professional wordsmith who agreed to not put me through the mill and give the text a light touch proofing. She came back in a day with corrections and the super kind words - 'wow, what a life. It's great.' My old friend Sarah Robinson also read the first draft for me and gave me great feedback on so many areas and was a real support through this crazy project of mine. Without her, I may not have found the energy to finish. To Chris and Sarah, thank you both.

Most of all I would like to thank the countless number of people and new friends I have made along the way. It is the kindness of strangers that is the most rewarding part of travelling. Wherever you are now, I thank you.

For anyone looking to put their own book together, the sorting of pictures took a month, the writing a month and laying out (using Scribus) a month. My motto throughout was that 'half a good plan finished is better than a perfect one never done.' It is not perfect, but it's done.

I was born on the Mornington Peninsula on Australia's southern coast. My family moved to the UK when I was sixteen and I attained the nickname Dingo, which has stuck ever since. I studied Engineering at Kings College London and have run a software company ever since graduating. When I am not travelling, I live in Cowes on the Isle of Wight in England, where I can mostly be found on or by the sea.

I welcome any questions or feedback at: david@updata.co.uk

I am grateful for a review on Amazon

Countries List

Andorra	Germany	Panama
Antigua and Barbuda	Greece	Poland
Argentina	Guatemala	Portugal
Australia	Honduras	Qatar
Austria	Hong Kong	Romania
Barbados	Hungary	San Marino
Belgium	Iceland	Scotland
Belize	India	Serbia
Bermuda	Indonesia	Singapore
Bosnia and Herzegovina	Ireland	Slovakia
Brazil	Italy	South Africa
Cambodia	Japan	South Korea
Canada	Jordan	Spain
Cayman Islands	Kenya	Sri Lanka
Chile	Laos	Sweden
China	Latvia	Switzerland
Costa Rica	Lithuania	Tanzania
Croatia	Malaysia	Thailand
Cuba	Malta	Tunisia
Czech Republic	Mauritius	Turkey
Denmark	Mexico	Uganda
Dominican Republic	Monaco	United Arab Emirates
Egypt	Morocco	United States of America
El Salvador	Myanmar (Burma)	Uruguay
England	Netherlands	Vatican City
Estonia	Nicaragua	Vietnam
Finland	Norway	Wales
France	Oman	

Countries visited - Countries to go to

Printed in Great Britain
by Amazon